Financial Management in the New Europe

Financial Management
in the
New Europe

Morten Balling

BLACKWELL
Oxford UK & Cambridge USA

First published 1993

Blackwell Publishers
108 Cowley Road
Oxford   OX4 1JF
UK

238 Main Street, Suite 501
Cambridge, Massachusetts 02142
USA

British Library Cataloguing in Publication Data

A CIP catalogue record for this book is available from the British Library.

Library of Congress Cataloging-in-Publication Data

Balling, Morten.
Financial management in the new Europe / Morten Balling.
p.   cm.
Includes bibliographical references and index.
ISBN 0–631–18294–2 (alk. paper). – ISBN 0–631–18295–0
1. Corporations – Europe – Finance.   2. Corporations – European Economic Community countries – Finance.   3. Corporations – Finance-Law and legislation – Europe.   I. Title.
HG4132.B35   1993
658.15'094 – dc20

Typeset in 10 on 12 pt Palatino
by Graphicraft Typesetters Ltd, Hong Kong

This book is printed on acid-free paper

Die Bundesbank wird in der Endstufe nur noch einen bescheidenen Einfluss auf die geldpolitischen Entscheidungsprozesse in Europa nehmen können. (In the final stage the Bundesbank will only be able to exert a modest influence on the monetary policy decisions in Europe.)

Helmut Schlesinger, Frankfurt, 18 May 1992.

Contents

Foreword

This is a book about financial management in a European environment. As a management book it is addressed to decision makers. Decision makers need knowledge and support in order to perform well. Their time is scarce. They do not have much time for reading books. Accordingly, the author has tried to write a concise text. It is the aim of this book to provide relevant knowledge to European financial managers in a concentrated way.

It might also be useful to state from the outset what the book is not. It is not a directory to the EC institutions although it has features in common with such directories. It is not a guide or road map to the European financial landscape or to the statistical and legal sources describing the environment although it has features in common with such guides. Neither is it a broad textbook in international or corporate finance although it covers subjects that are generally included in such books. Finally, it is not a European tax management guide although it deals with the importance of the diverse tax environments in Europe. Readers who are looking for directories, guides, articles and textbooks within the fields mentioned may, however, obtain some help through the many references to such publications in the relevant sections of this book. Most of the references are given to sources written in English. There are, however, also some references to essential publications written in German and French.

To write a book implies a tough selection process. Given the limited number of pages, the author must continuously decide what material to include and what to exclude from the text. The author of this book has tried consistently to ask the question: is this material essential to a financial manager in a European firm in the 1990s? Only when the answer is yes has the material been included.

The book you have in front of you is the result of the selection process. It has turned out to be a mixture of financial theory, financing techniques, economics, and legal and institutional material describing the European financial environment. The text crosses the boundaries between such well established fields as corporate finance, international finance, portfolio management, company law, tax management, financial markets and institutions, and international banking. There are excellent textbooks on the market in all these fields. This book cannot replace any of them. It can rather supplement them by adding a European dimension to the subject in question.

The focus of the book is on the company's financial environment. It is obvious to anyone that the European financial environment is changing rapidly. The plans for creation of an Economic and Monetary Union during the 1990s provided the original impetus for the book project. The implications for corporate finance of the possible establishment of an EMU and the accomplishment by the end of 1992 of the internal market in the EC are of course subject to much attention in the book. In June 1992, however, the ratification process for the Maastricht Treaty of December 1991 ran into trouble. It is therefore uncertain how the European political architecture will develop in the years ahead. Change is, however, also the name of the game in the more theoretical sections. The European financial manager must therefore be prepared to spend a considerable part of his time in updating his knowledge in all the fields mentioned. The book contains a lot of references to sources that are considered to be appropriate for such updating.

The author has received inspiration and support from many persons and institutions. First of all I am much indebted to my colleagues at the Department of Finance at the Aarhus School of Business, Denmark: Anders Grosen, Torsten Jacobsen, Svend Jakobsen, Peter Løchte Jørgensen, Peder Harbjerg Nielsen and Frank Pedersen. We have discussed a broad sample of the issues in the book over the years and they have kindly accepted the increased teaching burden that follows when a colleague goes on sabbatical in order to concentrate on writing. My colleague at the Department of Information Sciences, Hans Jørn Juhl, has carried out the statistical analysis which is presented in chapter 8.

As a personal member of the Société Universitaire Européenne de Recherches Financières (SUERF), I have participated in a number of meetings dealing with European capital market integration. Professor Niels Thygesen, University of Copenhagen, during his recent period as a president of SUERF, organized colloquia on aspects of financial integration that are directly relevant to the analysis here. I am also indebted to a number of libraries. I have benefited from the services of the libraries of the Aarhus School of Business, the Copenhagen Business School, the Institut Universitaire International Luxembourg, the Commission of the European Communities in Brussels, and the London Business School. I have visited the Centre of European Law in

London. I have had the opportunity to discuss subjects in the book with Karel van Hulle, Company Law Division of DG XV, and Mario Burgio, Taxation Division of DG XV of the EC Commission in Brussels. The largest professional debt of all, however, is to my friend Professor Arthur I. Stonehill, Oregon State University, who agreed to read the whole manuscript and suggested a number of improvements. The persons mentioned here are of course in no way responsible for the analysis in the book. I am indebted to the Vilhelm Kier Foundation, Aarhus. The Foundation supported the book project by allowing me to live in its apartment in London in the autumn of 1991, while I was working in the library of the London Business School.

Finally, I want to thank my wife Ellen because she has patiently accepted that my thoughts on many occasions have been occupied by the book project when they ought to have been centred on family affairs.

Morten Balling

1

Corporate Finance in
a European Environment

The aim of this chapter is to put financial management into a European perspective. The integration process in the EC has implications for most investment and financing decisions. Corporate goals are revised as the relative influence of different corporate stakeholders changes. The currency environment may be affected by the gradual transition from EMS to EMU. Company laws, tax laws and laws concerning securities markets are adapted to EC directives. The number of EC member states is expected to grow. In such an environment, the financial manager must be prepared for profound changes.

1.1 The European Perspective in Finance

This book is written from the point of view of a financial manager (FM) in a European firm. The representative undertaking in which he works will be referred to as 'Eurocomp'. The manager's job is to help to find answers to a number of basic questions with far-reaching implications for the future of the firm. Some of these questions concern the supply of capital to the firm: Who is going to supply capital in the future? What amount of capital will be appropriate? What kinds of capital will the firm need? What will the capital suppliers expect in return? What type of information should be disclosed to the investors? What should the balance be between debt and equity capital? According to what criteria should alternative capital sources be compared?

Other questions concern the firm's application of capital. What kind of assets are needed in order to operate the firm? Where should new physical assets be located? What should be the balance between financial and non-financial assets? What type of securities is it appropriate to include in the firm's portfolio? What criteria should be used to evaluate investment proposals?

When it is seen as the major aim of financial research to support the decisions of financial managers, it becomes interesting to ask how practical decision makers rank financial research areas according to relevance. Ramirez et al. (1991) have carried out a survey in which financial officers and middle managers were asked to rank financial areas for which more research would aid the decision maker. The financial managers gave the highest ranking to problems associated with ownership and changes in ownership of listed companies, regulatory problems including the influence of tax laws on financial decision making, and problems associated with long-term financing.

Satisfactory answers to financial management questions arising in companies resident in the European Community (EC) cannot be given today before the European perspectives have been taken into consideration. As national borders lose their former significance as barriers to trade transactions, European firms must evaluate their capital expenditures in new production facilities with a view to a single European market. The abolition of capital controls means that the European firm faces a much broader menu of investment and financing options than before. It means also that potential capital suppliers may be found among residents in all European countries.

The multiplication of possible sources and uses of capital does not make financial planning easier. Harmonization efforts in the EC can, however, contribute to transparency and limitation of complexity. The liberalizations that have been carried out so far in Europe have created many diversification opportunities. The continued Europeanization of the firm's financial environment can be expected to create further diversification opportunities, which may benefit investors as well as companies. The financial environment is moving. It is likely that the degree of integration of the financial markets will be higher in the future than today. Companies that understand the integration process will be able to gain from the arbitrage opportunities that are created (Lessard 1989) describes such opportunities from a global point of view.

1.2   Ownership, Residence and Corporate Goals

Business activity in Europe is carried out by a large number of undertakings which differ from each other with respect to ownership, residence, legal status and group affiliation. In the following, we will assume that financial management problems are seen from the point of view of a limited liability corporation. When reference is made to the representative financial manager, we assume that the person in question carries a responsibility for the financial performance of a company with residence in the Community.

For several years the possibility of setting up companies under a European company statute has been discussed (Van Hulle 1989). Trojan-Limmer (1991) has described the most recent amendments to the proposed European company statute. At the time of writing, companies still have to be based upon national company law in one of the EC member states. Company law harmonization has so far been one of the most successful areas of EC law approximation but there remain significant differences between company law regimes. In other areas covered by the EEC Treaty, the efforts to harmonize have been far less successful. This applies in particular to corporate tax regimes. It follows that it is essential to be explicit with respect to company characteristics when financial management problems are discussed.

In the literature on financial management, corporate goals have been analysed and discussed for many years. The most widely used textbooks in corporate finance tend to assume that corporate managers aim at stockholder wealth maximization (Brealey and Myers 1991: 73; Ross et al. 1990: 15; Van Horne 1989). There are a number of advantages to starting with this assumption. Decision rules become relatively simple. Investment decisions can be taken by means of the net present value criterion and corporate managers can be told to leave diversification efforts to the shareholders.

One should keep in mind, however, that most of the textbooks with a global circulation are written by authors coming from and therefore most familiar with the Anglo-Saxon world. A number of authors – some of them from continental Europe – tend to work with more diffuse corporate goals. Donaldson (1984) and Cornell and Shapiro (1987) are, however, outstanding examples of American authors working with multiple corporate goals. They see the decision making process in the company as an interplay between managers, owners, employees and possibly also other stakeholders or company interested parties (CIPs).

In multinational companies, stakeholders with actual or potential influence on the corporate goals are residents in several different countries. Such diversity can complicate the setting of goals considerably. Roth and Ricks (1990) have studied objective setting in companies with large international operations. Based on answers to a field study, they classify their sample of companies in two groups. The companies belonging to the so-called 'focused group' concentrated on relatively few objectives such as net profit, productivity and innovation objectives. Companies in the other group – the 'multifocal group' – emphasized several different objectives such as profit, rate of growth, market share, and penetration of international markets. A comparison of the economic performance of the two groups shows that the more narrowly focused companies outperformed the multifocused businesses in each and every performance dimension.

The motives of the different CIPs may be in conflict. Payments that are income from the point of view of one party are expenses from the point of view of the corporation. A CIP may in principle be in favour of cost reductions in the company provided that the reductions do not imply loss of income for himself. Corporate behaviour is thus determined by the balance of influence among the CIPs. The balance varies from country to country. It varies also within the individual European country. At one extreme, there are companies whose financial behaviour is dominated by a single strong owner-manager. The behaviour of such companies may correspond well with stockholder wealth maximization. At the other extreme there are public listed companies with hundreds of thousands of small shareholders whose behaviour is dominated by hired managers and professional board members with relatively small holdings of shares. Between these two extremes there are a large number of combinations of influence on goal setting and management practices.

In some European countries the employees have the right to elect members of the board of directors. That is for instance the case in Denmark, the Netherlands and Germany (Stonehill and Dullum 1990). It seems fairly obvious that there is a need to modify the goal assumptions on which financial management theory is based when employee-appointed board members have the opportunity to influence corporate investment and financing decisions. The influence of the employees is of course not restricted to cases where they are represented on the boards.

The CIPs that are involved with the company either through ownership or through occupation have two things in common: they want financial compensation from the company, and they want to some extent to be protected from the risks that are associated with the company. Each individual who is a CIP must in fact carry out a trade-off between expected income and risk in his economic relations with the company.

The shareholders benefit from the limited liability. Their maximum loss is the price they have paid for the shares. They want to be compensated for their investment through dividends and/or capital gains. If they find that the board of directors and the management show poor performance, they can sell their shares or they can use their voting power at the stockholder meeting in order to replace the directors who in turn select the management team.

The management and the employees want to be compensated for their services to the company by wages, pensions and job security. They may also show an interest in company cars, well equipped offices and travel to interesting cities abroad. They have an obvious interest in arrangements under which they can buy shares on favourable terms.

The banks and other creditors want to be paid for funds lent and financial services rendered and they try to limit their credit risk by demanding security for loans to and guarantees given on behalf of the company.

Wages to employees and management, compensation to directors, interest payments and fees to banks and dividend payments to shareholders have a currency dimension. So have the different measures of risk that are considered by the CIPs to be relevant. The trade-off between expected income and risk cannot be carried out before the currency of reference has been selected. The trade-off by company external groups must be based on the disclosure of financial information. Shareholders form their dividend and capital gains expectations by means of earnings figures and other data disclosed by the company. At present, financial company information is in general expressed in the currency of the company's residence country. Listed European companies are obliged to give supplementary figures denominated in European Currency Units (ECUs). This practice, which in most cases is authorized by national accounting laws, corresponds well with the fact that companies must be incorporated in a particular country and that the majority of the CIPs are residents in the same country and want to earn an income in the local currency and evaluate their risk and future buying power in terms of that currency.

1.3 The Currency Environment

At the time of writing, there are 11 separate currencies in the EC.[1] There are, however, close to 200 national currencies in the world. Any company with residence in Europe or elsewhere operates therefore potentially in a very complex global currency environment. Currencies can be identified by the so-called ISO-codes. Appendix A contains a sample of ISO-codes for European currencies and a few of the most important non-European currencies in the world. The ISO-codes are applied in all numerical examples in the book, except that ECU is used in preference to its code XEU.

The number of currencies in existence is not stable. The number increases when new independent states are formed, as has happened in Eastern Europe since 1989. The number of currencies falls when countries agree to form monetary unions. In December 1991 at Maastricht, the EC heads of state and government agreed on a draft Treaty on European Union. It was part of the agreement that a full Economic and Monetary Union (EMU) should begin for those member states judged eligible to participate, not later than 1 January 1999.

If this decision is carried out, it will imply a drastic simplification of the currency environment in Europe. At the time of writing, the prospects for the EMU are very uncertain. A decision to start an EMU will also have far-reaching consequences for corporate financial management. The number of currencies to include in foreign exchange risk management will fall. Corporate goals will be expressed in ECUs. The CIPs will formulate their expectations of income and risk in terms of the ECU. Wages, compensations, fees, pensions, interest payments and dividends will be paid in ECUs. Financial information disclosed by the companies will be expressed in ECUs. Local-currency-denominated assets and liabilities will be transformed to ECU-denominated assets and liabilities. Financial managers who expect an EMU to be formed must try to look ahead and evaluate what all these changes in the currency environment will imply for the company.

1.4   The Legal Environment

The present European environment is also characterized by many national differences in the tax treatment of interest, dividends and other kinds of capital income. In spite of ongoing harmonization efforts, it is likely that many of these differences will exist for some years. The FM must be aware of the implications of this for the after-tax returns to investors and lenders in different member countries. In the existing tax environment, it is necessary to carry out very complicated calculations in order to determine an 'optimal' European tax policy for the company. Again, harmonization of the tax systems can potentially result in drastic simplifications.

Company laws, banking laws, and stock exchange laws provide – in addition to the tax laws – the legal framework for corporate finance. At the time of writing, there are still considerable differences between the legal frameworks in the EC countries. The national rules have, however, been through a long series of adjustments owing to the harmonization efforts of the EC Commission, so that important parts of the legislation have converged towards common principles. In some areas, the rules are completely identical. The harmonization process must be expected to continue. The legal framework and the financial environment of Eurocomp will become more and more European.

It follows that there are many reasons to apply a European approach to corporate finance. In addition to the trade reasons in connection with the creation of the internal market, and the legal reasons, there are also reasons related to stockholder integration. It is particularly evident that there is a need for European thinking, if it is assumed that the shares in a European company are listed on one of the stock exchanges in Europe and owned by stockholders in almost all EC countries. Thurley and Wirdenius (1991) believe that European management approaches and styles will first become necessary in transborder organizations. It follows from the above assumptions that the company must disclose accounting information in accordance with the EC rules for listed companies. It follows also that translation of accounting figures to ECUs becomes an important part of the information flow from the company to the stockholders.

1.5   The European and Other Environments

The terms 'Europe' in the title of this book and 'European' in the heading of this chapter refer as a rule to the EC level. Considering the existence of non-member countries in the Eastern part of Europe and in Scandinavia, this use of the word 'European' is of course a simplification. Austria, Sweden, Finland, Switzerland, Cyprus and Turkey have applied for full membership and Norway, Hungary and other East European countries are expected to apply in the near future. One may therefore well ask, as Bernard Cassen (1991) has done: how large is Europe? Several scenarios are possible. A heightened institutional integration among the 12 countries that are EC members today might to some extent conflict with the future admission of new members. If one tries to give an evaluation of the long-run perspectives, one must therefore try to answer the question: will the EC become deeper or wider, or what mixture of deepening and widening should one expect? It is not inconceivable that there will be 20 EC member countries at the beginning of the next century. Expansion may take another form than admission of countries as full members. More countries than today may apply for and be accepted as associated countries. According to Hans Tietmeyer (1991), the EC can hardly turn its back on the Eastern European countries that want closer cooperation with the Community. A widening of the membership or the number of associated countries could put a brake on the integration process and imply a certain dilution of the political cohesion of the Community. The EC could become the European wing of an Atlantic free trade area, in which the US and Canada were also members. The British government of 1991 seemed to have some sympathy for this scenario. In the words of Norman Lamont (1991), the wider objectives for EMU, as for other Community policies, are that it should help build a Community that is outward looking. The Dutch and Italian governments seem to be more in favour of a scenario with deepening of the integration among the existing members (Poos 1991). Trade policy is obviously a very important aspect of every European scenario. It is only natural that non-European countries follow the integration process closely and try to use their influence in order to avoid a development which may be called 'fortress Europe' (Congress of the US 1990; Gyohten 1991).

The present institutional structure in Europe has developed over the years. The legal foundation of this development has been a series of amendments to the original treaties (OOPEC 1978). The institutional structure of the EC has so far reflected a quadripartite division of functions between the Parliament, the Council of Ministers, the Commission, and the Court of Justice. In describing the powers of the Council and the Commission, article 189 in the EEC Treaty distinguishes between regulations, directives, decisions, recommendations and opinions. A *regulation* has general application; it is binding in its entirety and directly applicable in all member states. A *directive* is binding, as to the result to be achieved, upon each member state to which it is addressed, but leaves to the national authorities the choice of form and method. A *decision* is binding in its entirety upon those to whom it is addressed. *Recommendations* and *opinions* have no binding force.

It follows from the definition of directives that they must be incorporated into the national legislation of a member state. Normally the national parliament must pass a law according to which the new rules are introduced. In many cases the rules in a directive are so specified that the only realistic option for the national parliament is to introduce the precise wording of the directive in the national law.

Contrary to the case of a directive, a decision can also be addressed to persons or companies. Examples of this may in particular be found in competition law, where the Commission has the power to make decisions concerning violations of competition rules.

Regulations are published in the *Official Journal of the European Communities* (*OJ*). Directives and decisions are notified to those to whom they are addressed, but they are also published in the *OJ*. It follows that the FM, in order to be up to date with respect to EC initiatives in company law, capital market regulation and corporate taxation, must follow both the official law journal or gazette of the parliament of his own host country and the *OJ*.

A firm whose host country is a member of the EC is in a political sense operating in institutional environments at at least five different levels: municipal, national, European, OECD and global. Additional levels may of course be relevant in member countries with an internal federal structure. It might be added that the term 'global' can be interpreted in several ways. Let us, however, for the sake of simplicity restrict ourselves to the five levels mentioned. This book focuses on the European level. The author is, however, aware that the European level cannot be studied in isolation from the four other levels. As will be discussed in chapter 2, some of the EC initiatives are implemented through national legislation in the member countries, and large contracts with local government authorities will often be covered by EC rules. It may be added that many EC institutions have a thorough cooperation with global organizations.

1.6 The Financial Manager's Working Situation

How will the working day of our representative European financial manager be spent in the years ahead? He or she will be busy. Every morning there will be external or internal mail to read and to answer. Colleagues and business connection will contact the FM by telephone or fax at irregular intervals during the day. They will assume that the FM is informed about the main news in the *Financial Times*, the *Wall Street Journal*, and probably also a local business newspaper. The FM will promise to come back with answers to their questions, perhaps in the form of written memos or reports. The FM will have to prepare for and participate in meetings. Depending on the organization of Eurocomp, the FM will contact dealers and credit officers in the bank or colleagues, who will be asked to carry out financial transactions or to solve current problems.

This short description illustrates that the FM cannot expect to have much time for studying and information gathering. The FM must, however, accept that everybody expects an FM to be well informed. Precise and prompt answers are appreciated both by busy colleagues and by external business partners. The FM has a tough time allocation problem.

One solution to cope with this problem is to arrange for a circulation system within the company for the most important journals and information letters. In the so-called *Social Science Citation Index (SSCI)*, economics and business journals are ranked according to the number of citations from all *SSCI* sources to articles published by those journals in recent years.[2] The *SSCI* ranking can be very useful for a university researcher who wants to allocate his time, but the coverage of the index is definitely too broad for a financial officer. In order to determine the journals to include in the company circulation system, the FM could select a small subset of the finance journals that are ranked highest by the *SSCI*, but the company's needs may be so specialized that the *SSCI* ranking is not relevant.

Abstracts are appropriate for busy managers. There are several excellent journals with abstracts on the market. The FM could include the *Journal of Economic Literature* and *World Banking Abstracts* in the company's circulation system.[3] All journals with abstracts are classified according to subject. The FM could make it a habit to spend a few minutes on the most relevant categories each time a new issue arrives on the desk.

The FM has to decide what balance he wants to maintain between articles on theoretical, legal, institutional and market subjects. Even within a narrow subset of finance-oriented journals, it is impossible to cover all areas in depth. There is an obvious need for an agreement with colleagues on the division of responsibility for keeping up to date in the different relevant subjects.

Journals differ with respect to levels of abstraction. They differ also with respect to what assumptions they make concerning the reader's mathematical and statistical capabilities. The FM's selection of articles for the circulation system must therefore also take into consideration the need for factual information and the quantitative background of the readers.

Information on the institutional development in the EC is of course very important in the present context. EC information sources are dealt with in chapter 2.

1.7   Information Costs

Scarcity of time is thus a very important part of the FM's working situation. Another crucial factor is the cost of acquiring information. Providers of financial information have a very long list of services to offer – many more than a typical European company can subscribe to. Again the FM and his colleagues must study the options and make choices which reflect the company's criteria of relevance. It is easy to state in broad terms that the company should acquire information until the benefits of the last piece of information correspond to its costs. It is much more difficult in practice to establish that such an optimization has been achieved. Nevertheless, in planning for the flow of financial information, the FM should consistently try to answer the question: will the company be better off if we buy the extra information, considering both the expected value of the information and the costs involved?

1.8   Be Prepared for Change

The reader is assumed to be or to want to become a financial manager. He or she should be aware that by taking a job as an FM, one accepts a commitment to a lifelong learning and training process. One of the reasons why an FM has to read selected finance journals systematically is that such reading will be essential to continued performance. Irrespective of the quality of the university or the business school from which the FM graduated, his or her knowledge has to be updated. This applies in the broadest sense. New theories and models are developed, the global financial environment changes, the European environment changes, the industry in which Eurocomp operates changes, and so does the structure and the functioning of the company.

The best advice an author can give a prospective FM is accordingly: be prepared for change. What does that mean for the education of financial managers? It means that students should learn about the factors that cause change. They should be trained in spotting changes that affect the financial environment of companies. They should learn how to evaluate the impact of such changes on their own company. Different kinds of exposure analysis are thus relevant in textbooks on financial management. Exposure analysis (see chapter 8) reflects a defensive attitude and is often followed by a description of hedging techniques that can protect the company against adverse impacts from the environment. Students should of course also be trained in the analysis of strategies that allow companies to exploit new positive opportunities in the markets.

Notes

1   The Belgian franc (BEF) and the Luxembourg franc (LUF) have identical values.
2   In 1988 the top 15 journals were: (1) *Journal of Economic Literature*, (2) *Journal of Financial Economics*, (3) *Econometrica*, (4) *Journal of Legal Studies*, (5) *Journal of Political Economy*, (6) *Quarterly Journal of Economics*, (7) *Brookings Papers*, (8) *Journal of Accounting and Economics*, (9) *American Economic Review*, (10) *Harvard Business Review*, (11) *Journal of Monetary Economics*, (12) *Journal of Economic History*, (13) *Review of Economic Studies*, (14) *Journal of Law and Economics*, (15) *Journal of Finance*.
3   The *Journal of Economic Literature* has a good guide to new books and articles and short abstracts of selected articles. It is published quarterly by the American Economic Association. Articles are classified according to subject. An FM could follow the categories (E) macroeconomics and monetary economics, (F) international economics, (G) financial economics and (K) law and economics. *World Banking Abstracts* is published six times every year by Blackwell Journals, Oxford, UK and Cambridge, USA.

2

Survey of EC Measures Concerning Corporate Finance

The aim of this chapter is to give an overview of and exact references to EC measures with implications for corporate finance. The overview follows the structure of the EC Treaty of Union. It covers right of establishment, free exchange of services, cross-border capital movements, rules of competition, initiatives in the field of taxation, company law harmonization, EC measures concerning stock exchanges and securities markets, and trade policy.

2.1   Coping with Big Quantities of Material

The quantity of EC documentation material relevant to corporate finance is impressive. To cope with it analytically is a challenge to everybody concerned. It is in fact impossible for an individual researcher to acquire and to maintain a detailed knowledge of all relevant material. A financial manager has even less time to read than the researcher. He may often be well advised to consult a firm of lawyers, each of whom may specialize in certain aspects of Community law. There are directories with names and addresses of suitable lawyers and consultants (Euroconfidential 1989). Another way for the manager to face the challenge is to become familiar with one of the currently updated documentation systems, and to apply the system whenever important financial decisions with a European dimension have to be made.

The Commission's own inter-institutional system is called the CELEX system. The name is derived from the Latin 'Communitatis Europae Lex'. It is a computerized documentation system on Community law (Bensch 1991). It has been accessible to the general public since 1981 as the OOPEC *Directory* (OOPEC 1991), published twice a year to describe the situation on 1 June and 1 December (Euroconfidential 1989). The CELEX system is put into a broader documentation context in Thomson (1989: 28) and Hanson (1991). The system may be approached through terminals in each of the official EC documentation centres in the member countries. The user can read on the screen the complete text of all indexed documents, including amendments made since the publication of the latest edition of the document. For each document the system provides the document number, title and reference to the *Official Journal of the European Communities (OJ)*, plus indications of possible changes with attached document numbers.

The documents in the CELEX system are classified into 17 chapters according to subject. In the widest sense, most chapters may contain material that could be considered relevant to financial management in European companies. In the present book, however, it has been decided to limit the scope to five of the chapters: 'Company law' (chapter 17 in the CELEX system), 'Competition policy' (8), 'Free right of establishment and free exchange of services' (6) 'Tax policy' (9), and 'Economic and monetary policy and free capital movements' (10).

There are other excellent documentation systems; see Ehlermann and Bieber (1991), a comprehensive guide published since 1956. If the reader wants to focus on tax management at the European level, the guides of the International Bureau of Fiscal Documentation (IBFD various years) can be recommended.

2.2 The Tree Structure of the EC Treaty of Union

Figure 2.1 is designed to make it easier for an FM to acquire an overview of the EC Treaty of Union, which is a very complicated document. At the time of writing, the Treaty amendments agreed upon in Maastricht in December 1991 still have to be ratified by some of the national parliaments. In a Danish referendum on 2 June 1992, a narrow majority voted against the Maastricht Agreement. The Danish parliament is therefore unable to ratify it. In the following text, however, it is assumed that ratification will eventually take place in a majority of the EC countries and the new provisions will enter into force in the years to come.

Considering the size of the EC Treaty and the number of related protocols and documents, it is out of the question to go into detail in all parts of figure 2.1 Instead an attempt is made to explain how selected Treaty provisions can be expected to affect corporate financial management in the years ahead. Rasmussen (1989) and Petersmann (1991) analyse constitutional aspects of European integration. Toth (1990) presents precise legal definitions of terms and concepts from European Community law as they are used in the treaties and acts of the institutions.

Figure 2.1 has an inverse tree structure with the root of the tree at

Figure 2.1 Structure of that part of the EC Treaty of Union consisting of amendments to the EEC Treaty

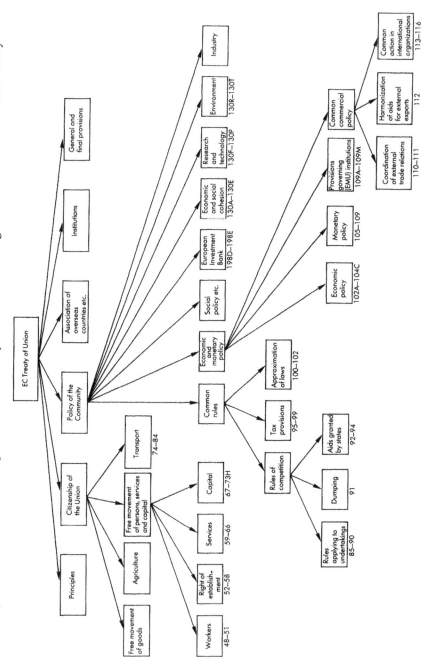

the top and the smallest branches at the bottom. In the text below, the tree structure is utilized to point out in a systematic way from which sections (branches) of the Treaty the various directives and regulations (twigs) are derived.

From a financial management point of view, it is appropriate to focus on two main branches of the EC Union tree: 'Citizenship of the Union' and 'Policy of the Community'. In the present book, the sub-branch 'Economic and monetary policy' is particularly interesting because it contains the EMU provisions. The citizenship branch is sub-divided into four so-called titles: 'Free movement of goods', 'Agriculture', 'Free movement of persons, services and capital', and 'Transport'. The provisions for free movement of goods deal with elimination of internal customs duties, the setting up of the common customs tariff and elimination of quantitative restriction between the member states. These provisions are of course fundamental for the integration of European markets for goods, but since most of them were implemented some years ago, it does not seem necessary to give them a thorough treatment in connection with financial management after 1992.

2.3 Right of Establishment

The branch 'Free movement of persons, services and capital in figure 2.1 deserves some discussion. According to articles 48 to 73 of the Treaty of Union, restrictions on such movements are abolished for *nationals* of the member states. In article 52 on the right of establishment, it is laid down explicitly that the abolition also applies to restrictions on the setting up of agencies, branches or subsidiaries by nationals of any member state established in the territory of any member state.

The provisions also apply to companies in Europe owned by investors in third countries. Such companies are thus considered to be nationals of the EC member country in which they have their residence. They have therefore the right to establish entities in other member countries on equal terms with companies that are owned by local investors. The common practice of US-controlled or Japanese-controlled parent companies of setting up a holding company in one EC member country and letting the holding company establish subsidiaries in other member countries should be evaluated in the light of the right of establishment rules of the Treaty.

Company law harmonization in the EC (discussed in more detail below) is primarily derived from article 54, which is one of the rules on right of establishment.

2.4   Free Exchange of Services

Restrictions of freedom for nationals to provide services from one member country to another are abolished according to article 59. There are many different kinds of service. In the context of financial management, the supply of cross-border financial services has special relevance.

In the 1985 White Paper on competition in the internal market, the Commission emphasized the importance of liberalization of financial services (Commission of the EC 1985). The Commission pointed out the relative growth of the service sector in the member countries in relation to the manufacturing sectors.

Among the financial products the exchange of which the Commission wanted to be facilitated at the Community level are insurance policies, home-ownership savings contracts, consumer credit, and participation in collective investment schemes. Harmonization should be guided by the principle of home country control. Supervisory functions should thus be taken care of by the competent authorities of the member state of origin, while the authorities of the member state of destination of the service should only have a complementary role.

The Council has adopted a number of directives concerning the supply of financial services. A complete list can be found in chapter 6 of the CELEX system (OOPEC 1991; see also Empel 1990; Commission of the EC (DG XV) annual).

2.5   Rules on Capital Movements

Chapter 4 of the Treaty deals with capital movements. At the time of writing, free movement of capital between persons and companies in different member states is based on the *Council Directive of 24 June 1988 for the Implementation of Article 67 of the Treaty* (88/361/EEC).[1] An appendix to the directive contains a nomenclature for the capital movements referred to in the directive. The provisions have been analysed by Oliver and Baché (1989).

Chapter 4 of the Treaty will be changed considerably by the 1991 Maastricht Agreement. With effect from 1 January 1994, articles 67 to 73 are to be replaced by the new articles 73B to 73G. Article 73B contains the new main rule on capital movements. Within the framework of the provisions set out in this chapter, all restrictions on the movement of capital between member states and between member states and third countries will be prohibited, and all payments between member states and between member states and third countries will be free of restrictions. According to the main rule in article 73B, there will from 1994 be no difference in the treatment by EC authorities or member state authorities of capital transactions of companies that differ from each other with respect to ownership or residence.

There are exceptions from the main rule however. Article 73C, paragraph 1, allows the continued application to third countries of any restrictions which exist at the end of 1993 under national law or under Community law adopted in respect of the movement of capital to or from third countries involving direct investment, establishment, the provision of financial services and the admission of securities to capital markets.

Companies with residence in third countries must therefore be prepared to deal with barriers of entry in the form of capital restrictions in some of the member countries, also after 1994. It is likely that non-EC parent companies that want to establish entities in the Community for the first time will find it appropriate to do so in two stages: in the first stage they will set up a subsidiary in one of the most open member countries, and in the second stage they will let the subsidiary establish sub-subsidiaries in the more closed member countries.

The provisions of article 73C will probably also have the effect that groups of financial companies with their parent company in the US or Japan will continue to provide financial services to European customers through subsidiaries in London, Luxembourg, Brussels or Frankfurt. In the financial services industry, the choice of group structure will still be under strong influence from the structure of EC law.[2]

The main rule in article 73B seems to correspond well with the goal of creating a Community which is more open to the outside world. It is, however, not completely out of the question that *new* Community restrictions on movements of capital to or from third countries will be introduced in the future. Thus article 73C, paragraph 2, provides for measures taken by the Council by a qualified majority on such capital movements if they involve direct investment, establishment, the provision of financial services and the admission of securities to capital markets.

Third country companies should probably not be too concerned that the new EC rules on international payments and capital movements could affect trade related payments. Non-EC companies must, however, design their plans for the establishment or acquisition of European companies and the financing of such transactions with due regard to the possible continued existence or reintroduction of restrictions.

The concern of the member states for the protection of their tax base is the background for the new article 73D. According to the provisions in the first paragraph of this, a member state will have the right to apply provisions in its tax law which distinguish between taxpayers according to their residence and the place where their capital is invested. Chapter 10 of this book gives a number of examples of rules discriminating according to country of residence and source country of capital income. Article 73D allows the countries to maintain tax systems with such features.

It is difficult to evaluate the effectiveness of the provision of article 73D, paragraph 3, according to which the allowed tax measures and procedures will not constitute a means of arbitrary discrimination or a disguised restriction on the free movement of capital and payments. The European Court can be expected to have difficult problems of interpretation when in the future it has to draw the line between acceptable tax measures that discriminate between income based on combinations of taxpayer residence country and income source country in order to protect the tax base of the country, and tax measures that restrict capital movements.

In the past, international capital movements have under exceptional circumstances caused crises in financial markets. The possible recurrence of such crises has caused the authors of the Union Treaty text to introduce an 'earthquake' clause in article 73F. According to the article, the Council may, acting by a qualified majority, take safeguard measures *vis-à-vis* third countries of limited duration in order to protect the operation of the EMU against movements of capital to or from third countries. Measures according to this earthquake clause are not confined to long-term capital transactions. Non-EC companies should therefore in their financial planning in principle allow for the possibility of temporary restrictions on almost all kinds of payments crossing the Community border occasioned by future international political and financial crises. The likelihood of the occurrence of such situations seems, however, to be comparatively small.

Finally, in article 73G the new rules on capital movements are connected with the provisions of the Union Treaty relating to the common foreign and security policy. According to article 228A, the Council can find it necessary to interrupt or to curtail economic relations with one or more third countries. The measures taken may concern both movements of capital and payments related to trade transaction. Member states are also, according to article 73G, paragraph 2, allowed to take measures on their own initiative for serious political reasons.

2.6   Rules of Competition

As illustrated in figure 2.1, the common rules of competition are grouped into rules applying to undertakings, dumping rules, and rules for aids granted by states. Companies are according to article 85 not allowed to make agreements with other companies which may affect trade between the member states or prevent, restrict or distort competition within the Community. Abuse of a dominant position by one or more undertakings is, according to article 86, prohibited in so far as it may affect trade between member states.

Chapter 8 of the CELEX system contains sections on competition principles, cartels, dominating positions, concentrations, state-owned companies, subsidies, dumping within the Community and national monopolies. The documentation system contains a long list of cases in which the Commission has decided to approve or to prohibit agreements between European companies based on an evaluation of their possible implications for efficient competition in the Community. The juridical literature is also dominated by decisions made by the Commission and by rulings from the European Court of Justice (Bellamy and Child 1987; Goyder 1988; Siragusa and Subiotto 1991). From a financial management point of view, the section on concentrations seems to be the most interesting. This part of the competition rules has direct implications for policy on mergers.

In 1989 *Council Regulation EEC 4064/89 on the Control of Concentrations between Undertakings* was issued (McDonald 1991). The regulation refers to articles 87 and 235. It became effective in September 1990. It gives the Commission control over large mergers. All the member countries have their own competition authorities. Zuleeg (1990) has analysed situations where community rules on competition and national rules are in conflict. The division of labour between the Commission (DG IV) and the national authorities with respect to merger control is regulated by a system of thresholds. Measures of the turnover of the companies involved must exceed certain amounts before the merger becomes the responsibility of the Commission. The thresholds cannot be assumed to be stable in the years to come; the Commission has already expressed an interest in lower levels.

One of the thresholds concerns the aggregate worldwide turnover. If this amount exceeds ECU 5 billion, the merger is a Community responsibility. Another threshold concerns the total turnover of the companies within the EC. Here the critical amount for the time being is ECU 250 million. If more than two-thirds of the aggregate Community-wide turnover is within one member state, the merger becomes a national affair. Mergers may be dealt with by the national authorities not only because they fall below the thresholds, but also because of the legitimate interests involved. Public security, plurality of the media and prudential rules are all mentioned in the merger control regulation.

In dealing with mergers, the Commission's main criterion is whether the merger will create a dominant position incompatible with effective market competition. The Commission should not be concerned if the market share of the merged venture is less than 25 per cent of the total in the Community. It follows that statistics on market shares may play a critical role in negotiations with the Commission on mergers.

Companies with plans for large mergers should know that prior notification to the Commission is mandatory. If the Commission has not reacted within one month of notification, the merger is automatically considered to have been approved. Violations of the merger control rules are subject to fines. Decisions made by the Commission and penalties charged can be appealed to the European Count of Justice.

Under the rules on competition in the Treaty, the Commission is committed to remove anti-competitive barriers to trade within the Community. Measures taken with that purpose may to some extent conflict with the Commission's trade policy and industrial policies (Kulms 1990).

Dumping is a kind of price discrimination under which the same good is sold abroad at a much lower price than in the domestic market. Article 91 allows member states that are injured by dumping to take protective measures. The use of anti-dumping measures has been on the agenda of the GATT negotiations on several occasions (Stegemann 1991). Twenty-five countries have signed the so-called Anti-Dumping Code which contains a list of conditions that should be fulfilled before a country applies anti-dumping duties. Lux (1992) has analysed the European Court's judgements concerning anti-dumping measures.

Aids granted by states may distort competition among undertakings in the Community. According to article 92, such aid is incompatible with the common market in so far as it affects trade between member states. Subsidies may also affect the location of new investments. This subject is discussed in chapter 4 of this book.

2.7   Tax Provisions

In April 1990, the EC Commission announced that it was changing its policy as to the harmonization of corporate taxation (Liebman and Patten 1991). The Commission withdrew its 1975 proposal for a standardized system and approximated tax rates and announced a less ambitious plan. The aim was now to coordinate the national tax policies of the member states in more general terms.

In the summer of 1990, two important directives were adopted. The first, the *Council Directive of 23 July 1990 on the Common System of*

Taxation Applicable to Parent Companies and their Subsidiaries in Different Member States (90/435/EEC),[3] has the aim of establishing a situation in which a subsidiary's profits are taxed only once. Corporate decisions on the location of new entities should therefore no longer be strongly influenced by tax considerations. The second, the *Council Directive of 23 July 1990 on the Common System of Taxation of Mergers, Divisions and Contributions of Assets taking place between Companies from Different Member States* (90/434/EEC),[4] has the aim of deferring taxation of any capital gains arising when companies merge across member state borders until the assets are subsequently disposed of.

In the summer of 1990, the member states also agreed on a *Convention on the Elimination of Double Taxation in Connection with the Adjustment of Profits between Associated Enterprises* (90/436).[5] The convention concerns cases in which member countries are involved in disputes about double taxation arising from transfer pricing practices of international groups of companies. It provides for an arbitration procedure to be applied when the states are unable to reach agreement.

The Commission has proposed a Council directive on a common system of taxation applicable to interest and royalty payments made between parent companies and subsidiaries in different member states,[6] and proposed a Council Directive concerning arrangements for the taking into account by enterprises of the losses of their permanent establishments and subsidiaries in other member states.[7] An adoption of the first proposal should ensure that withholding taxes on interest and royalty payments between parents and subsidiaries located in different member countries would be abolished. An adoption of the second proposal would allow companies to carry out Europe-wide consolidation so that losses incurred by entities in other member countries could be offset against the profits made by the parent company.

EC member states should impose indirect taxes in a non-discriminatory way. Formally, the provisions of article 95 only prevent the application of indirect taxes for protection against the competition of products from other member states, but in most cases the rules will probably also provide for non-discrimination *vis-à-vis* products originating outside the Community.[8]

The Council has adopted several directives on turnover taxes and excise duties. Only a few are mentioned here. One is the *Sixth Council Directive of 17 May 1977 on Harmonization of Memberstate Legislation on Turnover Taxes, the Common VAT System and a Uniform Basis of Calculation* (77/388/EEC).[9] This directive was amended or modified more than 15 times from 1977 to 1990. An important amendment was made in the Ninth Council Directive (78/583/EEC).[10] In 1990, the EC Commission proposed an amendment to (77/388/EEC) which abolishes the concept of exports and imports in intra-Community trade as from 1 January 1993.[11] It was adopted by the Council as (91/680/EEC). A transitional VAT arrangement based on the 'destination principle' is intended to expire not later than 31 December 1997 and will be replaced by a definitive arrangement based on the 'origin principle'. In 1991 it was agreed to set a standard rate of VAT equal to or higher than 15 per cent with effect from 1 January 1993. Lower rates (but higher than 5 per cent) can be applied to selected goods and services for social or cultural reasons.

Article 96 of the Treaty lays down the principle that repayment of internal taxation on products that are exported may not exceed the internal taxation imposed on them. The provision must be evaluated in the light of the rules on subsidies.

Chapter 10 of this book contains a survey of the tax systems in the member countries, and a more detailed discussion of the implications of the tax regimes for corporate financial planning.

2.8 Approximation of Laws

Articles 8A and 100A of the EC Treaty of Union were introduced into EC law in 1986 by the Single European Act. The provisions relate approximation of laws to the aim of establishing the internal market. The variety of rules among the member countries has caused large practical difficulties for business operations on a European scale. It was therefore stated as an aim to establish a situation at the end of 1992 under which products from one member country should be able to move throughout any other member country without meeting barriers in the form of different national rules.

Approximation of laws is essential to the integration of markets. The modern economic and technical world seems to be subject to a proliferation of government regulations. Consequently, the internal market programme included a long list of technical harmonization measures (Kendall 1991). The political motivation for the regulations may be consumer protection, concern for the environment or maintenance of health standards, but the regulations may in addition have effects on the competition between domestic and foreign producers. Some of the solutions to reduce the trade barriers created by incomplete approximation of laws are to extend the area covered by mutual recognition of texts, administrative authorizations, standardization of technical rules on the European level and the declaration of the equivalence of national rules (Vignes 1990).

2.9 Company Law Harmonization

The EC company law directives are based on article 54 of the Treaty. The directives must therefore be studied in the context of the above mentioned rules on right of establishment (Dine 1990).

The *First Company Law Directive* (68/151/EEC)[12] deals with the safeguards which, for the protection of the interests of members and others, are required by member states of companies or firms. It covers the capacity of a company and its directors, disclosure of certain information and publication of certain information including accounts. Owing to the adoption of the First Directive and the subsequent amendments of the national company laws, those safeguards should now be equivalent throughout the Community.

Article 7 of the First Directive makes persons who act on behalf of the company before it has been formed liable for the obligations arising from such action, if the company does not assume the obligations. The article is therefore relevant to corporate debt management in the early stages of a new company. Article 12 of the First Directive obliges the shareholders to pay up subscribed capital, to the extend that commitments entered into with creditors make it necessary.

The *Second Company Law Directive* (77/91/EEC)[13] lays down minimum requirements for the formation of public companies and the maintenance, increase and reduction of capital in such companies. The directive contains several rules of the utmost importance for the management of equity capital in European companies.

Article 6 specifies a common minimum capital originally at 25,000 European units of account (EUA). The EUA comprised a composite basket of fixed amounts of the currencies of the member states. The equivalent in national currency should be calculated initially at the exchange rate applicable on the date of adoption of the directive. According to article 8 of the Second Directive, shares may not be issued at a price lower than their nominal value, or, where there is no nominal value, their accountable par.

Article 15 limits the funds that can be distributed to shareholders. The article therefore creates, through its impact on the national company law, a framework for the company's dividend policy and capital structure. It is thus in general not allowed to pay dividends to the shareholders, if such payments would reduce the equity capital at the end of the financial year to a level below the subscribed capital plus those reserves which may not be distributed under the law or the statutes.

According to article 25, any increase in capital must be decided upon by the general meeting. The decision itself and the implementation of the increase in the subscribed capital are to be published in accordance with article 3 of the First Directive. Each member state is supposed to appoint a national gazette for that purpose.

Whenever the capital of the public company is increased by consideration in cash, according to article 29 the shares must be offered on a pre-emptive basis to shareholders in proportion to the capital represented by their shares. The right of pre-emption may not be restricted or withdrawn by the statutes or the instrument of incorporation. This may, however, be done by a decision of the general meeting. The management is required to present to such a meeting a written report indicating the reasons for restriction or withdrawal of the right of pre-emption, and justifying the proposed issue price. The rules also apply to securities which are convertible into shares or which carry the right to subscribe for shares, but not to the conversion of such securities, or to the exercise of the right to subscribe.

Articles 30–38 of the Second Directive deal with reduction of the subscribed capital. There are rules to protect the company's creditors whose claims antedate the publication of the decision to reduce the capital. They should, according to article 32, have the right to obtain security for claims which have not fallen due by the date of the publication.

The *Third Company Law Directive* (78/855/EEC)[14] concerns mergers of public limited liability companies. The directive makes a distinction between merger by acquisition and merger by formation of a new company. Merger by acquisition is defined as an operation whereby one or more companies are wound up without going into liquidation and transfer to another all their assets and liabilities in exchange for the issue, to the shareholders of the company or companies being acquired, of shares in the acquiring company and a cash payment, if any, not exceeding 10 per cent of the nominal value of the shares so issued or, where they have no nominal value, of their accounting par value. In a merger by formation of a new company the assets and liabilities of several companies are transferred to a new company that they set up. After the operation, the owners will own shares in the new company.

Merger decisions as a rule are to be made by the general meeting of the shareholders of each of the merging companies. The Third Directive prescribes a number of minimum requirements for the documents and information on which merger decisions are made. According to article 11, all shareholders are entitled to inspect at least

1   the draft terms of merger
2   the annual accounts and annual reports of the merging companies for the preceding three financial years

3   an accounting statement drawn up as at a date which must not be earlier than the first day of the third month preceding the date of the draft terms of merger
4   reports of the management bodies of the merging companies
5   expert reports.

Article 5 of the Third Directive provides a list of draft terms of merger. The share exchange ratio is the most important. Valuation of shares in a merger situation is at the same time very important for the wealth of the shareholders and very complicated. In acknowledgement of this, the legislators have in the directive provided for two reports, which are intended to explain in depth the draft terms of merger. Let us call them respectively the management merger report and the expert merger report.

Article 9 specifies the obligations of the management of each of the merging companies to draw up a detailed written report explaining the draft terms of merger and setting out the legal and economic grounds for them, in particular the share exchange ratio. According to article 10, experts, acting on behalf each of the merging companies but independent of them, appointed or approved by a judicial or administrative authority, must examine the draft terms of merger and draw up a written merger report to the shareholders. The experts must in any case state whether in their opinion the share exchange ratio is fair and reasonable. As a minimum, the expert merger report must indicate the method or methods used to arrive at the share exchange ratio proposed, and state whether the method or methods are adequate in the case in question, indicate the values arrived at using each method and give an opinion on the relative importance attributed to the methods in arriving at the value decided on. The companies are obliged to supply all relevant information and documents to the experts.

The Third Directive provides for the protection of interested parties other than the shareholders. Thus, according to article 13, the laws of the member states must provide for an adequate system of protection of the interests of creditors of the merging companies whose claims antedate the publication of the draft terms of merger and have not fallen due at the time of such publication. Holders of securities, other than shares, to which special rights are attached must, according to article 15, normally be given rights in the acquiring company at least equivalent to those they possessed in the company being acquired.

The *Fourth Company Law Directive* (78/660/EEC)[15] establishes minimum standards of financial reporting for individual companies within the EC. It deals with the presentation and content of the annual accounts and annual report of the management, the method of valuation used in annual accounts, and the audit and publication of these documents. The directive, which has been amended in certain respects in 1983 by the adoption of the Seventh Directive on consolidated accounts, has a very significant impact on the annual published accounts of most European limited liability companies.

According to article 2, the annual accounts comprise the balance sheet, the profit and loss account and the notes on these accounts. The accounts must give a 'true and fair view' of the company's assets, liabilities, financial position and profit or loss. The concept of true and fair view originates in the United Kingdom and Ireland and the requirement deviates significantly from the traditional continental approach to accounting (Andersen 1978). Accounts must be drawn up in accordance with standard formats set out in the directive. The prescribed standard formats mirror the traditionally highly codified practices in some of the continental member countries, for instance in Germany.

Article 31 of the Fourth Directive states the general principles of valuation. These include the principles that the company must be presumed to be carrying on its business as a going concern, that the methods of valuation must be applied consistently from one financial year to another, and that valuation must be made on a prudent basis. The concept of prudence implies that only profits made at the balance sheet date may be included and that account must be taken of all foreseeable liabilities and potential losses arising in the course of the financial year concerned or of a previous one, even if such liabilities or losses become apparent only between the date of the balance sheet and the date on which it is drawn up.

In article 15, fixed assets are defined as those assets which are intended for use in the company on a continuing basis for the purposes of the undertaking's activities. Movements in the various fixed asset items must be shown in the balance sheet or in the notes on the accounts. Fixed assets with a limited economic life are to be depreciated systematically over their lives. According to article 35, fixed assets must initially be valued at purchase price or production cost. Later those values must be reduced in a number of cases. Such downward value adjustments must normally be charged to the profit and loss account and disclosed separately in the notes on the accounts, if they have not been shown separately in the profit and loss account.

At the time of writing, the status of the *Fifth Company Law Directive* is that of an amended proposal.[16] It concerns the structure of public limited companies and the powers and obligations of their organs. There is also a number of new rules about the audit of annual accounts. If or when the directive is adopted, articles 33–36 will, through their incorporation into national law, to some extent change the framework for the shareholders' right to vote at the general meeting. The intense political discussion about the Fifth Directive has in particular concerned the proposed employee participation in the company's administrative organs. The negotiators from the UK have maintained that these types of provision are irrelevant to company law.

The *Sixth Company Law Directive* (82/891/EEC)[17] on division of companies supplements the Third Directive on mergers. While a merger reduces the number of existing companies, a division increases the number of companies. In article 2, division by acquisition is defined as an operation whereby, after being wound up without going into liquidation, a company transfers to more than one company all its assets and liabilities in exchange for the allocation, to the shareholders of the company being divided, of shares in the companies receiving contributions as a result of the division and possibly a cash payment not exceeding 10 per cent of the nominal value of the shares allocated or, where they have no nominal value, of their accounting par value.

Article 3 obliges the administrative or management bodies to draw up draft terms of division in writing. The rules are very similar to the rules on the draft terms of merger in the Third Directive. The similarity between the Division Directive and the Merger Directive is also evident in article 7 on the management division report and article 8 on the expert division report.

In article 21, division by the formation of new companies is defined as an operation whereby, after being wound up without going into liquidation, a company transfers to more than one newly formed company all its assets and liabilities in exchange for the allocation, to the shareholders of the company being divided, of shares in the recipient companies and possibly a cash payment not exceeding 10 per cent of the nominal value of the shares allocated or, when they have no nominal value, of their accounting par value. The documentation and information requirements are almost the same in divisions by the formation of new companies as in divisions by acquisition.

The *Seventh Company Law Directive* (83/349/EEC)[18] deals with consolidated accounts. Broadly speaking, it applies to all European parent companies that are themselves subjected to the Fourth Directive on annual accounts. According to article 1, a member state must require any parent undertaking governed by its national law to draw up consolidated accounts and a consolidated annual report. A company is considered to be a parent company if it has a majority of the shareholders' or members' voting rights in another undertaking; or has the right to appoint or remove a majority of the members of the administrative, management or supervisory body of another undertaking and is at the same time a shareholder in or member of that undertaking; or has the right to exercise a dominant influence over an undertaking of which it is a shareholder or member pursuant to a contract entered into with that undertaking or to a provision in its memorandum or articles of association; or is a shareholder in or member of an undertaking and controls alone a majority of shareholders' or members' voting rights in that undertaking.

Subsidiary undertakings may themselves be parent undertakings through majority shareholdings in other companies. According to article 3, any subsidiary undertaking of a subsidiary undertaking is to be considered a subsidiary undertaking of the parent undertaking, which is the parent of the undertakings to be consolidated.

Articles 16–35 provide detailed rules on the accountancy principles to be followed and the information to be included in the consolidated accounts. The rules create a common framework but leave considerable freedom for the member states to decide among alternative treatments. Article 36 deals with the consolidated annual report. In this report investors must be given a fair review of the development of business and the position of the undertakings included in the consolidation taken as a whole. They must be provided with information on important events that have occurred since the end of the financial year, on likely future developments, on research and development activity in the group companies, on the shares in group companies held by other group companies, and so on. From the point of view of the shareholders in a European parent company, the information in the consolidated annual report and the consolidated accounts is essential investor information.

There are international initiatives on consolidated accounts other than the EEC's Seventh Directive. Similar initiatives have been taken by the International Accounting Standards Committee (IASC), the Organization for Economic Cooperation and Development (OECD), and the United Nations (UN) Committee on Transnational Corporations (Andersen 1983: 59) Among the organizations mentioned there seems to be a broad consensus about the desirability of a high degree of comparability and increased disclosure of information from groups of companies. After the publication of the Seventh Directive, the IASC took action to modify its consolidation guidelines in order to get closer to the principles on which the directive is based. Differences remain, however. The long-run aim of the directive is to harmonize consolidation practices within the 12 EC member states. For political reasons, it was considered desirable initially to choose formulations that could cover existing practices. The text therefore contains many optional provisions – so many, in fact, that the achievement of uniform consolidation practices in the Community seems to be some years away (Lefebvre and Lin 1991). The UN and OECD have for many years demonstrated a keen interest in the activities of multinational groups of companies or transnational corporations (OECD 1984, 1986, 1987).

The *Eighth Company Law Directive* (84/253/EEC)[19] contains minimum qualifications for persons responsible for carrying out the statutory audits of accounting documents.

At the time of writing, the *Ninth Company Law Directive* is still under preparation. It is intended to define dominant and dependent undertakings (groups), to require further disclosure of significant shareholdings, and to provide for the interests of dependent companies and outside shareholders. The directive should be evaluated in connection with the Seventh Directive on consolidated accounts.

A proposal for a *Tenth Company Law Directive* (85/C23/08) on international mergers was submitted by the Commission to the Council in January 1985.[20] The directive should supplement the Third Directive, which deals only with mergers involving companies governed by the law of the same member state. As a rule, domestic and international mergers should be treated in the same way. Thus, according to the proposed article 2, member states would provide for cross-border mergers in accordance with the Third Directive, except where the Tenth Directive provides otherwise.

The *Eleventh Company Law Directive* (89/666/EEC)[21] regulates the obligations of foreign branches to provide information The rules on compulsory disclosure cover, for instance, the address and activities of the branch, the name and legal form of the company, the names of the persons who are authorized to represent the company in dealings with third parties and in legal proceedings, and accounting documents in accordance with article 3.

For branches belonging to companies in the EC, the disclosure requirements are determined by the laws of the company's host country. The compulsory disclosure of accounting documents is thus, according to article 3, limited to documents drawn up, audited and disclosed pursuant to the law of the member state by which the company is governed in accordance with the Fourth, the Seventh and the Eighth Directives. The host country of the branch may, however, according to article 4 stipulate that the documents must be published in another official language of the Community. If the company which owns the branch has its residence outside the EC, the disclosure requirements are regulated by the laws of the member country which is host country for the branch.

Article 11 of the Eleventh Directive has caused a small amendment to the rules on the contents of the annual report in the Fourth Directive: the existence of branches is now to be indicated in the report.

The *Twelfth Company Law Directive* (89/667/EEC)[22] concerns single-member private limited liability companies. Such companies are characterized by the fact that their shares are owned by a single person.

The proposal for a *Thirteenth Company Law Directive*[23] concerning takeover and other general bids will, if or when it is adopted and later incorporated in national law, have a profound impact on the way mergers and acquisitions in the Community will take place. Article 2 of the proposal presents a number of definitions. The 'offeree company' is defined as a company whose securities are the subject of a takeover or other general bid. The 'offeror' means any person or company, including where appropriate the directors of the offeree company, who launches a bid in accordance with the obligations set out in article 4 or on a voluntary basis. A fundamental principle of equal treatment of shareholders who are in the same position is established in article 3.

Article 4 contains an important threshold of $33\frac{1}{3}$ per cent of the voting rights in the offeree company. If a person aims to acquire a number or percentage of the shares which, added to any existing holdings, gives him a percentage of the voting rights above the $33\frac{1}{3}$ per cent threshold, he will be obliged to make a bid to acquire all the securities of the offeree company. Exempted from the provisions in article 4 are cases where the securities of the offeree company have not been admitted to official stock exchange listing or have not been the subject of a request for such admission at the moment when the bid is announced, and cases where the offeree companies are small companies in the sense of article 27 in the Fourth Directive.

According to the proposed article 10, the offeror will draw up an offer document in respect of the bid, stating among other things the names and registered offices of the parties involved; the securities for which the bid is made; the consideration offered for each security and the basis for the valuation used in determining it and, in the case of a cash consideration, the guarantees provided by the offeror regarding payment of that consideration; where appropriate, a statement concerning any future indebtedness of the offeree company to finance the bid; and where the consideration comprises securities, the date from which those securities will entitle their holders a share in the profits. The document will give the latest date on which the bid may be accepted; the steps to be taken by the addressees of the bid in order to signify their acceptance and to receive the consideration for the securities which they transfer to the offeror; and the intentions of the offeror, explicitly expressed, regarding the continuation of the business of the offeree company, including the use of its assets, the composition of its board and future of its employees.

The offer document will according to article 11, be either published in full in one or more national or mass circulation newspapers and in the national gazette; or made available to the addressees of the bid at addresses announced in notices in the newspapers and the gazette, or by equivalent means approved by the competent supervisory authority; or, where all the securities comprised in the bid are registered, circulated to all addressees of the bid. The period for accepting the bid will the less than four weeks or more than ten weeks from the date of publication of the offer document.

Article 13 specifies the conditions that must be fulfilled in order to withdraw a bid. The board of the offeree company will draw up a detailed report giving its views on the bid and setting out the arguments for and against acceptance. When the consideration offered comprises securities for which at the time of the bid no official stock exchange listing has been requested, the board's report will be accompanied by the report of an expert independent of the parties of the bid and appointed or approved by the competent supervisory authority. This report in all cases will state whether, in the expert's opinion, the consideration offered is fair and reasonable and will give the expert's views on the basis for valuation used to determine the consideration. The report will, in good time before the expiry of the period for acceptance, be made public. Once the period of acceptance has expired, the result of the bid will, according to article 18, be made public.

The *Fourteenth Company Law Directive* on dissolution and liquidation of companies is still under preparation at the time of writing.

A number of observations can be made on the contents of the company law directives. First of all it is apparent that the directives are primarily concerned with disclosure of accounting information to investors and other external information users, management of equity capital, and mergers and acquisitions. The Commission has for many years stressed the importance for the functioning of the common market of equivalent rules in the member states on the supply of information, on formation of companies, and on changes in company capital structure and ownership. The Commission's concern for the framework for mergers and acquisitions was also evident in the section above on competition policy.

Dine (1991) and Ellis & Storm (1991) are loose leaf publications covering EC company law. They are updated regularly.

2.10   EC Measures Concerning Stock Exchanges and Markets

The EC Council does not seem to be very interested in finding short names for its directives. Inspired by Warren (1990) and Tondkar et al. (1990), we will refer to the directives mentioned in this section as the Admission Directive, the Listing Particulars Directive, the Interim Reports Directive, the Major Holdings Transactions Directive and the Insider Trading Directive.

Capital flows between the member states are facilitated if the investors know that there are common minimum requirements when companies want to have their securities listed on a stock exchange. The aim of the *Admission Directive* is to remove obstacles to the interpenetration of securities markets that may be caused by divergent admission conditions. The official name of the document is *Council Directive of 5 March 1979 Coordinating the Conditions for the Admission of Securities to Official Stock Exchange Listing* (79/279/EEC as amended by 82/148/EEC).[24] The directive refers to article 54,3,g of the Treaty, i.e. one of the rules on right of establishment. Companies that want to list their equity securities on a stock exchange have to fulfil a number of requirements concerning market capitalization, publication of financial statements, negotiability of the securities etc. The directive requires each member state to designate an administrative and supervisory authority.

The *Listing Particulars Directive* prescribes a number of detailed disclosure requirements that must be fulfilled prior to approval of the listing. The requirements are stated in *Council Directive Coordinating the Requirements for the Drawing up, Scrutiny and Distribution of the Listing Particulars to be Published for the Admissions of Securities to Official Stock Exchange Listing* (80/390/EEC as amended by 82/148/EEC and 89/298/EEC).[25] The disclosure requirements include information on the persons responsible for preparing the listing particulars and for auditing the financial statements, the capitalization of the issuer, the principal business activities, assets and liabilities, profits and losses, business prospects etc. The *Interim Reports Directive* reflects the interest of the EC authorities in keeping investors informed regularly about the current development of listed companies. The official name of the document is *Council Directive of 15 February 1982 on Information to be Published on a Regular Basis by Companies the Shares of which have been Admitted to Official Stock Exchange Listing* (82/121/EEC).[26] Semi-annual reports must be published in widely distributed newspapers.

The *Major Holdings Transactions Directive* has as its aim to obtain publicity on transactions under which the control of listed companies can change between different investor groups. The name of the document is *Council Directive on Information to be Published when Major Holdings in the Capital of a Listed Company are Acquired or Disposed Of* (88/627/EEC).[27] There are a number of thresholds in the text that release the obligation to provide information to the public. The directive has implications for the discussion in chapter 9 on acquisition of companies.

The aim of the *Insider Trading Directive* is to prevent abuse of information asymmetries among the investors (Hopt 1990). The directive requires member states to prohibit any persons who have access to inside information from taking advantage of that information by trading in transferable securities. This directive, entitled *Council Directive Coordinating Regulations on Insider Trading* (89/592/EEC),[28] also prohibits insiders from using the information to recommend trades by third parties.

2.11 Statute for a European Company?

Company law harmonization in the Community has so far been quite successful. Nevertheless, financial managers in European groups of companies still have to cope with twelve diverse systems of company law. Subsidiaries in other member countries must be incorporated under the laws of the respective host countries. In order to promote cross-border business activities and economies of scale, and in order to facilitate cross-border mergers and acquisitions, the Commission has during the years from 1970 to 1992 proposed and reproposed the introduction of an EC-wide company statute. At the time of writing, the latest edition is *Proposal for a Council Regulation on the Statute for a European Company.*[29] Trojan-Limmer (1991) and Hauschka (1992) describe briefly the latest amendments of the proposal. Hauschka calls it a minimal solution. The proposal refers to the Treaty articles 54 and 100A. The proposed Societas Europea (SE) would enjoy limited liability and would have a minimum share capital of ECU 100,000. Its registered office would be located anywhere within the Community.

According to *Proposal for a Council Directive Complementing the Statute for A European Company with Regard to the Involvement of Employees in the European Company*, at least one-third and not more than one-half of the members of the supervisory board would be appointed by the employees of the SE or their representatives in that company. The political discussions concerning the structure of the SE have therefore many features in common with the difficult negotiations on the proposed Fifth Company Law Directive referred to above.

At the time of writing, it is not possible to evaluate if or when the EC Council would agree on an SE regulation.

2.12   Common Commercial Policy

In the EC Union Treaty tree in figure 2.1 the branch 'Economic and monetary policy' is subdivided into 'Economic policy', 'Monetary policy', 'Provisions governing (EMU) institutions' and 'Common commercial policy'. The first three twigs are dealt with in chapter 3 on the Economic and Monetary Union. In the present chapter, we will accordingly restrict ourselves to some comments on common commercial policy.

A common commercial policy is to be implemented. It is based on uniform principles with respect to changes in tariff rates, conclusion of tariff and trade agreements, export policy and measures to protect trade such as those to be taken in the case of dumping and subsidies. Negotiations with international organizations or third countries are conducted by the Commission within the framework of directives issued by the Council.

The Council has published numerous decisions based on the articles on commercial policy. Only two are mentioned here: *Council Decision of 16 December 1969 on Uniform Trade Agreements between the Member States and Third Countries and on Negotiation about Community Agreement (64/494/EEC)*[30] and *Council Decision of 23 September 1991 on authorization to Continuation of Certain Trade Agreements Concluded between Member States and Third Countries* (91/509/EEC).[31] These decisions are supplemented by a large number of Council regulations on common import arrangements concerning trade with third countries.

2.13   Other EC Measures

The list of EC measures concerning corporate finance dealt with in the present chapter is fairly long. It is, however, not complete. The list will be extended in some of the chapters to follow. Measures related to the Economic and Monetary Union are included in chapter 3. Measures concerning banks and other financial institutions are covered by chapter 5.

Several of the measures mentioned briefly above will of course be dealt with in more detail later. This reflects the central idea of the book that financial decisions made by managers of European companies must respect the existing complicated framework of rules and regulations. In the discussion of financial management to follow the legal environment will be confronted with corporate behaviour and financial instruments and institutions.

Notes

1   *Official Journal of the European Communities (OJ)*, C 26, 1 February 1988, 1.
2   Financial companies with residence in third countries may also benefit from the provisions of article 59 according to which the rules on free exchange of services may be extended by the Council to nationals of a third country who are established within the Community.
3   *OJ*, L 225, 20 August 1990, 6.
4   *OJ*, L 225, 20 August 1990, 1.
5   *OJ*, L 225, 8 August 1990, 10.
6   *OJ*, C 53, 28 January 1991, 26.
7   *OJ*, C 53, 28 February 1991, 30.
8   The GATT agreements contain also a number of provisions for non-discrimination.
9   *OJ*, L 145, 13 June 1977, 1.
10   *OJ*, L 194, 19 July 1978, 16.
11   *OJ*, C 176, 17 July 1990, 8.
12   *OJ*, L 65, 1968, 8.
13   *OJ*, L 26, 1977, 1.
14   *OJ*, L 295, 1978, 36.
15   *OJ*, L 222, 1978, 11.
16   *OJ*, C 240, 1983, 2.
17   *OJ*, L 378, 1982, 47.
18   *OJ*, L 193, 1983, 1.
19   *OJ*, L 126, 1984, 20.
20   *OJ*, C 23, 1985, 11.
21   *OJ*, L 395, 1989, 36.
22   *OJ*, L 395, 1989, 40.
23   *OJ*, C 64, 1989, 8.
24   *OJ*, L 66, 16 March 1979, 21; *OJ*, L 62, 5 March 1982, 22.
25   *OJ*, L 100, 1980, 1; *OJ*, L 124, 5 May 1989, 8; *OJ*, L 112, 3 May 1990, 24.
26   *OJ*, L 48, 1982, 1.
27   *OJ*, L 348, 17 December 1988, 62.
28   *OJ*, C 277, 1989, 13.
29   COM (89) 268 final SYN 219; COM (91) 174 final SYN 218 and 219.
30   *OJ*, L 326, 29 December 1969, 39.
31   *OJ*, L 272, 28 September 1991, 85.

3

From EMS to EMU?

The aim of this chapter is to describe European monetary cooperation. First, there are sections on the history, principles and effects of the existing EMS. The role of central rates, bilateral parity exchange rates and intervention rates is explained. Secondly, the actual and potential applications of the ECU are overviewed. Thirdly, the EMU development so far and the prospects for the years to come are discussed.

3.1   A Twenty-Year Perspective

Let us, initially, try to look at the European currency environment from a 20-year perspective. In the years from 1979 to 1999, the conditions for corporate financial management have undergone and will undergo fundamental changes. Gros and Thygesen (1991) have provided a very readable overview of the development of European monetary integration. The beginning of the period is marked by the start of the European Monetary System (EMS) in March 1979. The end of the period, January 1999, according to the Maastricht Agreement of December 1991 is the latest starting point for stage 3 of the Economic and Monetary Union (EMU). Thus, the 20-year period has been and will be a period of remarkable transition. European companies have had to and probably will have to adjust to a financial environment which is less and less national and more and more European.

So far, the transition process has been gradual. This will probably also be the case for the remaining part of the 20-year period. Financial managers should therefore have time to adjust their instruments and approaches to the steps taken by parliaments, governments, central banks and Community institutions and to the derived effects of these steps in the financial markets.

In the first part of the period, the extended central bank cooperation within the EMS was primarily felt by companies through a reduction in exchange rate volatility. The EMS implied a gradual shift in the focus of corporate exchange exposure management towards exposures in USD, JPY and other non-European currencies (for currency codes see appendix A).

Later, convergence of interest rates and inflation rates in the member states followed. This convergence had implications for investors and borrowers with assets and liabilities denominated in several European currencies. The effects of diversification of portfolios consisting of instruments denominated in EC currencies were reduced. Capital controls were lifted, financial markets became more integrated, and trade flows within the Community were growing. Companies experienced a Europeanization of their customer base, their investor base, their network of suppliers and of course their competitors.

In 1978–9, the European Currency Unit (ECU) was created as a basket of the EC currencies. The ECU was given an official role as the *numéraire* for the central rates of the EMS currencies, as a denominator for the claims and liabilities arising between the central banks as a result of intervention, and as a reserve instrument. Parallel to the official use of the ECU, an increasing number of private market participants chose to use the currency basket in their financial instruments and transactions. This applies in particular to the international bond market.

The EEC Treaty was amended by the Single European Act of 1986. The amendment required the member states, pursuant to article 102A, to cooperate in order to ensure the convergence of economic and monetary policies which is necessary for the further development of the Community.

In the middle of the 20-year period, in 1989, the Delors Report (CSEMU 1989) was published. The report described the steps that could lead to an Economic and Monetary Union. In December 1991 at Maastricht, the EC heads of state or government agreed on a draft Treaty on European Union, which included amendments to the Treaty of Rome concerning an EMU (Bank of England 1992; Deutsche Bundesbank 1992a). As described later, the EC governments agreed on a detailed statute for a European System of Central Banks (ESCB), embracing the existing national central banks and headed by a new institution, the European Central Bank (ECB). A timetable for the establishment of an EMU was included in the agreement.

The Maastricht Agreement cannot enter into force unless all EC member states ratify it. This condition will not be fulfilled because of the majority against the agreement in the Danish referendum of 2 June 1992. A majority of the other countries have, however, declared that they intend to continue their ratification procedures. It is therefore possible that they will sign a new treaty which contains provisions similar to the Treaty on European Union. The position of Denmark (and the UK) in relation to this 'alternative' Treaty on European Union is uncertain. In the following it is assumed that some kind of alternative Treaty will be signed and ratified by a majority of the EC member states.

If this assumption concerning ratification turns out to be realistic and if the agreed timetable for the EMU (perhaps in a modified form) is adhered to, European companies will have to adapt their management goals and techniques to further fundamental changes in the financial environment in the years to come. The prospect of a single European currency has received much publicity. Of course it deserves that publicity from a financial management point of view but there are many other relevant aspects. The prospect also raises a number of important questions whose answers are uncertain. Some of them will be discussed later. At this point, a few are mentioned in order to give the reader a realistic perspective of possible scenarios in the remaining part of the 20-year period. How many member countries will ratify the alternative Treaty and be able to fulfil the agreed convergence criteria and accordingly be eligible to participate in the single-currency scheme from the start? Will the single currency be defined by means of the basket ECU as we know it today or will it be subject to revision before the transition date? What kind of transitory intervention arrangement will be selected for member state currencies that continue to exist after the introduction of the single currency? Will a basket defined ECU continue to exist parallel with a single-currency ECU? At what exchange rates and when will existing claims and obligations denominated in national currencies be transformed to single-currency ECU-denominated assets and liabilities? The outcomes of many financial decisions that are taken today depend on how these questions are answered.

3.2   The History, Purpose and Principles of the EMS

The European Monetary System was formally established by the resolution of 5 December 1978 of the European Council. The system came into operation on 13 March 1979 according to an agreement between the central banks of the member states of the European Economic Community (CGCB 1979: 7–18). At the time of writing, the system is still in operation. According to the agreement on the draft Treaty on European Union concluded in Maastricht in December 1991, the EMS will be replaced by a stronger form of cooperation between the central banks known as an Economic and Monetary Union, in connection with the creation of a European System of Central Banks. Some of the technical aspects will, however, probably survive, and most of the EMS will probably remain in operation during the first two stages of the transition to the EMU. As mentioned above, stage 3 of the EMU is scheduled to start no later than 1 January 1999, but only for those member states that are judged eligible. It is therefore possible that the currencies of the remaining member states will still be managed under an EMS-type intervention arrangement at the start of the next century.

The declared purpose of the EMS was to provide a scheme for the creation of closer monetary cooperation leading to a zone of monetary stability in Europe (CGCB 1979: 43). The 1978 resolution provided that the European Currency Unit should be at the centre of the EMS. The ECU was defined as a basket of agreed amounts of each of the currencies of the member states. The ECU should be used as the denominator (*numéraire*) for the exchange rate mechanism, as the basis for a divergence indicator, as the denominator for operations in both the intervention and the credit mechanisms, and as a means of settlement between monetary authorities of the European Community.

In order to understand the exchange rate mechanism (ERM) of the EMS, it is useful to distinguish between four different types of rates: central rates, bilateral parity exchange rates, intervention rates and market rates quoted daily in the spot market for foreign exchange. According to the 1979 agreement, each participating central bank should initially notify the Secretariat of the Committee of Governors of the Central Banks of the member states of a *central rate* in terms of the ECU for its own currency. Adjustments of central rates are subject to mutual agreement by a common procedure which comprises all member countries and the Commission. Pairs of central rates are used to calculate *bilateral parity exchange rates* between the participating currencies. Around the bilateral parity exchange rates, fluctuation margins of ±2.25 per cent are established. These margins determine the *intervention rates* within which the spot *market rates* are allowed to fluctuate. Countries may temporarily use wider margins up to ±6 per cent. The opportunity to use wider margins was applied by Italy from 1979 to 1990. Spain and Portugal have 6 per cent margins at the time of writing.

The main principle in the exchange rate mechanism of the EMS is that of symmetrical mutual intervention. The intervention rates are calculated in such a way that obligations to intervene arise at the same time for the two central banks involved.

According to the 1978 resolution, interventions were in principle to be made in participating currencies, and intervention in those currencies was made compulsory when the market rates reached the intervention rates. These two rules were gradually modified by the developing intervention practice and subsequent amendments of the agreements. Within the framework of 'concerted action', it soon became common practice for the central banks to intervene also in third country currencies, in particular in USD. Owing to differences in size, it is possible for at least the small EMS countries to change the position of their own currency versus the other EMS currencies by intervening in the American dollar. In recent years, some central banks have to a limited extent intervened by selling or buying ECU-denominated instruments against their own currency (Louw 1991: 134).

Gradually, compulsory intervention on the intervention rates was partially replaced by 'intramarginal intervention'. This implies that the central banks intervene before the market rates reach the intervention rates. The technique makes it possible to smooth out short-term fluctuations in the foreign exchange market as far as EMS currencies are concerned. The formal recognition of the importance of intramarginal intervention was given in the Basle-Nyborg Accord in November 1987. The 'very short-term financing facility', which initially was intended to enable the central banks to finance compulsory intervention, was by the accord also made available, on a voluntary basis, for the financing of intramarginal intervention, thus providing central banks with further lines of credit.

In addition to the described symmetrical mutual intervention in the EMS, there are rules in the 1978 resolution about a 'divergence indicator'. The rationale of this indicator is to introduce an element of asymmetry by putting an adjustment burden on a single member country whose economic performance deviates considerably from the performance of the other countries. The divergence indicator is based on the market value of the ECU basket in terms of each member currency. The market value of the basket is calculated by means of the market rates of the component currencies in terms of the member currency in question. The movements of the relevant bilateral market rates are constrained by the intervention rates. These constraints imply in turn that there are also limits on the movements of the market value of the ECU away from the central rate. The 1978 resolution defines a 'divergence threshold' at 75 per cent of the maximum spread of divergence for each currency. Any movement of a currency beyond the threshold carries a presumption that appropriate action will be taken by the authorities concerned, and only by them. If adequate economic policy measures are not taken, the authorities must explain the reasons for this to the other authorities.

The calculations connected with the divergence indicator are quite complicated and the mechanism is difficult to understand. It may perhaps be a consolation that the indicator gradually lost importance, partly because of the increased reliance on intramarginal intervention. The evolving intervention practice has of course also reduced the importance of obligatory interventions at the intervention rates.

3.3   The Effects of the EMS

There is a very comprehensive academic literature on the performance of the EMS (see Haldane 1991; Cobham 1991). In a performance evaluation it is natural to compare the empirical evidence with the objectives that were formulated in connection with the establishment of the system. As described above, the goal of the EMS was to create a zone of monetary stability in Europe through closer monetary co-operation among the member states. Monetary stability is generally interpreted as having two dimensions, one of price and the other of exchange rate (McDonald and Zis 1989). Accordingly, most of the empirical studies have been concerned with respectively the inflation performance of the member countries and the volatility of exchange rates between the member currencies since 1979. The first group of empirical studies does in general demonstrate that the member countries have converged on lower and more stable rates of inflation, especially since 1983 (see for example Collins 1988). The other group of studies confirms in general an increasing level of stability in intra-EMS exchange rates (Gros 1987).

There has been some discussion of the exact role of the EMS in the decline and convergence of inflation rates in the member states. It has thus been pointed out that the OECD countries outside the EMS in the first half of the 1980s demonstrated an inflation performance similar to that of the EMS countries (Ungerer et al. 1986). The political interest in a convergence towards the inflation performance of Germany has, however, probably been stronger among the EMS countries than among non-participating countries. Pomfret (1991) points out the willingness of the individual member countries to sacrifice some monetary independence in order to support the economic integration process. It is therefore possible that a number of stability-directed measures would not have come into being in the high-inflation member countries without the EMS and the interest in its continued existence (Ungerer 1989).

Appendix B of the book contains the central rates, the bilateral parity exchange rates and the intervention rates of the EMS at 17 September 1992. The appendix shows rates for nine currencies: the Greek drachma (GRD) and the British pound (GBP) do not participate in the exchange rate mechanism, and the rates of the Belgian franc (BEF) and the Luxembourg franc (LUF) are identical. Until 17 September 1992 the British pound (GBP) did participate in the ERM, with ±6 per cent intervention limits. Table 3.1 is based on the mutual rates at 6 April 1992 of three of the most important currencies: the British pound (GBP), the German mark (DEM) and the French franc (FRF). By concentrating

Table 3.1 Exchange rates for three EMS currencies at 6 April 1992

		Frankfurt (DEM)	Paris (FRF)	London (GBP)
Central rate		DEM 2.05586/ECU	FRF 6.89509/ECU	GBP 0.696904/ECU
DEM 100	UIR		FRF 343.050/DEM 100	GBP 35.9970/DEM 100
	BPR		FRF 335.386/DEM 100	GBP 33.8984/DEM 100
	LIR		FRF 327.920/DEM 100	GBP 31.9280/DEM 100
FRF 100	UIR	DEM 30.4950/FRF 100		GBP 10.7320/FRF 100
	BPR	DEM 29.8164/FRF 100		GBP 10.1073/FRF 100
	LIR	DEM 29.1500/FRF 100		GBP 9.5190/FRF 100
GBP 100	UIR	DEM 313.20/GBP 100	FRF 1050.550/GBP 100	
	BPR	DEM 295.00/GBP 100	FRF 989.389/GBP 100	
	LIR	DEM 277.80/GBP 100	FRF 931.800/GBP 100	

DEM	German mark	UIR	Upper intervention rate
FRF	French franc	BPR	Bilateral parity rate
GBP	British pound	LIR	Lower intervention rate
ECU	European currency unit		

Source: Danish Central Bank

on these currencies, we can present a simplified explanation of what the EMS means for a European company.

Suppose that Eurocomp is a German company engaged in trade with France and the United Kingdom. Suppose that FRF and GBP are used as invoice currencies. The financial manager of Eurocomp will then be interested in the maximum and the minimum rates of exchange of FRF and GBP in terms of DEM. These figures may be found in the Frankfurt column of table 3.1. If Eurocomp has GBP-denominated accounts receivable, the FM will note that the exchange rate cannot be lower than DEM 277.80/GBP 100. If Eurocomp has FRF-denominated accounts payable, the FM will note that the exchange rate cannot be higher than DEM 30.495/FRF 100. If Eurocomp is resident in France or the United Kingdom, the rates in the columns for Paris and London may be used in the same way.

The preceding analysis is based on two conditions. The first is that the politically agreed EMS rates are stable within the relevant time horizon. The second is that the three currencies move all the way to the intervention rates. We are therefore in fact ignoring intramarginal intervention. The second condition can only be fulfilled if there is a change in the whole exchange rate structure between the EMS currencies.

Suppose now that the DEM moves alone. We assume again that Eurocomp is located in Germany. Table 3.2 illustrates the scope for exchange rate fluctuations. In the first column we find the current offer and bid exchange rates on 15 October 1991. These rates are market rates. UIR and LIR in the next column indicate respectively upper intervention rate and lower intervention rate from a Frankfurt point of view according to the EMS rates in force. The DEM intervention rates for FRF and GBP were also included in table 3.1. In the third column are indicated the distances from the current market rates to respectively the upper and the lower intervention rates. If a currency is strong in relation to the DEM, the percentage distance to the UIR in table 3.2 will be small. Suppose now that the DEM is depreciated unilaterally versus all the other EMS currencies, while the exchange rate structure among them is unchanged, as in the upper part of table 3.2. If this happens, the movement of the DEM will be stopped by intervention of the Belgian and German central banks, because the distance between the current market rate DEM/BEF and UIR is the smallest (1.95 per cent).

If a currency is weak in relation to the DEM, the percentage distance to the LIR in Frankfurt will be small. It is assumed in the lower part of table 3.2 that the DEM is appreciated unilaterally versus all the other EMS currencies, while their mutual exchange rate structure is

Table 3.2 Scope for fluctuations of three EMS rates against DEM on 15 October 1991

Current offer rate	UIR	% to UIR	Offer rate if max. DEM depreciation
DEM 291.70930/GBP 100	313.20	7.28	DEM 297.46802/GBP 100
DEM 29.37129/FRF 100	30.495	3.76	DEM 29.95111/FRF 100
DEM 4.86414/BEF 100	4.959	1.95	DEM 4.95930/BEF 100

Current bid rate	LIR	% to LIR	Bid rate if max. DEM appreciation
DEM 291.45313/GBP 100	277.80	4.62	DEM 289.55685/GBP 100
DEM 29.34399/FRF 100	29.150	0.65	DEM 29.15307/FRF 100
DEM 4.85437/BEF 100	4.740	2.35	DEM 4.82441/BEF 100

DEM   German mark   UIR   Upper intervention rate
GBP   British pound   LIR   Lower intervention rate
FRF   French franc
BEF   Belgian franc
Source: Unibank A/S, Copenhagen

constant. When this happens, the movement of the DEM will be stopped by intervention of the Banque de France and the Deutsche Bundesbank, because the distance between the current market rate DEM/FRF and LIR is the smallest (0.65 per cent).

If the FM of Eurocomp located in Germany believes that the exchange rate structure between the other EMS currencies will be unchanged in the short run, this can support expectations of a fluctuation margin which is somewhat narrower than the distance between UIR and LIR. On the day on which the data in table 3.2 were collected, the FM would expect the DEM/GBP market rate to fluctuate within the range DEM 297.46802/GBP 100 to DEM 289.55685 and the DEM/FRF rate between DEM 29.95111/FRF 100 and DEM 29.15307/FRF 100.

3.4   Actual and Potential ECU Applications

Pursuant to Council Regulation (1971/89/EEC) of 19 June 1989, the ECU is at present defined as the sum of the components in table 3.3. The present definition causes some problems in connection with its use in contracts among private market participants. The basket structure is according to Council Regulation of 5 December 1978, article 2(3), subject to revision every five years. It follows from the definition as a

Table 3.3 ECU components as at June 1989

Currency[a]	Amount
DEM	0.6242
GBP	0.8784
FRF	1.332
ITL	151.8
NLG	0.2198
BEF	3.301
LUF	0.13
DKK	0.1976
IEP	0.008552
GRD	1.44
ESP	6.885
PTE	1.393

[a] For codes see appendix A.
Source: Danmarks Nationalbank, *Annual Report*

basket with specified amounts of currencies that the weight of each currency depends on the market exchange rates. Devaluing currencies lose weight in the basket while revaluing currencies gain weight. In 1978 it was feared by some of the high-inflation member countries that their currencies would experience declining weights in the ECU, while the German mark would become more and more dominating. The revisions with five-year intervals should prevent such a development, and in 1984 and 1989 the weights of the appreciating currencies were indeed reduced roughly in proportion to the magnitude of their increases due to realignments during the previous five years (Steinherr 1990). When the ECU is used in a private contract, revisions of the basket imply changes in the value of the claims and obligations among the contracting parties. The ECU basket may also be changed in connection with the admission of new member countries to the EC.

In spite of possible concerns over the rules for revision, the number of applications of the ECU has been growing ever since the unit was introduced in 1979. So has the extent of the individual applications. The growth process must be evaluated in the light of the fact that several member countries maintained institutional barriers which limited private lending and borrowing in ECU-denominated instruments (Britton and Mayes 1990). In countries like Denmark, France, Greece, Ireland and Italy, the ECU was treated as a foreign currency and ECU transactions were consequently subject to the remaining foreign exchange restrictions. In Germany, the private use of the ECU was inhibited by an article in the Currency Act which prohibited residents from entering into indexed debt unless explicitly authorized by the Bundesbank (Masera 1987: 9). Since the beginning of stage 1 of the EMU in the summer of 1990, most inhibitions against the private use of the ECU have been abolished. It seems likely that the increase in the use of the ECU will continue into the twenty-first century.

Table 3.4 lists a number of actual and potential ECU applications. (Most of the statistical data on ECU applications in the text may be found in CGCB 1992.) The reader should keep in mind that it is conceivable that there will exist more than one type of ECU in the future. The applications are classified into five main groups: (1) central bank and Community institution applications, (2) financial market applications, (3) commercial and corporate management applications, (4) company law and investor information applications and (5) other applications.

3.4.1   *Central Bank and Community Institution Applications*

As described above, according to the 1979 central bank agreement, the ECU basket is used as the basis for calculation of bilateral parity rates and intervention rates in the EMS. This is application 1.1 in table 3.4. The use of the market value of the ECU basket as a divergence indicator is referred to as application 1.2.

Interventions in the EMS cause credit operations among the central banks. The fact that these credits are denominated in the ECU is called application 1.3. Finally, it is also an original official use of the ECU that settlements of debts between the central banks arising from interventions may take place in ECUs. In addition to this use, application 1.4 also covers the practice that central banks deposited 20 per cent of their gold and 20 per cent of their USD holdings with the European Monetary Cooperation Fund. The central banks received ECU-denominated claims in return for the deposited amounts.

Since 1990, the EC has provided medium-term financial assistance to Eastern and Central European countries. The reason for the inclusion of these arrangements in table 3.4 as application 1.5 is that the loans are predominantly denominated in ECU. In addition, the unit is applied in the Community's support mechanism for member states' balance of payments problems.

The European Investment Bank (EIB) uses ECU in several ways. In table 3.4 these are referred to as application 1.6. The capital of the institution is denominated in ECU and a majority of the member states who are the shareholders have replaced their original capital contributions in national currencies with contributions in ECUs (Orbañanos

Table 3.4 ECU applications

1 *Central bank and Community institution applications*
   1.1 Basis for definition of intervention obligations
   1.2 Basis for calculation of divergence indicator
   1.3 Denominator for credits among central banks
   1.4 Reserve instrument and means of settlement among central banks
   1.5 Community assistance and support arrangements
   1.6 European Investment Bank applications
   1.7 Denomination of the Community budget etc.
   1.8 EC structural funds and the European Development Fund
   1.9 Exchange rate peg for non-EC currencies
   1.10 Link to international exchange rate system
   1.11 Notes and coins

2 *Financial market applications*
   2.1 Bank deposits and loans
   2.2 Clearing system for payments
   2.3 Bonds
   2.4 Treasury bills
   2.5 Commercial paper
   2.6 Currency and interest rate swaps
   2.7 Currency and interest rate futures
   2.8 Currency and interest rate options

3 *Commercial and corporate management applications*
   3.1 Prices for goods and services
   3.2 Contract and invoice currency in foreign trade
   3.3 Means of commercial payments
   3.4 Internal accounting unit for groups of companies

4 *Company law and investor information applications*
   4.1 Minimum capital requirements
   4.2 Unit in disclosure of accounting information
   4.3 Denomination of equity capital
   4.4 Unit in stock exchange quotations

5 *Other applications*
   5.1 Means of tax payments
   5.2 Unit in land registers

1991). The EIB's borrowing and lending activities in ECU are covered by the statistics referred to under financial market applications below in section 3.4.2. The recently established European Bank for Reconstruction and Development applies ECU in almost the same ways as the EIB (Dunnett 1991).

The budget of the EC is denominated in ECU. Application 1.7 is governed by a so-called Financial Regulation which provides for the use of the ECU as a unit of account but does not accord it the function of unit of denomination or means of settlement. The Commission has proposed that all financial rights and obligations of the Community could be expressed in ECU. This principle has so far been accepted by the Council in relation to application 1.8, the EC structural funds. Since 1990, payments under the structural funds have been executed in ECUs. The Commission pays experts and consultants and finances external aid programmes, research and cooperation with third countries in ECUs. In 1990, 22.7 per cent of the EC General Budget gave rise to payments in ECUs.

In October 1990, Norway decided to link the Norwegian krone (NOK) to the ECU. In May and June of 1991, Sweden and Finland took the same step. In September 1992, the Finnish government decided to let the FIM float. According to the Hungarian Minister of Finance Mihaly Kupa (1991), application 1.9 is seriously considered by some East European countries as well.

Article 109 of the EC Treaty of Union contains rules according to which the Council under certain conditions may conclude formal agreements on an exchange rate system for the ECU in relation to non-Community currencies. In the absence of an exchange rate system, the Council may formulate general orientations for exchange rate policy in relation to non-EC currencies. The provisions, which are referred to here as application 1.10, demonstrate clearly that in stage 3 of the EMU the ECU will play a very decisive role in prospective international exchange rate agreements with the United States, Japan and other non-EC countries.

The public has an inclination to identify money with its physical representation in the form of coins and notes (Louw 1991: 130). These means of payment are traditionally provided with pictures of kings, queens or other national symbols and the prospect of their disappearance in connection with a transition to EMU gives rise to strong feelings. In fact, notes and coins represent only a small share of the money supply in most modern countries. In technical terms, it is conceivable that interchangeable ECU notes and coins will circulate in the Europe of the year 2000 bearing the heads of different national worthies (Johnson 1990).

Article 105A of the EC Treaty of Union gives the ECB the exclusive right to authorize the issue of bank notes within the Community. The ECB and the national central banks may issue such notes, which are proposed to be the only notes to have the status of legal tender within the Community (Louis and De Lhoneux 1991). The bank notes will be denominated in ECU, and this is referred to here as application 1.11. The European Monetary Institute (EMI) is in article 109F given the task of supervising the technical preparation of ECU bank notes.

3.4.2 *Financial Market Applications*

ECU transactions play a considerable role in international bank inter-mediation. The share of the ECU may be assessed on the basis of outstanding amounts or on the basis of flows through the banking system. In its most recently published statistical review, the BIS pre-ferred to look at the outstanding stocks (CGCB 1992: 5). The ECU's share of bank liabilities and bank assets in the foreign currency sector has risen modestly to a level of approximately 4 per cent at the end of the third quarter of 1991. On the liabilities side, the ECU has moved up to third place behind USD and DEM. On the assets side it ranks as number four behind JPY.

The BIS statistics illuminate a number of structural features of ECU application 2.1 in table 3.4. Interbank claims and obligations dominate in banks' ECU balance sheets as they do in items denominated in other currencies. The share of non-banks has, however, increased to a level of approximately 26 per cent at the end of the third quarter of 1991. The degree of internationalization is measured by the share of cross-border business. This share is about 80 per cent in the interbank sector and about 60 per cent in the non-bank sector. With respect to the geographical distribution of ECU bank intermediation, it seems to be companies and investors resident in Italy, the UK, France, Spain and Belgium/Luxembourg who are the most active borrowers and depositors in the market for ECU bank loans and deposits.

At the end of the third quarter of 1991, the banks covered by the BIS statistics on international banking developments had ECU-denominated liabilities of approximately ECU 150 billion, a considerable part of it deposited in sight accounts. In order to be able to apply amounts de-posited in ECU sight accounts for payment purposes, it is necessary to have a clearing system. Clearing of ECU payments was in 1991 performed by 45 commercial banks belonging to the ECU Banking Association (EBA) under the aegis of the BIS and with support from the Society for Worldwide Interbank Financial Telecommunication (SWIFT) (Haberer 1991). The number of cleared transactions was approximately 120,000 per month, representing a volume of ECU 800 million.

The SWIFT network is used for the transmission of payment orders denominated in many different currencies. ECU payment orders are copied automatically and stored in one of SWIFT's computers in Belgium. Once every day, data from the ECU payments are used by SWIFT to calculate the net debit or credit position in ECUs of each clearing bank towards all the others. Each participating bank is informed of its own balance and the BIS receives a complete survey. The BIS keeps a record of the credit and debit positions and carries out the daily settlement operations. Originally, the settlements were based on ECU deposits given by the clearing banks and taken by the BIS, but gradually the settlement of balances has been facilitated by overnight borrowing. The ECU clearing system is a 'wholesale' system designed for the handling of big payments. An increase in the commercial applications of the ECU will necessitate reforms of the clearing system and links with the national payment systems (Louw 1991: 140).

The growth of the issue of ECU-denominated bonds – application 2.3 – is impressive. From the end of 1987 to the third quarter of 1991, the outstanding stock of ECU-denominated bonds in the international bond market grew from ECU 31.5 billion to ECU 72.2 billion. The latter figure corresponds to 5.8 per cent of the total outstanding. In addition, the issue of ECU-denominated securities grew on the domestic capital markets. One of the ECU characteristics that makes application 2.3 attractive from the point of view of borrowers and investors is the relative stability of the value of the basket in relation to the individual member state currencies (Salojarvi 1991).

The distribution of ECU bond issues by category of borrower shows that EC governments have issued about 45 per cent, borrowers in the business sectors (both EC and other) about 33 per cent, and EC institutions 11 per cent. The remaining issues were made by non-EC governments, non-EC institutions and international organizations. The geographical breakdown of ECU bond issues shows that the biggest amounts are issued by borrowers resident in Italy, France, the UK, Greece and Belgium/Luxembourg. The EC Secretariat collects information on the turnover of Eurosecurities from Euroclear and CEDEL. The turnover-based ranking of the most important currencies of denomination was in 1991 USD, ECU, DEM, JPY and GBP.

The issue of ECU-denominated government securities comprises not only long-term bonds but also short-term securities like treasury bills. The governments of France, Italy, Ireland and the United Kingdom have all included application 2.4 in their public debt. The British government manages a programme of regular monthly issues of ECU treasury bills. Ariane Obolensky (1991) has explained the reasons why the French government has expanded the issue of ECU-denominated securities.

Note issuance facilities have to an increasing extent enabled borrowers to issue commercial paper or Euronotes denominated in ECU. According to data compiled by the BIS, the ECU's share of outstanding Euronotes at the end of the third quarter of 1991 was ECU 9.5 billion or 8.6 per cent. It seems likely that big European companies with geographically diversified operations and a high credit standing will expand their use of application 2.5 as a convenient and flexible way of short-term financing.

The International Swaps Dealers Association (ISDA) compiles statistics on swaps. The currency swaps in which the parties acquire the right to receive or the right to dispose of a series of ECU payments – application 2.6 – were in 1990 in most cases linked to ECU bond issues. The opposite payments were mainly in USD and DEM. The most active market participants were financial institutions, national governments and supranational institutions.

An ECU interest rate swap is an interest rate risk management instrument. Typically, the instrument is applied by a market participant who wants to change a commitment to pay a series of payments determined by a fixed ECU interest rate to a series of payments linked to a variable ECU interest rate or vice versa. The most frequent maturities range, according to the ISDA statistics, from one to five years.

On the French futures exchange MATIF and on LIFFE in London, there is a considerable turnover in futures contracts with ECU-denominated bonds as underlying assets or based on the three-month ECU interest rate. The statistics on the futures exchanges shows that application 2.7 is growing.

The market for options that provide the holder with the right to buy or to sell ECU-denominated assets is fairly new. On MATIF, an options contract on ECU futures was introduced in April 1991 (Pezet 1991).

3.4.3 Commercial and Corporate Management Applications

Application 3.1 covers the publication by companies of price lists in ECU. At the time of writing, this application is definitely the exception. The main rule is that companies with Europe-wide operations publish price lists in the most important national currencies. The frequency by which such lists have to be revised depends on inflation rates and exchange rate changes. As explained later, a transition to one currency in the Community will make the market for goods and services much more transparent and thus simplify marketing procedures. The statistical data on the use of the ECU for invoicing in international trade are limited and incomplete. According to foreign trade data gathered by BIS, application 3.2 remains stable but low. The combined percentage share of ECU-denominated foreign trade was below 1 per cent in 1991, but in the export figures from Spain, Italy and Portugal the shares were higher. The share of ECU-denominated transactions is higher in the current-account flows than in the trade-account flows because of Community transfers in ECUs and interest payments.

The existing private ECU clearing system was described briefly in connection with application 2.2. It was characterized as a wholesale system for large payments. Through the participating banks, it is possible to settle debts denominated in ECU. There is, however, a long way to go before smaller European companies can use ECUs for their mutual commercial payments, i.e. application 3.3.

Travellers in Europe have for some years had the opportunity to use credit cards and traveller's cheques in ECU, and other cheques may also be denominated in ECU. The actual payment must, however, normally take place in national currency.

International groups of companies may consider the ECU as a unit for internal accounting and reporting purposes. There seems to be a tradition for the application of the parent company's home currency as currency of reference for the group, but groups with entities in several European countries could consider the advantages of application 3.4.

3.4.4   Company Law and Investor Information Applications

As mentioned in chapter 2, the Second Company Law Directive (77/91/EEC) with later amendments contains minimum capital requirements expressed in ECU. In the administration of the national company laws into which these provisions are incorporated, the capital requirements are translated into national currency, but companies could in the future be authorized to denominate their capital and to issue their shares in ECUs (Louw 1991: 140).

The Fourth and the Seventh Company Law Directives (78/660/EEC and 83/349/EEC) with later amendments both contain provisions for the publication of accounts in ECU. The Council Directive of 8 November 1990[2] exempts small and medium companies from some of the disclosure obligations. From the point of view of stock market efficiency, the increased transparency and comparability due to ECU-denominated company information are beneficial. Companies that want to broaden their investor base in Europe can probably see that it is in their own interest to disclose such information, i.e. application 4.2.

If companies are allowed to issue shares in ECU, the next logical step in the direction of increased stock market transparency would be to allow stock exchanges to apply the unit in their official quotations.

3.4.5 *Other Applications*

Today, taxes are calculated in and must be paid in national currency in all EC member states. After the transition to stage 3 of EMU, taxes will have to be paid in ECUs. One might expect that national governments will gradually increase the use of ECU in official documents and allow their taxpayers to pay their taxes in ECUs, i.e. application 5.1. The realism of the idea should be evaluated in connection with the ongoing process with an increasing use of ECU-denominated public debt. Many member state authorities are already involved in large amounts of financial ECU transactions. At a certain stage, it will probably also be appropriate to consider the use of the ECU as a unit in land registers (application 5.2) or in other registers of important assets.

3.5   The First Stage of EMU

In its report of April 1989, the Delors Committee recommended a transition to an Economic and Monetary Union in three stages (CSEMU 1989). At its meeting in Madrid in June 1989, the European Council decided that the first stage of the realization of the EMU should begin on 1 July 1990. The legal framework for the closer coordination it was intended to bring about was laid down by the Council of Finance Ministers in March 1990 in a decision on the attainment of progressive convergence of economic policies and performance (90/141/EEC). The 1990 decision replaced a council decision of 1974 on economic convergence (74/120/EEC). Later in Dublin in the summer of 1990, the European Council agreed that an intergovernmental conference of EC member states should be convened on 13 December 1990 to discuss the amendments of the EEC Treaty necessary for the completion of the EMU. According to the published timetable, the amendments of the EEC Treaty agreed upon by the EC governments at Maastricht in December 1991 should be ratified by national parliaments before the end of 1992. As mentioned earlier, it has become impossible for the Danish Parliament to ratify the treaty amendments after the June 1992 referendum.

The 1990 decision applies the principle of multilateral surveillance. At least twice a year, the Council of Ministers will evaluate all aspects of economic policy in the member states. The surveillance encompasses economic performance, the compatibility of economic policies within the Community and the impact of global economic fundamentals. In addition to the general surveillance of developments in the Community, regular country reviews of national economic conditions and prospects and the policies of individual member states are also envisaged. With respect to fiscal policy, a review of the size and financing of budget deficits is to take place ahead of national budgetary planning. The aim should be to reduce excessively high deficits and avoid monetary financing. The importance of fiscal discipline has been stressed again and again, in particular by the Deutsche Bundesbank (1990).

During the first stage of the EMU, the member states are in fact taking part in a training process. The Council is given the right to make economic policy suggestions and recommendations to them individually, and their reactions to this will give strong indications of the strength of the will to integrate further within the Community. The 1990 Council decision provides for an annual report that is to be drawn up by the Council on the overall economic situation in the Community. After consulting the European Parliament and the Economic and Social Committee, the report will be adopted by the Council.

The role and functions of the Committee of Governors of the Central Banks have been extended by an amendment on 12 March 1990 to the Council Decision (64/300/EEC) on cooperation between the central banks of the EC member states. The new Council decision gives explicit priority to the goal of domestic price stability. The Committee is to hold consultations not only on the general principles and broad lines of central bank policy, but also on issues affecting the stability of financial markets and financial institutions to the extent that these issues fall within the competence of central banks. The central banks are to exchange information regularly about their most important measures. If major decisions are to be taken, such as the annual setting of national money supply and credit targets, the Committee is normally to be consulted in advance. Coordination of member states' monetary policies is to be promoted with the aim of achieving price stability as a necessary condition for the proper functioning of the EMS and the realization of its objectives of monetary stability.

The Committee has studied ways of establishing a common system of surveillance over monetary policies. One of the difficulties of presenting conceptional comparable intermediate targets is that monetary aggregates vary among countries, partly because the structures of national financial markets differ widely.

In the Protocol on the Statute of the European Monetary Institute which the member state governments agreed upon in Maastricht, it was laid down that both the Committee of Governors and the European

Monetary Cooperation Fund should be dissolved. The functions of the two bodies are to be transferred to the EMI which will later be replaced by the European Central Bank. During the transition period the task of strengthening the coordination of the monetary policies of the member states will therefore be the responsibility of the EMI. Tietmeyer (1990) has described some of the conditions that should be fulfilled before a European System of Central Banks can be established.

3.6   Convergence Criteria and EMU Timetable

At the Maastricht meeting in December 1991, the EC heads of state or government agreed on an EC Treaty of Union. The Treaty contains a long series of amendments to the most important of the three existing EC Treaties, namely the EEC Treaty of 1957 (The Treaty of Rome). The provisions for an EMU are included in articles 102A–109K. The draft Treaty was signed on 7 February 1992. The Treaty was scheduled to enter into force on 1 January 1993 but it seems likely that it will be delayed owing to ratification problems.

The second stage of EMU should start on 1 January 1994. Before that date, the member states are expected to initiate so-called programmes of convergence in order to ensure the sustainable economic convergence which is necessary for the realization of EMU. The programmes aim in particular at a reduction of the inflation rate and of government deficits. From the beginning of stage 2, the member states have to adapt their fiscal policies to a number of rules. It will no longer be permissible to finance government deficits by borrowing in the central bank. According to article 104A, the Community will not be liable for or assume the commitments of central governments, regional or local authorities or public undertakings of any member state, and a member state will not be liable for or assume the commitments of governments or other public authorities of another member state. The provision has been called a 'no-bail-out clause'. The aim of the clause is of course to maintain fiscal discipline. Gros and Thygesen (1991: chapter 8) have discussed the temptation for weak governments to refrain from unpopular cuts in public expenditures or tax increases when the financing of external deficits becomes easier in EMU.

At the start of the second stage, the European Monetary Institute will be established and take up its duties. The EMI will, as mentioned in the previous section, replace the Committee of Governors of the Central Banks of the member states.

If by the end of 1997 the date for the beginning of the third stage has not been set, the third stage will, according to article 109F, paragraph 4, start on 1 January 1999. But the heads of state and government may decide by qualified majority, on the basis of recommendations by the Council and after consulting the European Parliament, that a majority of member states fulfil the necessary conditions, and set an earlier date for the start of stage 3.

These provisions imply that the starting date for stage 3 is uncertain. So is the number of member states that will participate from the beginning. Much depends on the criteria which will be applied by the EC institutions and on the political will of the governments and parliaments (Hoffmeyer 1992). The Deutsche Bundesbank has warned against a softening of the criteria for participation in the monetary union owing to political considerations (Tietmeyer 1992).

Article 109F of the Treaty obliges the Commission and the EMI to report to the Council on the progress made in the fulfilment by the member states of the criteria for participation in stage 3 of the EMU. There will be two main subjects in the reports. The first is the compatibility between a member state's legislation, in particular with regard to the status and role of its central bank, and the provisions of the treaty relating to ECB and national central bank independence. The second subject is the fulfillment by each member state of a set of convergence criteria. At Maastricht, a separate protocol on the convergence criteria was signed. Table 3.5 summarizes the four convergence criteria.

Figure 3.1 illustrates the convergence situation at the end of 1991. According to the data applied, which are not completely correct in view of the protocol, only two countries, Luxembourg (L) and France (F), fulfilled all the convergence criteria at that time. This is illustrated geometrically by the fact that all four points relating to the economic performance of each of Luxembourg and France lie inside the so-called 'convergence rectangle' (points are not shown in the third and fourth quadrants for Luxembourg because that country had a government surplus on 1991). The rectangle is demarcated by the price inflation criterion line (PICL), the interest rate criterion line (IRCL), the government deficit criterion line (GDCL) and the (public) debt criterion line. According to the Danish central bank, which provided the data for the figure, the Danish performance would have been reflected in all DK points lying within the convergence rectangle if the data had been completely adapted to the provisions in the protocol.

The performance of the other member states can be described with reference to the number of points lying outside the convergence rectangle. Many outliers far from the sides of the rectangle reflect a considerable need for macroeconomic adjustment for the country concerned. The points for Germany (D) lie outside the GDCL but inside the other three lines, i.e. the German government deficit is a little too

Table 3.5 The 1991 protocol on convergence criteria

Criterion on inflation
The criterion means that member states shall have a price performance that
is sustainable and an average rate of inflation, observed over a period of
one year before the examination, that does not exceed that of at most the
three best performing member states in terms of price stability by more
than 1.5 per cent. Inflation is to be measured by the consumer price index
on a comparable basis, taking into account differences in national
definitions.

Criterion on the government budgetary position
The criterion means that at the time of the examination the member state
is not the subject of a Council decision as referred to in article 104B,
paragraph 6, that an excessive deficit exists for the member state
concerned. Article 104B refers to a special protocol on the excessive deficit
procedure. The protocol specifies two reference values: 3 per cent for the
ratio of the planned or actual government deficit to gross domestic product
(GDP) at market prices, and 60 per cent for the ratio of government debt
to GDP at market prices. Government means general government. Deficit
means net lending as defined in the European System of Integrated
Economic Accounts. Debt means total gross debt at nominal value
outstanding at the end of the year and consolidated between and within
the sectors of general government.

Criterion on participation in the ERM
The criterion means that a member state has respected the normal EMS
fluctuation margins without severe tensions for at least the last two years
before the examination. In particular the member state will not have
devalued its currency's bilateral central rate against any other member
state's currency on its own initiative for the same period.

Criterion on interest rates
The criterion means that observed over a period of one year before the
examination a member state has an average nominal long-term interest rate
that does not exceed that of at most the three best performing member
states in terms of price stability by more than 2 per cent. Interest rates are
to be measured on the basis of long-term government bonds or comparable
securities, taking into account differences in national definitions.

---

*Source: Protocol of 11 December 1991 on the Convergence Criteria as Mentioned in article
    109F of the EC Treaty of Union*

Figure 3.1 Convergence rectangle at the end of 1991

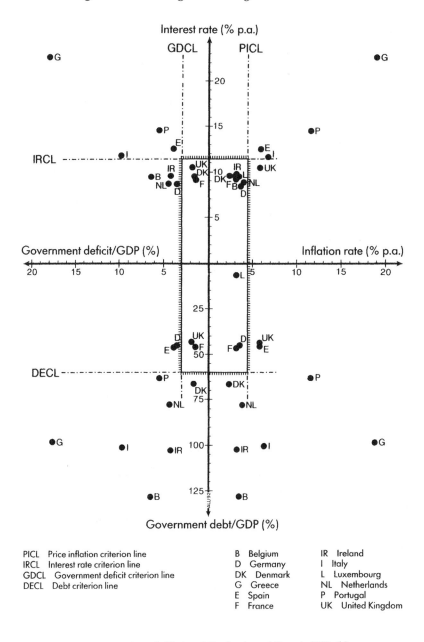

PICL   Price inflation criterion line
IRCL   Interest rate criterion line
GDCL   Government deficit criterion line
DECL   Debt criterion line

B   Belgium
D   Germany
DK   Denmark
G   Greece
E   Spain
F   France

IR   Ireland
I   Italy
L   Luxembourg
NL   Netherlands
P   Portugal
UK   United Kingdom

Source: Danish National Bank, *Annual Report*, 1991, 14

large in relation to the German GDP, but the country is fairly close to fulfilment of the convergence criteria. The performance points for the Netherlands (NL) lie outside the GDCL and the DECL, i.e. both the government deficit and the government debt are too large in relation to the GDP to fulfil the criteria. The adjustments needed seem, however, to be modest. The United Kingdom (UK) and Spain (E) did not at the end of 1991 fulfil the criterion on participation in the ERM (see table 3.5), which is not included in figure 3.1. An evaluation of the macroeconomic performance of these two countries based on figure 3.1 shows, however, that their points are only partly outside the convergence rectangle. The UK points lie outside the PICL line but inside the other three lines. The Spanish performance points lie outside the PICL, IRCL and GDCL lines but inside the DECL line. The points of Ireland (IR) and Belgium (B) lie inside the PICL and IRCL lines but outside the GDCL and DECL lines. Both countries have a remarkably high government debt in relation to their GDPs.

Finally, there are member countries whose macroeconomic performance is characterized by the observation that they did not at the end of 1991 fulfil any of the convergence criteria. That applies to Greece (G), Italy (I) and Portugal (P). These countries have to go through a very thorough adjustment process before they can be deemed eligible to participate in stage 3 of the EMU. In 1991 Robin Leigh-Pemberton, Governor of the Bank of England, in a speech in Italy expressed in a polite way that the Italian government had important structural and budgetary problems to cope with.

In evaluating the European macroeconomic convergence process in the years to come, one should keep in mind that the size of the convergence rectangle depends on the development of the three best performing member countries. If their inflation rates converge towards zero, the right hand side of the rectangle moves to the left. If their interest levels decrease, the upper border of the rectangle will move downwards. Such reductions of the rectangle will of course make it more difficult for the other member countries to fulfil the convergence criteria. Should the performance of the core countries deteriorate, however, this will facilitate the adjustment task of the authorities in the high-inflation member countries.

3.7 Macroeconomic Benefits and Costs of EMU

It seems appropriate to conclude the chapter with a summary of the expected macroeconomic advantages and disadvantages of the transition to EMU. One of the best sources at hand is the Commission's own monumental report (Commission of the EC 1990a) which contains a thorough appraisal of the likely economic effects of the move to EMU. Emerson and Huhne (1991) have written a popular version of the Commission's report. Goodhart (1991) has produced an excellent and short overview of the main points in the Commission's report, as have Carré and Johnson (1991).

We must of course first ask what kind of final situation the transition process is supposed to end with. The fundamental premise of the Delors Report and the Maastricht Agreement on EMU is that monetary union is the final objective. A monetary union is, in accordance with the 1970 Werner Report, defined as an area in which there is total and irreversible convertibility of currencies, complete liberalization of capital transactions and full integration of financial markets, and elimination of margins of fluctuation and irrevocable locking of exchange rate parities. At the time of writing, the convertibility condition and the liberalization condition were already fulfilled or about to be fulfilled with the completion of the internal market programme (Leigh-Pemberton 1990). There are, however, many steps to take before the exchange rate policy condition is fulfilled.

The Delors Report was not very specific with regard to the transition process (Giovannini 1990). The time schedule was left to be decided by the national governments. According to the Committee, economic and monetary union form two integral parts of a single whole. They should therefore be implemented in parallel, and the speed of monetary convergence should be adapted to the development of economic convergence. It takes time to implement competition and structural policies and to coordinate macroeconomic policies, so the Committee preferred not to set up a rigid timetable, which would probably have to be discarded because of unforeseeable events. In contrast, the European Parliament in its 1989 resolution on Economic and Monetary Union set out a precise timetable (Jacobs 1991). As mentioned above, the Maastricht Agreement specified a timetable with some flexibility with respect to the transition to stage 3. At the time of writing, it is an open question to what extent the agreed timetable will be kept.

In its 1990 report on the implications of an EMU, the Commission stresses the importance of establishing a clearly structured conceptual framework within which the effects can be analysed (Commission of the EC 1990a: 18). The effects are classified into systemic changes, policy changes, behavioural changes and final economic impacts. In connection with *systemic changes*, the Commission mentions changes to the economic constitution. This involves a new single currency (called ECU), a new central banking system, a completed single market, and rules for national government budgets. *Policy changes* are not confined to monetary policy but encompass also other kinds of economic policy. The new central banking system should play a decisive role in the management of monetary policy. Fiscal policy, still conducted by the national authorities, should gradually be subjected to agreed constraints. *Behavioural changes* refer to the decisions of firms, households, trade unions and financial institutions. These private agents will go through a learning process during which they will adapt not only to the single market, the single currency and other systemic changes but also to a new mechanism for setting of political priorities. When the Commission applies the term *final economic impacts*, it refers to microeconomic efficiency, macroeconomic stability, and equity between countries and regions.

The benefits and costs of EMU are according to the Commission generated by the 16 mechanisms listed in table 3.6. Referring to mechanism 1, which is the first of four concerning efficiency and growth, the Commission points out the remaining volatility between the EC currencies. On a monthly basis this volatility is estimated to be 0.7 per cent for the currencies participating in the exchange rate mechanism. The EMU could therefore potentially eliminate this volatility and consequently reduce exchange rate uncertainty. Andersen and Sørensen (1991) explain how exchange rate uncertainty causes interest rate differentials among the EMS currencies and how the EMU can contribute to a further reduction of those differentials.

Transaction costs in the foreign exchange market (mechanism 2) vary substantially depending on who the agents are and on the size of the transactions. Large interbank transactions have very small transaction costs, while costs are higher in connection with small bank transfers and transactions in bank notes. After having taken into consideration the in-house costs for companies involved in intra-European trade, the Commission estimates overall transaction costs to amount to approximately 0.5 per cent of GDP. At the time of writing, this corresponded to close to ECU 20 billion per year. The potential savings on transaction costs will be relatively larger for residents in small countries with less widely used currencies. The counterpart to these savings for companies engaged in intra-Community trade etc. will be a reduction in the gross income of the financial services sector.

Mechanism 3, building on 1992, concerns that part of the economic union which goes beyond the internal market. The Commission finds it appropriate to assign more economic policy functions to the Community level wherever this is necessary to achieve all the economic gains from market integration. Competition policy, trade policy, and control of state subsidies are mentioned as relevant areas. The transfer

Table 3.6   Economic mechanisms generating benefits and costs of EMU

Efficiency and growth
  1   Exchange rate variability and uncertainty
  2   Exchange transaction costs
  3   Extending 1992 to economic union
  4   Dynamic gains

Price stability
  5   Price discipline
  6   Institutions conducive to stability-oriented monetary policy
  7   Transitional costs of disinflation

Public finance
  8   Autonomy, discipline, coordination
  9   Lower interest rate costs (less seigniorage losses)
 10   Public sector efficiency

Adjustment without exchange rate changes
 11   Loss of nominal exchange rate instrument
 12   Adjustment of real wage levels
 13   Lesser country-specific shocks
 14   Removal of external constraints

International system
 15   ECU as international currency
 16   Improved international coordination

Source: One market, one money, *European Economy*, 1990, no. 44, Brussels: Commission
    of the European Communities

of economic policy functions to the Community level should of course
take place in the light of the principle of subsidiarity, i.e. that tasks
should be assigned to the lowest level of government unless welfare
gains can be reaped by assigning them to a higher level.

From a national point of view, the transfer is often called 'loss of
sovereignty' (Gaddum 1992). Those who oppose moves in the direction of a more unified and centralized Europe will of course not classify mechanism 3 as an EMU benefit. Eltis (1991) has expressed serious
concerns with respect to a transition to monetary policy decision
making at the Community level.

Mechanism 4 in table 3.6 refers to gains that go beyond the once and
for all gains due to step improvements in economic efficiency and
welfare. The diminished exchange rate risk and the improved price
transparency in the EMU may thus stimulate investment with positive implications for economic growth (Baldwin 1990). It is also

conceivable that the EMU should reduce the overall uncertainty that affects investment in the Community.

Mechanisms 5, 6 and 7 are all related to price stability. The primary objective of the European System of Central Banks is to be to secure price stability. Referring to mechanism 5, the Commission rejects the traditional theory that there is a trade-off between high inflation and low unemployment. As the Commission sees the evidence, the post-war macroeconomic experience of the industrialized world suggests that, on average, high-inflation countries have a higher unemployment rate and a lower income per capita than low-inflation countries. Despite the difficulties in establishing an overall analytical basis on which to measure the costs of inflation there is, according to the Commission, wide agreement that inflation does cause considerable costs. The costs depend on the extent to which the inflation is anticipated by the market participants. Higher inflation and therefore also higher variability of inflation lead to higher variability in relative prices and may cause welfare losses in much the same way as exchange rate volatility (Neumann and Von Hagen 1991).

Mechanism 6 concerns institutional factors conducive to price stability. It will improve the credibility of the monetary policy that the ESCB is given a statutory mandate to aim at price stability. An open issue in this context is the definition of the price index which the ESCB should stabilize. At the European level, prices can diverge much more than inside each of the member countries. A choice will have to be made for instance between a consumer price index and a producer price index. Having made that choice, the next step must be to select a weighting system which in an appropriate way represents the economic importance of the underlying transactions in the Community.

There is an important connection between the mandate of the ESCB with respect to price stabilization and mechanism 15 on the role of the ECU in the international monetary system. In stage 3, the ESCB will take over the responsibility for interventions in the foreign exchange market. The choice of exchange rate regime as such should, according to article 109 of the EC Treaty of Union, be left to the appropriate democratically legitimated Community institutions, but in order to be able to pursue the goal of price stability, the ESCB will have to have some independence in its management of the exchange rates versus third country currencies. The day-to-day intervention must respect the limits implied by the exchange rate regime that has been decided at the political level.

Disinflation can be associated with temporary losses of output. The economies of high-inflation countries have to go through a transitional period in order to achieve a low-inflation environment. In connection with this mechanism 7, the Commission stresses the importance of a strong political commitment to a central banking system, which itself has a reputation for price stability. It is essential to change the inflation expectations of the market participants (Jaillet 1991).

Mechanism 8 is the first of three concerning public finance. As monetary policy instruments are gradually transferred from the national to the Community level, the need for national fiscal policy instruments increases. This need may well conflict with the need to intensify budgetary discipline. Financial market integration gives national authorities access to borrowing in a much broader financial market, and the external current account disappears as a direct financial constraint. In its discussion of the matter, the Commission emphasizes the effectiveness of market discipline, i.e. the ability of markets to evaluate correctly default risk premiums and to trigger the appropriate response in the case of government borrowing (Commission of the EC 1990a: 112). The Commission fears that market discipline will not be sufficient, owing to expectations of Community assistance to member states with a high debt ratio and/or inadequate response of government to market signals. The conclusion is therefore that there is a case for addressing the risk of failures of market discipline through Community rules and procedures. As described above, fiscal discipline has been included in the convergence criteria in the Maastricht Agreement.

Mechanism 9 concerns the combined effect of lower interest rates on public debt servicing and seigniorage, i.e. the profits from the issue of currency. When, in the EMU, issue of currencies at the national level will be replaced by issue of ECUs at the Community level, rules for the distribution of this profit to the member states will have to be established. Seigniorage is only a major source of government revenues in high-inflation economies. Calculations made by the Commission on data from the end of the 1980s suggest that revenue losses will primarily be a concern for Greece, Portugal, Spain and Italy.

If the ESCB should prove a strong anchor for price stability, there are good reasons to expect interest rates to be lower. Nominal interest rates will reflect lower expected inflation. The disappearance of concern for future realignments between the EMS currencies will put a downward pressure on the interest level in the high-inflation member countries.

EMU will intensify competitive pressures on taxes on mobile factors and perhaps also on certain public expenditures. In connection with mechanism 10, the Commission uses a basic model in which goods, capital and citizens can and do move freely across national frontiers. Citizens are assumed to have full information, and private as well as non-private goods and services are produced under competitive conditions. Under such idealized circumstances, citizens could 'vote with their feet' by moving from one jurisdiction to another in order to select the package of goods and services and related taxation that suits them best. The mobility factor will therefore subject the public sector to a requirement of efficiency.

The model raises the issue of externalities. In the tax field, the possible migration of tax bases must be taken into consideration. While labour mobility can be expected to remain relatively low within the Community at least across language frontiers, capital mobility and mobility of goods will be very high. Consequently mechanism 10 will in particular be relevant in the case of capital income taxation, corporate taxation and indirect taxation (Giovannini 1989). In the absence of coordination, such externalities would put pressure on member countries to choose relatively low tax rates on mobile tax bases.

Mechanisms 11 to 14 concern adjustment without exchange rate changes. The Commission raises in the 1990 report the question of how serious it is for the member states to lose the exchange rate as a policy instrument. The Commission's own answer to this question is in relation to mechanism 11 that the fixing of exchange rates within the Community represents, at worst, only a very limited loss. It will still be possible for the Community as a whole to change the exchange rate of the ECU with respect to the rest of the world. The EMS member countries have more or less already adjusted to the fixed bilateral parity exchange rates. As the Commission sees the evidence, changes in nominal exchange rates within the EMS have historically primarily served to offset differences in inflation rates. However, other observers conclude that the realignments of the EMS have not served to maintain competitiveness between the member countries (Edison and Fisher 1991).

Adjustments in competitiveness can take place through prices and wages instead of through exchange rates (mechanism 12). The flexibility of the labour market is essential in this connection. It is the Commission's expectation that the EMU is likely to increase real wage flexibility in the Community.

The ongoing economic integration will make the occurrence of country-specific shocks less likely (mechanism 13). The Commission expects integration as a result of the internal market and EMU to lead to changes in industrial structures in the direction of deeper intra-industry trade and investment relations. A consequence of this is that most countries become involved in both exporting and importing the products of many industries. Old-style comparative advantage, in which countries specialize their production in distinct commodities, is expected to become less important.

Mechanism 14 is called removal of external constraints. The external constraint is defined by the Commission as the extent to which for a particular country or economic region there exists limitations on the net acquisition of foreign financial assets and liabilities. Such constraints may be the result of capital controls, transaction costs, information costs, discriminating tax laws and real exchange rate uncertainty. When external constraints are removed due to liberalization of capital movements and reduced exchange rate volatility, the allocation of capital inside the Community will be improved. What is left is essentially long-run solvency constraints of companies, households and governments. From the lenders' point of view, the nationality of the borrowers is unimportant. What matters is the ability of the borrowers to service their debts.

Creation of an EMU may have implications for the representation of EC countries in international monetary institutions. Negotiations within the IMF about future global exchange rate arrangements will of course be different if the number of European currencies falls as a consequence of the establishment of an EMU. It is also possible that a single European currency will gradually develop into a major world currency in competition with the USD. These two effects are expressed as mechanisms 15 and 16 in table 3.6. Dornbusch (1991) has made a strong plea for the establishment of an EMU because he finds it sensible that the European countries speak more with one voice in world financial affairs.

Note

1   *Official Journal of the European Communities (OJ)*, L 317, 1990, 57.

4

Investment Patterns and Decisions in a Single European Market

The aim of this chapter is to present evidence on trade and investment patterns in Europe. Direct foreign investment in different forms plays a significant role in European economic integration. Cross-border trade and investment are most intense between neighbouring member states. Decisions on the location of new business entities are affected by the establishment of the internal market. EC policies concerning trade with third countries and state aid are also of great importance.

4.1 European Trade and Investment Patterns

The degree of integration of the Community economy is reflected in the observed trade patterns and investment patterns. Changes in these patterns over time illuminate important aspects of the integration process. Unfortunately, it is not possible to describe the patterns exactly. Different definitions, errors and omissions cause empirical difficulties. Rough patterns are, however, better than no patterns. Let us therefore take a look at the trade patterns in table 4.1.

National statistical offices produce trade figures in local currency. These figures are later translated by the International Monetary Fund (IMF) to USD. In preparing table 4.1 the figures have been translated to ECU by means of the spot exchange rates at the end of 1990. The IMF publication contains figures for cross-border trade from the exporting country as well as from the importing country. Data collected in county X on exports to country M in a given year do not correspond exactly with data collected in country M on imports from country X. Discrepancies can be due to differences in the treatment of costs, insurance and freight and different timing because of transportation and storing time etc. The values presented in table 4.1 are averages of data from country X and country M for the registered mutual 1990 trade flows. The observed pattern of trade flows should therefore be interpreted with caution.

The first observation to make about table 4.1 is that in 1990 the

Table 4.1 EC trade patterns 1990 (ECU million)

Exporting country	B/L	DK	D	G	E	F	IR	I	NL	P	UK	EC	US	J	World
B/L	—	765	18,237	531	2,016	16,165	323	6,197	12,149	680	7,458	64,521	3,593	1,165	85,755
DK	537	—	5,025	193	496	1,512	133	1,298	1,158	160	2,844	13,356	1,281	837	25,433
D	21,345	5,307	—	2,940	10,554	35,087	1,248	27,669	24,142	2,661	25,325	156,278	21,183	8,185	298,770
G	127	56	1,451	—	152	569	14	1,088	200	19	474	4,150	366	83	5,837
E	1,198	238	5,739	299	—	8,222	155	4,166	1,661	2,560	3,773	28,011	2,477	562	40,286
F	14,050	1,229	28,106	1,190	9,613	—	657	18,135	7,846	2,048	14,690	97,564	9,612	4,259	157,968
IR	644	175	2,087	87	426	1,639	—	829	895	81	5,903	12,766	1,369	390	17,359
I	4,093	953	23,586	2,233	6,383	19,974	369	—	3,656	1,799	8,719	71,765	9,626	3,288	124,055
NL	14,714	1,483	26,028	946	2,444	9,667	595	6,986	—	884	11,703	75,450	3,838	837	95,969
P	353	263	2,076	60	1,621	1,998	67	475	623	—	1,484	9,020	610	139	11,954
UK	7,289	1,790	17,020	826	4,817	13,270	6,801	7,130	8,653	1,369	—	68,965	16,137	3,638	135,172
EC	64,350	12,259	129,355	9,305	38,522	108,103	10,362	73,973	60,983	12,261	82,373	601,846	—	—	998,558
US	5,736	1,196	15,192	545	4,554	11,902	2,022	6,298	8,369	691	17,710	—	—	—	286,967
J	2,328	831	14,184	729	2,303	5,651	766	2,791	3,720	449	8,352	—	—	—	210,005
World	87,172	23,048	252,916	14,449	63,820	171,156	15,330	132,660	91,887	18,430	162,819	1,033,687	377,425	171,774	—

B/L   Belgium/Luxembourg
DK   Denmark
D   Germany
G   Greece
E   Spain
F   France
IR   Ireland
I   Italy
NL   Netherlands
P   Portugal
UK   United Kingdom
EC   European Community
US   United States
J   Japan

Source: Direction of Trade Statistics, Yearbook 1991, Washington, DC: International Monetary Fund

foreign trade of the EC countries combined, measured either on aggregate exports or on aggregate imports, amounted to approximately ECU 1000 billion. The corresponding figures for the US and Japan, measured on global exports, were respectively ECU 287 billion and ECU 210 billion. The EC is therefore the world's largest trading region in terms of what is registered as foreign trade. This observation must of course be evaluated in the light of the very high share of intra-EC trade in the figures. About 60 per cent of the total export from EC countries is intra-EC trade.

The relative importance of intra-EC trade varies among the EC countries. Intra-EC trade represents a very large share of the total foreign trade of the small continental member countries. In the Netherlands, Belgium/Luxembourg and Portugal the shares are respectively 78, 75 and 75 per cent measured on exports. The intra-EC trade shares are lower in the UK, Denmark and France at 51, 53 and 62 per cent, but still high. The United Kingdom and France have relatively strong trade relations with their former colonies. Denmark has traditionally a large trade with the other Nordic countries.

The EC as a whole had a near balance between global exports and global imports in 1990. The balance was, however, the net result of large surpluses and deficits in the member countries. The trade surplus countries included, in that particular year, Germany, Denmark, Ireland and the Netherlands. Belgium/Luxembourg, Greece, Spain, France, Italy, Portugal and the United Kingdom had trade deficits.

Most of the member countries have a deficit in their trade with Japan. Relatively large deficits are observed for Germany, Greece, Spain, Ireland, the Netherlands, Portugal and the UK. France and Italy have modest deficits, while Denmark has a near balance between exports to and imports from Japan. The pattern of trade between the EC and the United States is more mixed. Germany and Italy have relatively large trade surpluses with the US. Denmark, Portugal and the UK are almost in balance, while there are deficits with the US in the trade balances of Belgium/Luxembourg, Greece, Spain, France, Ireland and the Netherlands.

The pattern of surpluses and deficits changes considerably over time. There are, however, some structural trade patterns that are more stable. Intra-EC trade is thus more intense with neighbours than with distant member countries. In table 4.1 this is illustrated by the strong trade relations between the Netherlands and Germany. Dutch exports to German customers represent 34 per cent of exports to the EC area and 27 per cent of the country's global exports. Trade with the United Kingdom dominates Irish foreign trade: exports to the UK represent 46 per cent of Irish exports to the EC and 34 per cent of the country's global exports. Belgian/Luxembourg exports to Germany and France combined represent 53 per cent of the two countries' EC exports.

By definition, trade patterns illustrate the significance of cross-border trade. Companies engaged in foreign trade can alternatively choose to supply foreign markets through foreign entities. *Direct foreign investment* (DFI) is therefore another important factor in European economic integration (international portfolio investment is discussed in chapter 8). EC member countries gather information on DFI as part of their balance of payments statistics. Eurostat publishes balance of payments data received from the central banks and national statistical offices (Eurostat monthly). Capital flows in the form of DFI are registered in the receiving as well as in the country of the investor. Owing to methodological divergencies between the member countries, there are large differences in the recorded capital movements.

In 1991, Eurostat published a report on DFI in the Community in the period 1984–8 (Eurostat 1991a). The main author of the report was Christine Spanneut. She explains for each member country the methodological differences from the OECD definition of DFI which is chosen as a benchmark. According to the OECD definition, inward and outward direct investment statistics should cover all directly and indirectly owned subsidiaries, associates and branches, where

1 A *subsidiary* is an incorporated enterprise in which the foreign investor controls directly or indirectly (through another subsidiary) more than half of the shareholders' voting powers or has the right to appoint or remove a majority of the members of this enterprise.
2 An *associate* is an entity in which the direct investor and its subsidiaries control not more than 50 per cent of the voting shares or have an effective voice in the management of that enterprise.
3 A *branch* is an unincorporated enterprise in the host country, which can be a permanent establishment or office, a partnership or joint venture, real estate, immovable equipment and objects, non-financial intangible assets (such as patents or copyrights) directly owned by foreign investors, or mobile equipment operating within an economy for at least one year.

In addition, all construction and installation work abroad, except if the installation is carried out by employees of the enterprise who go abroad to do the work and this work is completed in less than one year, should be considered as being undertaken by a direct investment enterprise. Included in the registered direct investment flows should, according to the OECD definition, be the following items: for subsidiaries and associated companies,the direct investor's share of the company's reinvested earnings, his net purchases of the company's shares and loans in the period, plus the net increase in trade and other short-term credits given by the direct investor to the company; for branches, the increase in unremitted profits plus the net increase in funds received from the direct investor.

Thus, DFI data covers acquisitions of existing foreign companies plus mergers with such companies and funds used in connection with the establishment of new foreign entities. It appears that a large and growing part of intra-EC DFIs represents cross-border acquisitions by European companies. In the present book, mergers and acquisitions are dealt with in chapter 9, while the establishment of new foreign entities and the expansion of such entities are covered by the present chapter.

None of the member countries has in 1991 based its balance of payments statistics exactly on the OECD benchmark of DFI. The United Kingdom and the Netherlands are, however, fairly close to it. In preparing the statistical tables in the Eurostat report on DFI, a lot of corrections had to be made. The data resulting from all these corrections is referred to as 'harmonized'. The reader is warned again that the harmonization is far from complete.

Although the description of the pattern of DFI in the Community is very rough, a number of interesting observations seem to be justified. First, it is shown that the EC taken as a whole has been a net investor in terms of DFI. Companies in the EC have consistently made direct investments in third countries that exceeded the direct investments received from non-EC investors. Japan has also had larger outward DFIs than inward investments but, in contrast to the Community, Japan received almost no DFIs in the period under consideration (1984–8). The US was a net receiver of DFIs in the period.

There has been a clear long-term trend of growth in both outward and inward DFIs in the Community. Intra-Community DFI is defined as investment made by a company resident in one member state in another company etc. resident in another member state. It does not include investment internal to each member state. Intra-Community DFI increased from about ECU 4 billion in 1984 to about ECU 20 billion in 1988.[1]

Corporate structures with holding companies cause difficulties when a geographical breakdown of European DFI is attempted. In the balance of payments accounts, capital flows with a holding company are normally attributed to the country in which the holding company is situated. The member countries apply in general the so-called 'foreign parent group criterion'. There is also a risk that capital flows passing through a holding company can be counted twice if they are reinvested in an enterprise in a third country. Thus, global DFI statistics

Table 4.2   Shares of EC member states in direct foreign investments
outside the Community in 1988 (ECU million)

Country	Outward	Inward	Net
Belgium/Luxembourg	1,870	1,276	594
Denmark	294	347	−53
Germany	5,284	−1	5,285
Greece	9	65	−56
Spain	552	1,799	−1,247
France	3,957	1,813	2,144
Ireland	622	190	432
Italy	1,142	3,063	−1,921
Netherlands	3,214	963	2,251
Portugal	2	203	−201
United Kingdom	13,765	4,562	9,203
European Community	30,711	14,278	16,433

Source: *European Community Direct Investment 1984–88*, 1991, Luxembourg: Eurostat,
     34–6

show that the Netherlands Antilles, the Bahamas, the Cayman Islands
and other offshore centres have very large DFI flows: inward when
the holding company is established or its capital increased, outward
when it acquires shares or make loans to other companies belonging
to the group.

The Eurostat report demonstrates that direct investment flows are
concentrated among the industrial countries. More than 75 per cent of
the inward and outward DFI flows of the EC were carried out with
other Western industrialized countries including Japan. The main
destination for outward DFI is the United States. In the observation
period, more than 65 per cent of outward DFI went to the US. The
European Free Trade Association (EFTA) countries play a significant
role in inward DFIs in the Community. Also Japanese firms invest to
a considerable extent in companies in the EC. Community companies
seem to have only modest DFIs in the EFTA and almost none in Japan.

In table 4.2, 1988 DFI figures are provided for each of the EC member countries. Companies resident in the UK are by far the most active
participants in DFI transactions with partners outside the Community.
The British DFI figures for non-EC transactions show net capital exports in each of the years under consideration. The dominant role of
the British investors probably reflects London's status as an international financial centre. The complete absence of inward DFIs in

Germany is certainly not typical. It is, however, characteristic of the German DFI flows to non-EC countries that outward investments over the years have been much larger than inward DFIs. The same applies to the Netherlands although on a smaller scale. Greece, Portugal and Spain receive much larger DFIs than their companies invest abroad. Nicolaides and Thomsen (1991) look at direct investment in Europe from a global and long-term perspective. They present evidence of the dramatic growth of DFI in Europe during the second half of the 1980s. Japanese and American firms and firms resident in the EFTA countries have acquired existing EC companies and invested in new plants in the Community on a large scale. The third country firms have through these transactions made their important contribution to the reshaping of the European economy. Among the motives for investment in the EC by non-EC companies are the business opportunities in an expanding and integrating market and the desire to be 'within the walls' if the prospect of a 'Fortress Europe' should turn out to be realistic. Nicolaides and Thomsen have, on the other hand, a moderately sceptical view of the role played by the internal market programme. The main reason for Japanese and American direct investment in Europe is according to their analysis the size and growth prospects of the market. Shapiro (1991) sees the investment activity as providing companies with the flexibility to respond to whatever surprises 1992 may yield.

Dunning (1991) reviews the extent and pattern of transatlantic production and contrasts the evidence on American DFIs in Europe with that on European DFIs in the United States. The internal market programme has revitalized US investment in the EC but European companies have certainly also increased their participation in firms resident in the US. The importance of both ownership relations and strategic alliances has increased.

Data for intra-EC DFIs in 1988 are presented in table 4.3. The source is again the Eurostat (1991a) report. Owing to incompatibility of data from investing and receiving member countries, the authors gave up the idea of producing a DFI matrix comparable with the foreign trade matrix in table 4.1. In stead they use the aggregated and partly estimated DFI flows declared by respectively the receiving country and the investing country.

It is natural that companies resident in the big countries play a large role in the intra-EC DFI flows. Usually, companies and investors resident in the UK have the largest DFI transactions in both directions. In 1988, very large Dutch transactions surpassed the British flows. Germany and Denmark are consistent net capital exporters in terms of intra-Community DFIs, while Greece, Ireland, Portugal and Spain are

Table 4.3 Shares of EC member states in direct foreign investment inside the Community in 1988

Country	(1) Outward[a] (million ECU)	(2) Inward[b] (million ECU)	(3) Net (million ECU)	(4) Outward (ECU per capita)	(5) Inward (ECU per capita)
Belgium/Luxembourg	1,631	3,477	−1,846	159	339
Denmark	231	126	105	45	25
Germany	2,094	917	1,177	34	15
Greece	6	84	−78	1	8
Spain	229	1,914	−1,685	6	49
France	4,852	4,200	652	87	75
Ireland	221	301	−80	62	85
Italy	1,135	1,214	−79	20	21
Netherlands	6,469	3,701	2,768	441	252
Portugal	30	314	−284	3	31
United Kingdom	5,855	2,472	3,383	103	43
Not allocated	238	179	59	—	—
European Community	22,976	19,076	3,900	71	59

[a] As reported by receiving country.
[b] As reported by investing country.
Source: European Community Direct Investment 1984–88, 1991, Luxembourg: Eurostat, 39–45

net receivers of intra-EC DFIs every year in the period under consideration. The net DFI flows of the other member countries change sign from time to time. In columns 4 and 5 the DFI amounts have been divided by the number of inhabitants in the country. The calculation gives a rough adjustment for the size of the country. These per capita measures show that companies and investors in the Netherlands, Belgium/Luxembourg and the UK are the most active in intra-EC DFI transactions.

In comparing tables 4.2 and 4.3 it should be kept in mind that capital flows carried out between subsidiaries or holding companies resident in Europe but owned by investors with domicile in third countries are recorded as intra-EC FDIs. Many of the big US multinationals have had entities in Europe for more than 25 years and the European cross-border investments of these entities will be included in table 4.3. The presence in the UK and the Benelux countries of many American and Japanese entities probably contributes significantly to the impressive DFI figures for these member countries.

The Eurostat (1991a) report provides some data on the sectorial distribution of DFIs. Energy and industry sectors represented around

60 per cent of Community outward DFIs while credit and financial institutions covered approximately 35 per cent of non-EC inward DFIs. Thus, the internationalization of the financial sector has a strong influence on the observed investment pattern. The sectorial breakdown of intra-Community DFIs demonstrates that finance and banking, energy and real estate are important sectors.

The investment patterns can be analysed by means of data other than balance of payments statistics. Dunning and Cantwell (1987) survey alternative data sources. In spite of the great data difficulties, they demonstrate that the importance of international groups of companies in the Community has been increasing over time. Similar observations are made in Hansen et al. (1992: chapter 4). This development can be illustrated by a number of case studies. In 1990, the EC Commission published a monumental *Panorama* study of the largest industrial companies in the EC (Commission of the EC 1990b). One of the results of the *Panorama* study is that the large European groups in the 1980s have registered a significantly faster growth than the economy as a whole. This probably also implies that the share of intra-EC trade accounted for by trade among entities belonging to the same group of companies has increased. The observed trade patterns in table 4.1 reflect to an increasing extent the marketing, production and sourcing strategies of the international groups. The EC publication contains separate sections on such main industrial sectors as steel, chemicals, electrical equipment, automobiles, and food and drink. The strategies of the large industrial groups are described and their performance is compared with competitors within and outside the Community. The serious concern of European managers for the importance of Japanese competition is for instance reflected in the section on the automobile industry. The Japanese car makers have in recent years acquired production facilities in Europe in accordance with their internationalization strategy. In contrast, some of the big European car makers have reduced their extra-European ambitions. Volkswagen decided to withdraw from the North American market in 1988. The aim of the EC *Panorama* study, which will be updated from time to time, is to facilitate analysis of future market trends. Corporate readers will probably be quick to find the sections of the study in which the strategies of the big players in their own industry are described.

Bownas (1991) examines the strategies of some of the big Japanese companies in the 1990s with special emphasis on their European operations. Among the main motives of Japanese executives are the desire to evade European protectionism and to get as close as possible to the European consumer. The author expects a dramatic increase in the volume of FDI in Europe from Japanese investors in the 1990s.

4.2 Domestic or Foreign Production?

Investment proposals do not come as revelations from heaven. They emerge rather as suggested solutions to practical problems for which corporate managers have been given the responsibility. Production managers have to meet production targets, technical requirements, and specifications in sales contracts. In their struggle to find feasible solutions they come up with investment proposals. If the suggested projects imply cash outlays beyond certain limits, approval by the top management or the supervisory board will normally be needed.

Investment proposals must to a large extent reflect the company's adaptation to changes in its environment. The environment has at least three relevant dimensions; market, technological, and legal or regulatory. An FM must keep in mind that the profitability of Eurocomp's capital investments depends on whether the trends in these three dimensions of the environment are properly understood by the management.

Suppose that Eurocomp has its residence in country R – one of the original six EC member countries – and that the company has existed at least since 1957. In that case, the company has been forced to adapt to a legal environment in which most of the customs duties and quantitative restrictions within the EC were removed before the introduction of the common external tariff in 1968. If the company's host country joined the Community later than 1968, the adjustment to the Community environment has taken place during a more recent transition period. The point to make here is that practically all manufacturing companies with residence in one of the 12 EC member countries are used to operating under international competitive conditions. Many of them have experienced competition not only from companies located in other EC member countries but also from companies in non-EC countries.

The establishment of the single European market is accordingly not a change in the legal and regulatory environment which brings European companies from a completely protected to a completely competitive situation. It is rather a change which intensifies an international competition that already existed and establishes a new situation which has fewer barriers to movements of goods, services and factors of production but is not completely without barriers (Jacquemin and Sapir 1989). Investment proposals have therefore probably for several years reflected and should also in the future reflect that the company has potential customers and competitors not only in country R – the residence country – but in other EC countries as well and probably also in third countries.

Decisions on where to locate new production facilities can be a very important part of a corporate investment project. Most companies prefer domestic investments. By selecting such investments, the management can avoid a long list of difficulties and costs in connection with differences in technical and environmental requirements, in contractual relationships with the employees, in taxes and in language and culture. If they choose to invest in the home country and at the same time expect to sell their products to customers in other EC countries or in third countries or to buy raw materials or components in those countries, they must prepare for cross-border trade. The companies may alternatively carry out direct investments in production facilities abroad.

The decision whether to produce domestically and engage in cross-border trade or to produce abroad depends on several factors. There is no unique widely accepted theory of DFIs. There are rather various hypotheses emphasizing different factors. Lizondo (1991) has produced an excellent survey of theories concerning the determinants of DFIs. Among the theories are industrial organization theory, internalization theory, eclectic approaches, product cycle theory, theories based on oligopolistic reaction, theories based on capital market imperfections, theories based on (in)stability of the political environment, and theories based on differences in national tax systems or government regulation.

Dunning (1988), who is mentioned by Lizondo as the father of the eclectic approach, enumerates a number of advantages that may follow from the establishment of production facilities abroad. The so-called locational advantages can be savings in transportation costs, access to cheaper factors of production, closeness to customers or suppliers, the presence of well educated workers, the quality of communications, transportation and power and water supplies or perhaps establishment in a research environment. Winters (1991) discusses the special variant of closeness to customers in connection with public procurement, which has been and to some extent still is biased in favour of firms with local presence. Culem (1988), Scaperlanda and Balough (1983) and Veugelers (1991) have studied locational decisions with special emphasis on country characteristics. In addition to the advantages enumerated above, the studies indicate that many companies seem to have a preference for direct investments in neighbouring countries and in countries in which cultural or language barriers are insignificant. Both trade integration as reflected in table 4.1 and ownership integration seem to be stronger between markets that are close to each other in geographical terms.

In all the EC countries there seem to be improvements from year to year in most of the conditions that have importance for business investments. Public investments in infrastructure and education make private investments more attractive. The speed of the improvements may differ from country to country and Eurocomp will accordingly have to re-evaluate the potential host countries for new ventures from time to time. There is also a tendency towards stricter government regulations in some areas. Consumer protection and protection of the environment can thus imply more costly business investments.

4.3 Eurocomp and the Internal Market

The completion of the internal market is bound to affect Eurocomp's performance in a number of ways. The structure of production in the whole Community will be changed and trade intensity will increase. Neven and Röller (1991) try to evaluate the impact of European integration on trade flows. They focus on the manufacturing sectors in Germany, France, Italy and the UK. Intra-EC trade, which according to table 4.1 constitutes the main part of the registered foreign trade of the EC countries, will gradually lose its character as foreign trade. The enlargement of markets from the national level to the EC level will enable some firms to exploit the opportunities for economies of scale more successfully. The uncertainties generated by possible exchange rate fluctuations will no longer interfere with producers' DFI decisions when a single currency has been adopted (Louw 1991: 136).

The impacts felt by Eurocomp will depend on how the company is positioned in the restructuring processes in the Community. In order to evaluate that position, the management could try to answer the following questions:

1 What kind of market barriers are presently relevant to Eurocomp?
2 To what extent are Eurocomp's sales, purchases and investments presently impeded by such market barriers?
3 To what extent are Eurocomp's sales, purchases and investments presently protected by such market barriers?
4 What can be expected with respect to the relevant internal market barriers and what are the implications for Eurocomp?
5 What can be expected with respect to the relevant external market barriers and what are the implications for Eurocomp?

In answering question 1, a distinction must be made between barriers with implications for intra-EC trade and barriers with implications for trade between EC companies and companies in third countries. They will be called respectively 'internal market barriers' and 'external market barriers'. The internal market programme concerns of course the first group of barriers. The programme aims at a removal of all intra-EC barriers to the free flow of goods, services, capital and labour. The programme does not directly aim at the external market barriers but it has important implications for many of them.

Emerson et al. (1988: 21) suggest a grouping of market barriers in five categories:

tariffs
quantitative restrictions (quotas)
cost increasing barriers
market entry restrictions
market distorting subsidies and practices.

Tariffs may affect the EC-external operations of Eurocomp, but apart from the agricultural sector where monetary compensation amounts can produce similar effects, tariff barriers to the EC-internal trans-actions should now be eliminated. This does not mean that all companies resident in the Community can disregard tariffs. The common external tariff is evidently a concern for companies that import from third countries. The operations and investments of such companies can also be affected by EC anti-dumping measures. The EC Commission has for instance occasionally imposed minimum local value-added restrictions on Japanese firms that had started operations in Europe after anti-dumping duties had been levied on their exports from Japan (Stegemann 1991). It may therefore be necessary for Japanese-owned companies resident in the Community to source themselves locally. Rules of origin can thus have an effect on investments and on the choice of suppliers in Europe (Nicolaides 1991).

Quantitative restrictions should also be absent in connection with intra-EC trade. Some restrictions of that kind can, however, still be found in connection with the enforcement of certain bilateral trade quota regimes that member countries maintain with third countries.

Thus, what is left for further discussion are the cost increasing barriers, the market entry restrictions and the market distorting sub-sidies and practices. In 1987, the EC Commission carried out a survey based on a questionnaire which was sent to about 20,000 enterprises with residence in the 12 member countries. The purpose of the survey was to find out how the European enterprises evaluated the serious-ness of the different categories of barriers. The results of the survey provide a lot of interesting details on some of the cost increasing bar-riers and market entry restrictions. It turned out that differences in technical standards and regulations plus administrative barriers were ranked by the enterprises as the most serious barriers. Government procurement restrictions, capital market controls and value-added-tax differences were ranked somewhat lower. There were, however, interesting variations in the ranking among industries and among countries. The presence of disparate technical standards and regulations seemed to be particularly important in engineering industries, while government procurement restrictions were considered to be serious barriers to producers of railway equipment and electrical equipment for power stations. Administrative barriers and frontier delays were indicated as relatively serious market barriers at the borders of Portugal, Spain and Greece, while the responding enterprises had experienced only small problems of that kind at the borders of Germany, France, the UK, Denmark and the Netherlands (Emerson et al. 1988: 32–3).

Distorting state aid is, according to article 92 of the EEC Treaty, incompatible with the common market unless derogations are granted. Thus, some state aid is allowed. Eurocomp may be in a position in which it may benefit from state aid. It may also be in a position where it has to fight with competitors that benefit from state aid. Governments do in general welcome investments in new companies and plants within their territories. Such investments create employment and income for the resident population. It is therefore quite natural that the EC member countries to some extent compete in order to attract new investments. Local governments within the same country occasionally behave in the same way.

The trend and patterns of state aid in the Community has been studied by Lehner and Meiklejohn (1991). Based on data from 1986 to 1988, the authors demonstrate that state aid is given primarily to the transport sector (mainly railways), the coal industry, agriculture and fisheries. Measured as a percentage of GDP, state aid to manufacturing is highest in Greece, Portugal, Ireland and Spain.

In answering question 1, the management of Eurocomp will have to go through the list of all potential barriers and to select for further study those barriers that have special importance for a company in that particular industry with residence in country R and with trade that crosses certain borders. The list of relevant market barriers is therefore company specific. So is the evaluation of the impact of the existing barriers on Eurocomp's sales, purchases and investments, as demanded by questions 2 and 3.

Questions 4 and 5 concern the likely development of internal and external market barriers. The development of the legal and regulatory environment has both a commercial policy and an industrial policy dimension. Geroski and Jacquemin (1989) are proponents of a rather ambitious European industrial policy by which the market conditions will change significantly. Other authors are more cautious. Nedergaard (1991) tries to evaluate the trends in EC trade policy by means of the political economy of protection and strategic trade policy.

There is a considerable amount of inertia in investments in new plants. The FM must therefore try to look some years ahead. He must try to evaluate the speed at which the relevant market barriers will be removed, and he must try to imagine what the environment will look like up to the year 2000. The legal and regulatory trends depend on political negotiations on several levels. Whereas the EEC Treaty envisages the complete abolition of all internal frontiers and obstacles to the free movement of goods under article 8A, at the external frontier the requirement is for equal treatment rather than for the abolition of barriers to entry. With respect to trade with third countries, the commitment to dismantling trade restrictions is derived from the Community's participation in the GATT negotiations and reciprocal agreements rather than directly within the legal regime established in the EEC Treaty itself (Cremona 1990). Thus, the outcome of the ongoing GATT negotiations has far-reaching implications for the degree of discrimination between EC companies and non-EC companies. The successful rounds of negotiations in the past within the GATT framework have contributed significantly to a reduction of the discrimination implied by the common external tariff.

This is not only a concern for companies that have to choose between investments within and outside the Community. The discrimination also has implications for EC companies that potentially have customers, suppliers or partners both inside and outside the Community. Environmental changes in relation to third countries may affect both the marketing conditions and the sourcing conditions behind an investment project.

When the internal market programme has been completed, the common commercial policy of article 113 of the EEC Treaty will have displaced member state commercial policies. At the time of writing, member states still have elements of their own trade policy; these arrangements reflect a patchwork of member state foreign policy interests and pressure from domestic constituencies. The same forces can, according to O'Cléireacáin (1990), be expected to be involved in the continued process of removing barriers and reducing discrimination. Authorized deviations from a common commercial policy based on article 115 are the main legal instruments presently used to prevent the free circulation of goods which enter the EC from third countries.

All the EC countries have signed the GATT agreements. They have therefore accepted a number of principles and rules for tariff policy and international trade. A main principle in the GATT agreements is that tariffs etc. should be used in a non-discriminatory way. There are two exceptions to this main rule: customs unions and free trade areas. When countries cooperate under such regional arrangements they are allowed to discriminate between member countries and non-member countries. The EC is based on a customs union (article 9 of the EEC Treaty). The EC countries are therefore under the GATT rules allowed to apply some of their market barriers in a way which favours EC residents and hurts non-EC residents. Under the GATT rules, it has also been possible for the 12 EC member countries to conclude the Lomé Convention, a preferential trading arrangement with 66 developing countries in Africa, in the Caribbean and in the Pacific. Many of the countries concerned are former colonies of France and the UK. Almost half of their exports to the EC have entered duty-free under the Lomé Convention (Gatt 1990).

4.4 Investment Incentives

Within the framework provided by the EEC Treaty, all EC member countries have an investment incentive policy. By an investment incentive is understood any government measure designed to influence private investment decisions by increasing the expected profitability or by decreasing the risks (OECD 1983). A potential direct investor should compare the menu of investment incentives in all potential host countries before important locational decisions are made.

In table 4.4, investment incentives are classified into three groups: fiscal, financial and non-financial. The effect of *fiscal incentives* can be felt directly on the government budget. Private investment projects are supported through a reduction of the investor's tax burden. The relief can be given initially during the period in which the building of a new plant is carried out or subsequently during the first years of operation. Chapter 10 gives an overview of the many forms in which fiscal incentives can be provided. The contents of double taxation agreements may have special importance in connection with DFI decisions. *Financial incentives* may take the form of grants or loans directly from the government or guarantees for loans provided by others. Most of the EC member countries provide financial incentives in connection with business investments in backward regions with large unemployment. The list of available *non-financial incentives* is long but it cannot be considered exhaustive. It covers the provision of a number of service facilities, supplies and tangible factors of production at preferential prices. In connection with the planning of large direct investments, it is common for the investing company to negotiate with local authorities on the purchase of land, construction of roads, access to ports, railways and airports, public investments in power and water supplies, sewage systems, education and transportation of employees, telecommunications and other kinds of public or semi-public service facilities.

Table 4.4 Investment incentives

Fiscal	Financial	Non-financial
Accelerated depreciation	Grants	Land at preferential prices
Preferential tax rates	Loans at preferential	Industrial buildings at low
Tax exemption	terms	rents
Tax credit	Guarantees	Power and water supplies
R&D expenditure allowance	Loans repayable only in	Telecommunications
Tax-free investment	the case of successful	facilities
	outcome of the	Transportation facilities
	investment	Training and technical
	Government equity	assistance
	participation	Consulting services and
		research support
		Government development
		contracts

Investment incentives may be conceived of as an integral part of the host country's regional policy or industrial policy. These policies are monitored by the EC Commission because they must be managed in accordance with the EEC Treaty and adapted to the related Community policies. The Organization for Economic Cooperation and Development in Paris also monitors the industrial policies of the member countries (OECD 1991a). Some of the investment incentive programmes aim at the so-called strategic industries. In recent years, the member countries have in particular given government support to the production of semiconductors, computers, telecommunications, consumer electronics, aircraft construction, automobiles and biotechnology (OECD 1991b).

4.5 Concluding Remarks

The statistics referred to in this chapter indicate that there has been a very significant growth in DFI in Europe since 1980. The high level of cross-border investment flows has been seen as one of the results of the increasing economic integration in the Community. It is probable that some features of the observed investment patterns will also be present in the years to come. The net flow of capital to the southern member countries can thus be expected to continue. The benefits from internalization of markets across boundaries such as avoidance of bargaining and buyer uncertainty, better coordination of operations, and reduction of time lags will still motivate formation of international enterprises.

There are, however, forces that may cause new trends. One of the motives for DFI discussed is the wish to have production facilities within existing trade barriers. When these barriers are reduced or removed as part of the internal market programme, there might be a dampening effect on DFIs within the Community. Eurocomp and other enterprises will probably have to base investment decisions more and more on economic factors in the environment and less and less on the regulatory aspects.

Note

1   Inward and outward DFIs for Spain and Portugal are included in the data for all the years 1984 to 1988 although the two countries did not belong to the Community before 1986.

5

European Financial Institutions and Markets

The aim of this chapter is to provide an overview of financial institutions and markets in the EC. References are given to important statistical sources. Main figures are presented and comparisons between the national financial markets are made. A number of financial instruments are defined and their importance illuminated

5.1 Classification of Institutions and Markets

A financial system in a country can be considered from a market perspective and from an institutions perspective. Markets are characterized by the traded types of financial assets, instruments and services. Institutions are characterized by their organization, by the types of financial services they provide and by their operations on the asset and liability sides.

There are a number of definitions of institutions and types of financial transactions in the EC directives concerning the financial sector. A distinction is made between credit institutions and financial institutions. *A credit institution* is defined as an undertaking whose business is to receive deposits or other repayable funds from the public and to grant credits for its own account. A *financial institution* is an undertaking, not being a credit institution, whose principal activity is to grant credit facilities (including guarantees), to acquire participations or to make investments.[1] The distinctive feature of a credit institution is evidently that it takes deposits from the public. The EC definition of a financial institution has a residual character: it comprises institutions whose main activity is to provide credit but which do not receive deposits from the public.

All firms have financial transactions and most of them grant credit to their customers. Big industrial firms can have financial transactions on a much larger scale than small banks. In the present chapter we will restrict ourselves to European firms whose main activity is financial. The demarcation is broader than the EC conception of credit

Table 5.1   Financial intermediation: categories in NACE

---

65   *Financial intermediation, except insurance and pension funding*
   65.1   Monetary intermediation
        65.11   Central banking
        65.12   Other monetary intermediation
   65.2   Other financial intermediation
        65.21   Financial leasing
        65.22   Other credit granting
        65.23   Other financial intermediation NEC[a]
66   *Insurance and pension funding, except compulsory social security*
   66.01   Life insurance
   66.02   Pension funding
   66.03   Non-life insurance
67   *Activities auxiliary to financial intermediation*
   67.1   Activities auxiliary to financial intermediation, except insurance
       and pension funding
        67.11   Administration of financial markets
        67.12   Security dealing activities
        67.13   Activities auxiliary to financial intermediation NEC[a]
   67.2   Activities auxiliary to insurance and pension funding

---

[a] NEC: not elsewhere classified.
Source: Explanatory Notes to NACE, 1991: revision 1, Luxembourg: Eurostat

institutions and financial institutions. It corresponds rather to groups 65 to 67 in the EC industrial classification system 'Nomenclature générale des activités économique dans les Communautés Euro-péénnes' (NACE).[2] The NACE categories of financial institutions are presented in table 5.1. The NACE codes are mandatory for the official statistical offices in the EC member countries from 1 January 1993. The implication is that in the years ahead it should be easier for users of statistics concerning the financial systems in all EC member countries to find data if they are familiar with the categories in table 5.1.

The classification is based on a conception of the division of labour between different types of institutions in the financial sector. Within category 65, 'Financial intermediation, except insurance and pension funding', a distinction is drawn between 'Monetary intermediation' and 'Other financial intermediation'. Deposit taking is the decisive criterion. Credit institutions and institutions whose main activity is 'Other monetary intermediation' seem therefore to be almost identical groups. Central banks, commercial banks, savings banks and postal giro systems that take deposits are all classified under 'Monetary intermediation'. Financial firms whose main activity is investment in shares, bonds, bills, unit trust units etc. are classified under 65.23 'Other financial intermediation NEC'. The same applies to firms whose main business is to write swaps, options and other hedging arrangements. Traditionally, the division of labour between different types of financial firms has been regulated by law in most member countries. It has for instance been common to prohibit banks from offering insurance services. The deregulation trend has changed the situation. Today, the institutions can cross most of the traditional frontiers between financial markets. This implies in table 5.1 that institutions classified in a group according to their main activity very often will also be active in other fields. Shifting frontiers in financial markets cause problems not only for supervisory authorities but also for the institutions responsible for financial statistics.

In table 5.2 are shown the 14 business activities which according to the Second Bank Coordination Directive (89/646/EEC) are considered to be integral to banking and thus within the scope of mutual recognition.[3] The length of the list reflects the financial innovation process: banking in the 1990s is much more than deposit taking and lending. Article 1 in the directive refers to the list in table 5.2 in order to enumerate the main activities of financial institutions. The main activity should be either to acquire participations in other companies or to carry out the activities 2 to 12 on the list. In countries with a universal banking system, credit institutions are normally active in the markets for all 14 activities.

Ideally, the institutional classification in table 5.1 and the market classification in table 5.2 should be cross-classified for each financial system. The FM could try to do this for the most important host countries in order to obtain an overview of which institutions are operating on the individual markets.

Statistics are necessary for an FM who tries to get an overview of the capital markets. Relevant financial statistics are produced by the BIS in Basle, by the OECD in Paris, by Eurostat in Luxembourg and by the national statistical offices and central banks. In addition, the Federation of Stock Exchanges in the EC (FSEC) in Brussels collects and publishes data from the individual stock exchanges in the member countries. The Banking Federation of the European Community (BFEC) collects statistics on the banking sector, while the Comité Européen des Assurances (CEA) produces statistics which describe the profile of European insurance. The choice of statistical source depends on how specific the information needs to be. In the following, the European financial markets are described only briefly by means of information from the BIS, the OECD, Eurostat, the FSEC and the BFEC. In many situations, the FM will have to use the more detailed national statistical sources in order to meet the information requirements.

Most of the financial institution categories given in table 5.1 may be

Table 5.2   Financial activities integral to banking

---

1   Deposit taking and other forms of borrowing
2   Lending[a]
3   Financial leasing
4   Money transmission services
5   Issuing and administering means of payments (credit cards, traveller's cheques and bankers drafts)
6   Guarantees and commitments
7   Trading for own account or for account of customers in:
   (a)   money market instruments (checks, bills, CDs, etc.)
   (b)   foreign exchange
   (c)   financial futures and options
   (d)   exchange and interest rate instruments
   (e)   securities
8   Participation in securities issues and the provision of services related to such issues
9   Advice to firms concerning captial structure, industrial strategy and related problems and advice and services concerning mergers and acquisitions
10   Money broking
11   Portfolio management and advice
12   Safekeeping and management of securities
13   Credit reference services
14   Safe custody services

---

[a] Including in particular consumer credit, mortgage lending, factoring and invoice discounting, and trade finance (including forfaiting).
Source: Directive (89/646/EEC), *Official Journal of the European Communities*, L 386, 12

found in the financial systems of each of the EC member countries. Their names differ according to language differences, and their relative market importance and ownership structure vary considerably. The OECD has published an overview of regulations of ownership of financial institutions in the OECD member countries (OECD 1991c). In most countries there are regulations applying to bank mergers and ownership linkages with non-financial companies. Mergers and interbank participations are often subject to prior approval of a banking supervisory office, the central bank or the minister of finance. In some countries, the central government owns a considerable share of the stock in banks or other financial institutions. Such institutions can be considered by an FM as private financial institutions if they primarily operate under market conditions.

In the following, we try by means of tables 5.1 and 5.2 to give a rough picture of the financial system as it looks from the point of view of a European FM. In the presentation by means of the NACE EC framework, it is necessary to point out some structural differences between the financial systems in the EC countries which can potentially affect the financial decisions made by the FM. The author's idea is that the framework may serve as a guide to financial institutions which is not country specific. The idea can be criticized. An obvious objection is that there are such big differences in the roles played by banks, for instance, in Germany and the United Kingdom that it is misleading to discuss these financial systems within the same framework. Germany has a universal banking system under which the banks are allowed to hold minority and majority stakes inside and outside the financial sector and to use the voting rights to influence the decisions of their corporate customers. In the UK, anonymous organized markets play a much greater role and the majority of the financial institutions are more or less specialized (Hellwig 1991).

The non-financial firm Eurocomp may be active on both the supply side and the demand side of the different financial markets. The company may be interested in buying bonds in some periods and in selling bonds in other periods. The company's funds profile depends on the rhythm in its capital investments and on the maturity structure of its debt. The professional dealers and market makers quote bid and offer prices with a spread which on average allows them to earn money, and Eurocomp should therefore expect the bid–offer spread in the market to work against the company. The tougher the competition in the market, the narrower the spread.

The European financial markets are partially integrated. There can therefore in principle be participants from several countries in the markets for all financial instruments and services in table 5.2. Investors and borrowers should therefore remember the global context in which the price formation in many of the financial markets takes place. The increasing market integration means that the competition between the financial institutions becomes stronger and that the prices of financial services in different countries are interrelated to an increasing extent.

Relations between the markets occur also because of the existence of multinational groups of financial companies. Most of the big European banks and insurance companies have branches and subsidiaries abroad (Klein 1991). The foreign entities may offer the same type of financial services as the parent company but they may also be specialized to some extent.

Eurocomp is assumed to be a potential buyer of financial services in several European countries. The FM is therefore assumed to be looking at table 5.1 as a first step in a search process with the aim of finding the best and the cheapest supplier of financial services in the Community. Suppose now that Eurocomp has identified a financing need, a need for short-term investment of funds or a need for other financial services. Suppose further that the appropriate type of financial instrument or service has been chosen (the balance between debt and equity financing is dealt with in chapter 6). Within the framework of table 5.2 these assumptions imply that a certain category has been selected. The FM then has to use table 5.1 to find the right institution in the financial sector which can offer the instrument, loan or service in question on the best terms. Statistics and directories can be used to identify the relevant institutions. The contents of prospectuses and offering circulars can give the FM an idea of the kinds of background information required by investors and institutions. Finally, the current data on the market in question in the information systems of banks illustrate the kinds of input which can be applied in calculations of yields and financing costs etc.

Central banks are included in table 5.1 under group 65.11. Central banks in general do not deal with non-financial companies. They have probably been included in the NACE grouping of the financial sector because of the importance of their transactions in particular in the markets for bank deposits and bonds. Their transactions are motivated by monetary policy or exchange rate policy considerations. A considerable part of the official international reserves of industrial countries are held in the form of bank deposits and short-term government bonds denominated in USD, DEM, JPY and ECU (IMF 1992: 81). In some EC member countries there are government-owned financial institutions that do not operate under market conditions. Most of them belong to the government sector in NACE.

5.2 Markets for Banking Services

Eurocomp is assumed to look at the markets for banking services from a corporate customer's point of view. The company buys the different financial services which according to table 5.2 are integral to banking. It belongs therefore to the duties of the FM to evaluate the costs and risks of these services. In the 1990s, the conditions according to which Eurocomp can use the banking services are strongly influenced by EC measures. When the Single European Act was signed in 1986, the EC member states committed themselves to integrate not only the markets for goods from the end of 1992 but also the markets for financial services (Knebel 1992). Originally, the Council primarily tried to use harmonization in the banking sector in order to achieve market integration, but owing to slow progress a new approach was adopted by the mid 1980s (Strivens 1992) The new approach to the liberalization of the financial services sector was based on three key elements: (1) harmonization of essential standards for prudential supervision and for the protection of investors, depositors and consumers, (2) mutual recognition of the way in which each member state applies those standards and (3) home country control and supervision of financial institutions operating in other member states. Wils (1991) and Key (1989) have both written very clear analyses of the concepts of mutual recognition and reciprocity.

The *Second Bank Coordination Directive* (89/646/EEC),[4] which was adopted by the Council in 1989, provided for freedom of establishment and cross-border supply of financial services. According to the so-called single licence system, a bank which has obtained a charter in one member state is allowed to set up branches and to supply financial services in other member states. The activities of the bank are supervised by the authorities of the bank's home country. Some of the articles in the directive impose, however, a number of administrative formalities that are likely to make the implementation of the cross-border activities quite burdensome for the banks.

Nevertheless, in the years to come it will gradually become easier for Eurocomp to buy banking services from banks with residence in other member states. It is not only the administrative formalities that will put a brake on the increase in the cross-border supply of banking services and on the establishment of branches in other member countries. Language differences, unfamiliarity with different national payment systems and legal rules concerning debt relations (Steiner 1992) will contribute to a continued segmentation of the European market for banking services. In 1990, the EC Commission issued a recommendation (90/109/EEC)[5] with the aim of making cross-border financial transactions more transparent. According to the recommendation, banks should inform their customers in detail of the commission fees and charges in their invoicing and of the exchange rates applied.

If Eurocomp acquires deposits in or shares issued by foreign banks, the company should be interested in the credit standing of these institutions. Several EC measures have the aim of harmonizing the protection of investors and customers. The *Directive on the Own Funds of Credit Institutions* (89/299/EEC)[6] and the *Directive on a Solvency Ratio for Credit Institutions* (89/647/EEC)[7] are based on capital adequacy considerations. Rudolf (1989) and Mast (1989) explain how the EC rules are derived from the work done by the so-called Cook Committee. The solvency of the European banks is, after the implementation of the directives, subject to a detailed ongoing regulation and supervision.

An adjusted total of risk assets is computed as a linear function of the quantities of assets in different classes with the risk weights specified in the regulations. It is the duty of the board of directors in each bank and the supervisory authorities to ensure that at all times the own funds exceed a minimum level which is calculated as 8 per cent of the risk-weighted assets. Schaefer (1989) has compared the linear approach of the regulators with risk measurement according to the modern theory of finance. He finds that there is no explicit statement by the regulators on what theory or view of the world their rules are based on.

The Commission has in 1986 recommended a *deposit insurance system* (86/63/EEC).[8] At the time of writing, the Commission is working on a proposal for a directive concerning a common deposit insurance system. According to the preliminary text, there will be a maximum compensation that depositors can receive in the case of a bank's failure. Hottner (1992) has criticized the proposal because it does not provide protection for bank depositors at the same level as the German system in force.

For practical purposes all European firms and investors own deposits in banks or other credit institutions. National and international statistical sources show that the volume of deposits is very large. The Bank for International Settlements (BIS) in Basle publishes statistics on the international deposit markets (BIS 1991a).

In the 1960s, the term 'Eurodollar market' became popular (Machlup 1970; Swoboda 1968; Johnson 1981). A Eurodollar was defined as a dollar deposited in a bank outside the US. This segment of the deposit markets worldwide attracted a considerable interest in the years characterized by restrictions on international capital movements. After the liberalizations of the 1980s, it has become common practice for banks all over the world – not only in Europe – to take deposits denominated in foreign currencies. The terminology has accordingly been adjusted. The expression 'the international interbank market', although not completely synonymous, seems gradually to have replaced 'Eurocurrency market' in the publications of BIS and other institutions that analyse the development.

It is not easy to work with statistics on the deposit markets. The BIS statistics are based on data reported by banks in the Group of Ten countries plus Luxembourg, Austria, Denmark, Finland, Ireland, Norway, Spain, the Bahamas, Bahrain, the Cayman Islands, Hong Kong, the Netherlands Antilles and Singapore and by the branches of US banks in Panama. Since France, Germany, Italy and the United Kingdom belong to the Group of Ten, most of the EC is covered by what BIS calls the 'reporting banks'. Only the banks in Greece and Portugal are not included.

Table 5.3   BIS reporting banks: international positions at end of March
1991 (ECU billion)

			External assets	External liabilities
A	Total		4857.8	5001.8
	1	Outside area countries	585.3	569.0
		(a) Non-banks	326.0	255.0
		(b) Banks etc.	259.4	314.0
	2	Inside area countries	4149.0	4158.1
		(a) Non-banks	868.3	784.5
		(b) Banks etc.	3280.7	3373.7
	3	Unallocated	123.3	274.6
B	Total local foreign currency		1028.3	849.3
		of which non-banks	519.9	211.2

Source: table 1 in *International Banking and Financial Market Developments*, August
    1991, Basle: Bank for International Settlements

The international positions of the BIS reporting banks are shown in
table 5.3. All the amounts represent cross-border claims. More than 80
per cent of the external liabilities of approximately ECU 5000 billion
are deposits etc. taken from market participants in the inside area
countries. Interbank deposits are much bigger than deposits taken from
non-banks. Both on the asset side and on the liabilities side approximately 80 per cent are accounted for by lending between banks. In
the BIS statistics, the reporting banks in ten EC countries have together
external assets of ECU 2085.9 billion corresponding to more than 40
per cent of the total. The interbank business is, however, concentrated
in London, Frankfurt, Paris and Luxembourg. The banks in London
report by far the biggest deposits among the European banks. Several
BIS tables give a currency breakdown of the reporting banks' cross-
border positions. Ranked according to their importance on the liability
side of banks in industrial reporting countries in 1991, the six most
important currencies were USD, DEM, CHF, JPY, ECU and GBP.

Banks lend short-term funds to each other on a very large scale.
They do this in both the domestic money markets and the international
money market. The individual transactions are large. The transactions
of the individual bank – let us call it Eurobank – must be considered
in relation to the customers' payments transactions. Customers with a
net cash inflow tend to increase their bank deposits. If they expect to
have the funds for some time, they will negotiate the terms with
Eurobank which takes the deposit. The interest income to the customer
of such deposits is of course an interest expense from the point of

view of the bank. Eurobank will therefore try to acquire an interest bearing asset. An obvious alternative is to place the money in the interbank market. There is accordingly a close relationship between the interest rate given by Eurobank to deposit giving customers and the rate offered by the bank in the interbank market.

Customers with a net cash outflow can borrow in Eurobank. This creates a funding need for the bank which can be covered in the interbank market. It is common practice for banks to fund even large loans with maturities of several years by taking deposits in the interbank market. The so-called *roll-over loans* have variable interest rates that are adjusted with a time interval corresponding to the maturity of the deposits used for funding. There is accordingly a close relationship between the loan interest rate paid by customers to Eurobank and the bid rate quoted by Eurobank in the interbank market. The outstanding claims in the deposit markets are enormous from the point of view of an average European non-financial firm. The FM should remember that they are enormous also from the point of view of an average European bank. The implication of this is that the level of interest rates in the deposit markets is also given for the bank management.

The banks follow a number of conventions in their interbank transactions. Interest rates are quoted on a per annum basis. A three-month quote by Eurobank on ECU deposits of 9.62–9.75 indicates therefore that Eurobank is willing to take ECU deposits with a three-month maturity from other banks at an annual rate of 9.62 per cent, while it is willing to give ECU deposits with that maturity to other banks at an annual rate of 9.75 per cent.

Bank deposits are given within established lines. They specify the maximum amount which the deposit giving bank is willing to have outstanding with each individual deposit taking bank in the market. Dealers are not allowed to place funds with other banks before the bank's board has approved the appropriate lines. The size of the lines depends on the creditworthiness of the deposit taking bank. There are conventions in the interbank market that lines are unadvised and uncommitted. 'Unadvised' means that the borrowing bank does not know how large its line is. 'Uncommitted' means that the lending bank is under no obligation to provide any funds. The utilization of lines is followed closely by the bank management, and the level of lines is subject to periodic review.

The overall activity in the interbank market is also managed by means of country limits. While bank lines reflect an evaluation of credit risk in relation to the individual bank, country limits reflect an evaluation of political risk. Some banks may adjust their classification

Table 5.4 Money supply in the EC countries in 1990 (ECU billion)

	M1	M2	M3
Belgium	33.4	125.6	188.5
Denmark	37.1	48.7	—
Germany	237.4	383.6	650.8
Greece	8.8	—	44.2
Spain	108.1	170.5	266.6
France	244.5	425.6	720.4
Ireland	4.1	—	16.5
Italy	303.5	574.6	757.8
Luxembourg	1.7	9.8	—
Netherlands	53.9	103.5	—
Portugal	12.9	34.1	—
United Kingdom	62.8	360.5	669.7
Total EC	1108.2	—	—

Source: Money and Finance, 1991, no. 3, Eurostat, 90–1

of countries according to the risk categories applied by the official export credit institutions.

The relative size of the deposit markets in the EC countries can be illustrated by means of money supply figures. The definitions applied by Eurostat (1991b: 10) are:

M1: currency (notes and coin) in circulation outside banks plus sight deposits held by the private sector with the banking system
M2: M1 plus certain less liquid financial instruments, mainly savings deposits and other short-term claims on monetary institutions
M3: M2 plus certain placements in a potentially liquid form such as deposits at statutory notice, placements with contractual maturity over one year, etc.

Table 5.4 shows the available money supply figures at the end of 1990. These reflect not only the relative size of the domestic economies of the member countries, but also that foreign investors hold deposits in the EC banks. BIS data seem to indicate that the international component of bank deposits is higher for banks in the United Kingdom and Luxembourg than in most other EC countries.

The relative importance of commercial banks varies from member country to member country. Rough comparisons of banking systems can be made by means of the data in table 5.5. At the end of 1989, there were 2179 commercial banks in the Community. They had 71,743

Table 5.5 Comparative European banking statistics at end of 1989

	(1) Number of banks	(2) Number of branches	(3) Staff	(4) Total assets (ECU billion)	(5) Assets/GDP	(6) Staff/ population (%)	(7) Population/ branch	(8) Average assets/bank (ECU billion)
Belgium	85	3,618	52,917	279.8	1.97	0.53	2,743	3.29
Denmark	80	1,940	35,534	99.4	1.02	0.69	2,641	1.24
Germany	321	6,607	192,500	509.9	0.46	0.32	9,236	1.59
Greece	32	1,866	44,367	46.3	0.99	0.44	5,366	1.45
Spain	146	16,623	157,056	298.2	0.86	0.40	2,349	2.04
France	418	9,888	223,805	824.8	0.93	0.40	5,651	1.97
Ireland	33	696	22,456	37.1	1.18	0.64	5,083	1.12
Italy	232	9,864	240,137	554.9	0.71	0.42	5,823	2.39
Luxembourg	166	300	15,190	268.7	40.71	4.06	1,247	1.62
Netherlands	88	4,000	111,836	364.0	1.75	0.76	3,690	4.14
Portugal	29	1,741	58,132	55.8	1.39	0.56	5,978	1.92
United Kingdom	549	14,600	444,090	1,683.5	2.43	0.78	3,909	3.07
Total EC	2,179	71,743	1,598,020	5,022.4	0.72	0.49	4,527	2.30

Sources: *Banking Federation of the European Community, Annual Report 1990; National Accounts, Paris: OECD*

branch offices and employed 1,598,020 persons. The relative importance of the banks can be illustrated by a few key figures and ratios. The total assets divided by the gross domestic product in column 5 varies from 0.46 in Germany to 40.71 in Luxembourg. The ratio is a very rough measure and it is influenced by the omission of savings banks and postal offices from the statistics, but the observed pattern indicates nevertheless that banking is a relatively important industry in Luxembourg, the UK, Belgium and the Netherlands.

In column 6, there is information on the percentages of the population employed in the banks. The Community average is 0.49 per cent. Once again, Luxembourg, the UK and the Netherlands stand out as member countries with many resources engaged in banking. In column 7, the average number of inhabitants per branch office is shown. The Community average is 4527 per branch; this is fairly high, but the number of persons per branch would of course be smaller if the branches of savings banks and postal offices were included. By this measure, Germany is at the top with 9236 persons per branch while Luxembourg has the lowest number at 1247.

The average of assets per bank in column 8 should be interpreted with caution. Member countries like the UK and Germany have a few very big banks and a large number of small and medium banks. The average of bank assets is not very informative when the industry is very concentrated. It turns out that the dispersion of the country averages in column 8 around the Community average of ECU 2.30 billion is modest.

Eurocomp cannot expect the observed structure of the European banking industry to be stable. Recently, a large number of bank mergers and acquisitions have taken place and further restructurings can be expected. Dermine (1990) has explained how economies of scale and economies of scope in financial firms can be expected to affect the structural adjustments of the European financial services industry. Dermine (1991) contains the evaluations of a number of experts of the influence of EC proposals on the future structure of the banking industry in Europe. Some recent restructurings in the financial industry have been motivated as adjustments to the new competitive situation in the internal market (Leonard et al. 1992). Other restructurings should probably be evaluated in the light of the relatively low profitability in European banking in recent years (OECD 1992a). To some extent, the low earnings reflect over-capacity in the industry. Some mergers may therefore be initiated by managements and boards with the aim of reducing capacity and costs. Emerson (1991) has given a fairly pessimistic evaluation of the banks' ability to defend the market for banking services in the 1990s.

What are the likely implications of mergers and acquisitions activity in the financial sectors for corporate bank customers? First, customers can expect to continue to benefit from the strong competition among financial institutions and firms which is closely related to mergers and acquisitions activity. The impacts on the supply side of the decrease in the number of independent financial institutions will probably be counterbalanced by the increase in the supply of cross-border financial services. The improved price transparency and telecommunications facilities will make it easier for corporate customers to choose the most cost-efficient providers of financial services. The formation of financial groupings comprising banking, real estate mortgage, insurance and pensions will be mentioned briefly in section 5.5.

5.3   Bond Markets

European bond investors have access to a very broad menu of securities. The Federation of Stock Exchanges in the European Community publishes statistics on listed fixed interest securities. The statistics comprise both bonds issued by public authorities and bonds issued by private institutions and companies. All types of bonds can potentially be included in Eurocomp's bond portfolio. Only private bonds can be issued by the company itself or on behalf of the company.

Table 5.6 illuminates some aspects of the European bond markets. The total number of listed fixed interest securities was 33,662 at the end of 1990. Approximately 37 per cent of the total number is listed on the German exchanges. Domestic private bonds play an important role in the German capital market. The number of listed bonds is also high in Luxembourg. This stock exchange is, however, dominated by international bonds which constitute more than 98 per cent of the number 7424. The exchanges in Denmark, Greece, Italy, Portugal and Spain are dominated by domestic bonds. There is, however, a clear tendency on most exchanges that the proportion of international fixed interest securities is increasing. The tendency is obviously related to the ongoing integration process.

Table 5.7 gives data on the value of the listed bonds. The aggregate par value of the 33,662 fixed interest securities listed amounted to ECU 3145 billion at the end of 1990. The international bonds listed in Luxembourg give this exchange a leading position among the European bond markets. The total par value is also high in the German exchanges and in Milan, London and Paris. The market turnover in fixed interest bonds reached ECU 1950 billion in 1990. The London Stock Exchange has the highest market turnover in fixed interest securities, followed by the German exchanges, Paris and Copenhagen.

Table 5.6 Number of listed fixed interest securities on European stock exchanges in 1990

	Overall total	Domestic			International		
		Total	Public	Private	Total	Public	Private
Amsterdam	1,166	998	159	839	168	—	—
Athens	86	86	73	13	0	0	0
Brussels	134	129	103	26	5	0	5
Copenhagen	2,274	2,225	90	2,135	49	3	46
Dublin	105	97	62	35	8	5	3
German exchanges	12,552	11,509	220	11,289	1,043	—	—
Lisbon	374	371	86	285	3	2	1
London	4,343	2,722	215	2,507	1,621	174	1,447
Luxembourg	7,424	104	31	73	7,320	—	—
Madrid	1,087	1,052	494	558	35	35	0
Milan	1,322	1,303	1,197	106	19	19	0
Paris	2,795	2,515	1,073	1,432	280	4	276
Total	33,662	23,111	3,803	19,298	10,551	242	1,778

Source: Statistical Yearbook 1990, Brussels: Federation of Stock Exchanges in the EC, 76

Table 5.7 Aggregate par value and market value turnover in fixed interest securities on European stock exchanges in 1990 (ECU billion)

	Par value			Turnover			Par value/GDP (%)
	Total	Domestic bonds	International bonds	Total	Domestic bonds	International bonds	
Amsterdam	129.4	121.9	7.5	40.9	40.4	0.5	56.0
Athens	19.2	19.2	0.0	0.3	0.3	0.0	44.3
Brussels	98.2	95.8	2.4	5.3	5.3	—	61.9
Copenhagen	162.8	148.0	14.8	232.3	221.3	11.0	145.8
Dublin	16.9	16.9	—	23.4	23.4	—	61.9
Germany	716.3	615.4	100.9	441.9	419.2	22.7	51.6
Lisbon	7.3	7.2	0.1	0.9	0.9	0.0	15.5
London	393.6	257.8	135.8	746.4	709.6	36.8	33.9
Luxembourg	764.0	1.9	762.1	0.4	0.0	0.4	27.7
Madrid	42.0	39.3	2.7	1.6	1.6	—	10.2
Milan	430.3	428.7	1.6	24.7	24.6	0.1	50.7
Paris	364.6	346.3	18.3	432.3	431.9	0.4	38.0
Total	3144.8	2098.5	1046.3	1950.5	1878.6	71.9	

Source: Statistical Yearbook 1990, Brussels: Federation of Stock Exchanges in the EC, 80 and 99

In the last column of table 5.7, the total par value of the listed domestic fixed interest securities has been divided by the gross domestic product (GDP) of the country in question. The resulting ratios give a rough impression of the relative roles of the bond markets in the EC member countries. Copenhagen distinguishes itself with 145.8 per cent, an indication of the traditional large role of the Danish bond market in the financing of residential buildings, industry, agriculture and the government. By the same measure, the markets for domestic bonds seem to play a relatively modest role in the economies of Spain and Portugal.

The nominal value of outstanding bonds has expanded considerably in recent years. There are several reasons. In some EC countries the expansion has been connected with large public sector deficits. Italy is an outstanding example. Financial institutions have a dominant position among the private issuers of bonds in most of the EC countries (BIS 1991b: 21). In the so-called Eurobond sector, the expansion is also connected with the establishment some years ago of an efficient trading infrastructure. There are two clearing systems, Euroclear and CEDEL, which enable market participants to transfer bearer bonds through a book entry system rather than through a procedure of physical movement of the bonds. The Association of International Bond Dealers has agreed on a common set of trading conventions.

The term 'Eurobonds' has traditionally been applied to bonds issued, and largely sold, outside the country of the currency in which they are denominated (Chester 1991). Additional characteristic features are that they are bearer bonds underwritten by an international syndicate of banks and exempt from withholding taxes. The growing integration of bond markets has gradually eroded the distinction between Eurobonds and domestic and foreign bonds. Benzie (1992) has analysed the convergence between the international and the domestic bond markets. Withholding tax regimes have been dismantled in several OECD countries, and bearer bonds are issued in a number of domestic capital markets. In addition, the settlement systems have been improved also for domestic and foreign bonds. The BIS still uses the words 'Eurobonds' and 'Euronotes', but the tendency seems to be that 'the international securities markets' is gaining ground.

A number of structural features of the international bond markets can be illuminated by the statistics from BIS. Table 5.8 gives a picture of the outstanding bonds with respect to type and currency of denomination. *Straight issues* are bonds without attached conversion options or warrants and without embedded options. Most straight bonds are issued with fixed coupons. A considerable part of the volume of issuance is within the maturity range five to ten years. According

Table 5.8   Structure of international bonds and notes at end of March 1991

Bond type and currency		Stocks (ECU billion)
Straight fixed rate issues		*806.9*
USD	266.9	
JPY	129.5	
CHF	88.9	
DEM	78.7	
ECU	60.0	
GBP	49.8	
Other	133.1	
Floating rate notes		*162.8*
USD	94.5	
GBP	32.7	
DEM	15.6	
Other	20.0	
Equity related issues		*205.7*
USD	141.0	
CHF	38.8	
Other	25.9	
Total		*1175.4*

Source: International Banking and Financial Market Developments, 1991, Basle: Bank for International Settlements

to table 5.8 USD remains the most important currency of denomination. ECU and JPY are, however, used to an increasing extent. Sovereign borrowers are very active in the ECU sector of the bond market. Since 1989, the majority of European governments have issued ECU-denominated bonds. Obolensky (1991) has explained the reasons why the French government has borrowed large amounts in the ECU market. The French Treasury ECU OAT is often used as a benchmark for the pricing of other ECU issues. The popularity of ECU in public borrowings may reflect partly that the financing costs are lower than for borrowing in domestic currency, and partly that such issues can support the government's image as 'good Europeans' (Euromoney 1991: 7).

Floating rate notes (FRNs) pay their holders a coupon that is adjusted periodically at a spread over a well known money market rate. Most FRNs are linked to the London interbank offered rate (LIBOR) for deposits denominated in the currency of denomination. Table 5.8 shows that the relative role of GBP is much greater in FRNs than in fixed rate bonds.

There are several types of *equity related bonds. Convertible bonds* give the investor the option to convert his bonds into equity in the issuing company. If exercised, the investor exchanges his bonds for shares. Because the option is traded at a premium in the market, the issuing company can pay a lower coupon than on a straight issue with similar characteristics. Warrants are also options; *bonds with equity warrants* therefore resemble convertible bonds. The difference is that warrants are detached from the bonds and traded separately. If the warrants are exercised, the investor will have to pay new money to the company. At the date of exercise, the investor must pay an amount corresponding to the exercise price written in the warrant. *Bonds with embedded options* may be related to stock indices, exchange rates or commodity prices. In connection with a loan issued by the Danish government in 1990, put warrants based on one-fifth of the Japanese stock index Nikkei were issued. The issued warrants give the holders the right in a three-year period to receive the difference between the exercise price and the underlying market price, if and only if the Nikkei index falls. The government covered its obligations under the warrant arrangement by means of a contract with Goldman Sachs (Ministry of Finance 1990).

Deutsche Bundesbank (1992b) provides a survey of some recent financial innovations related to bonds that are traded in Frankfurt.

5.4   Stock Markets

Chapter 2 contains a survey of the EC measures concerning stock exchanges. We referred to them as the Admission Directive, the Listing Particulars Directive, the Interim Reports Directive, the Major Holdings Transactions Directive and the Insider Trading Directive.

Eurocomp can issue stock in the domestic or in a foreign stock market in order to finance the company's expansion. It can also include stocks issued by other companies in its portfolio. After the incorporation into national stock exchange laws of all the directives mentioned, the company must carry out its investment and financing decisions within the EC created legal framework. The FM can contact banks, investment banks, stockbrokers and portfolio managers when stock transactions are contemplated. Walter and Smith (1991) assess the role investment banks can be expected to play in restructuring in Europe in the 1990s.

Statistics from the Federation of Stock Exchanges in the EC can also illuminate the role of the stock markets in Europe. Table 5.9 presents some key data. The total number of companies listed on European stock exchanges amounted to 6730 at the end of 1990. Table 5.9 reveals that the total consisted of 5042 domestic companies and 1688 international companies. International companies are defined as companies

Table 5.9 Numbers of companies with shares listed on European stock exchanges in 1990, including investment companies, funds and trusts

	Total	Domestic	International	Of which
Amsterdam	498	260	238	135 ICs
Athens	140	140	0	8 ICs
Brussels	343	180	163	—
Copenhagen	268	258	10	—
Dublin	71	51	20	12 ICs
German exchanges	647	413	234	—
Lisbon	152	152	0	—
London	2559	1946	613	245 ITs
Luxembourg	732	550	182	521 IFs
Madrid	431	429	2	—
Milan	220	220	0	—
Paris	669	443	226	—
Total	6730	5042	1688	

IC investment company; IT investment trust; IF investment fund.
Source: Statistical Yearbook 1990, Brussels: Federation of Stock Exchanges in the EC, 53

with their main office in another country. London Stock Exchange is by far the largest stock exchange in the EC in terms of the number of listed companies. The dominance of London is evident in both domestic and international companies. The international companies play a substantial role also in Amsterdam, Brussels. Germany and Paris.

The growth of the European equity markets depends on trends in the incorporation of private companies, on the privatization of government-owned undertakings and on the investment policies and asset growth of pension funds and other institutional investors (Euromoney 1992).

5.5   Insurance and Pension Markets

The activities of European insurance companies are regulated according to national laws that incorporate a number of different EC directives. The most important directives are the First Council Directive (79/267/EEC) as amended by the Second Directive (90/619/EEC)[9] on the coordination of laws and administrative rules concerning direct life insurance and on provisions which can facilitate the free exchange of services etc. The Second Directive (88/357/EEC) of 22 June 1988 with later amendments[10] related to the coordination of laws and rules concerning direct insurance except life insurance and on provisions which can facilitate the free exchange of services etc. In the spring of 1992, the Council reached a 'common understanding' with respect to the contents of a third non-life insurance directive. Council Directive (87/343/EEC)[11] deals with credit insurance and introduced technical exceptions from the previous non-life insurance directive (73/239/EEC).

Insurance companies and pension funds play a key role in the capital markets of the Community. A considerable part of the regular savings of the population is channelled through these institutions and their portfolio managers accordingly buy large amounts of stocks and bonds every year. There are investment rules in most national insurance laws. Typically, the rules provide a list of admissible assets to represent technical reserves. It has been proposed that the investment rules should be harmonized. A harmonization would prevent the member states from favouring securities issued by domestic companies and borrowers. Considering the size of the portfolios owned and managed by insurance companies, a harmonization would represent an important contribution to the European integration of markets for bonds and shares.

Table 5.10 gives a rough picture of European insurance patterns in 1989. On average, the EC inhabitants paid ECU 395.5 per year in non-life insurance premiums and ECU 355.3 in life insurance premiums. The total annual premiums for non-life and life insurance represented 2.93 and 2.63 per cent of GDP respectively. These percentages are significantly lower than the figures from the US, namely 5.13 and 3.65 per cent of GDP for non-life and life insurance respectively. In Europe, the propensity to insure is relatively high in the UK, Ireland, the Netherlands, Germany and France. Conversely, the propensity to buy insurance is low in Greece, and with respect to life insurance in Portugal and Italy.

The divergent insurance pattern is interesting from the point of view of a company with Europe-wide operations. The observed differences reflect a large number of underlying factors, some of which have implications for the costs of operating companies in the individual member countries. Demographic trends such as the age distribution of the population are important for savings behaviour and the demand for pension products. The standard of living of the population has implications for the level and structure of insurance premiums. Thus, the relatively high propensity to buy non-life insurance in the northern EC member countries must be evaluated in the light of the widespread ownership of houses, cars, household appliances and other durable goods which are exposed to fire, theft, accidents etc. (CEA 1991). The pattern of life insurance must be studied in the context of the social security systems in the individual member countries.

Table 5.10   Insurance premiums in Europe in relation to population and GDP in 1989

Country	(1) Non-life premiums/ population (ECU)	(2) Life premiums/ population (ECU)	(3) Total non-life premiums/GDP (%)	(4) Total life premiums/GDP (%)
Belgium	416.3	178.4	2.84	1.22
Denmark	515.3	330.9	2.71	1.74
Germany[a]	649.6	396.5	3.61	2.20
Greece	39.6	26.4	0.84	0.56
Spain	196.6	87.3	2.23	2.05
France	443.0	506.2	2.79	3.20
Ireland	347.8	583.5	3.89	6.53
Italy	258.0	84.3	1.88	0.62
Luxembourg	512.1	212.8	2.79	1.16
Netherlands	570.4	508.9	4.05	3.62
Portugal	93.9	24.4	2.45	0.64
United Kingdom	408.8	716.5	3.41	5.97
Total EC	395.5	355.3	2.93	2.63

[a] The *Länder* in former East Germany are not included.
Sources: Dansk Forsikringsaarbog, 1991, 55; Sigma, 1991/2

The traditions in the member countries are somewhat different with respect to private and social insurance concerning persons. In the majority of the European countries, the social security systems have been reformed in recent years and future reforms can be expected. People tend to look at private and social insurance as partly substituting types of cover. The implication is that improvements in the social security system tend to be followed by reduced demand for private insurance and individual retirement benefit schemes. One report (Andersen 1990a) presents the opposite view that private sector provision of pensions has surged because several states in Europe have reduced their commitments to providing for old age. From a company cost point of view it is of course important to gather information on the extent to which the company will have to contribute to the financing of compulsory insurance for employees.

Insurance companies offer non-financial companies protection against a long list of risks. To some extent, insurance companies compete with banks in providing risk management instruments. Risks in connection with cross-border trade in Europe were earlier covered by official export credit institutions on a substantial scale. The official institutions often charged premiums that did not correspond to the risks involved, and it was accordingly difficult for private credit insurance companies to compete. The efforts within the OECD and the EC to reduce government subsidies in connection with exports have partly succeeded. If Eurocomp wants to cover credit risk related to intra-Community trade, the company will probably have to buy cover from a private credit insurer. It must expect the premium to reflect the insurer's assessment of the risks involved.

Insurance and other financial services tend to converge (OECD 1992b; Laboul 1992). Moves in Europe across traditional borders between markets for different financial products have been made by many parties. Insurance companies have made some strategic investments that cross the borders of markets for other financial products. Banks have for their part sought new openings in order to defend market shares and to offset declining profitability in the market for banking services. Some of the initiatives seem to reflect efforts to utilize distribution networks with over-capacity. Moves have been based on an assumed complementarity of products which have traditionally been marketed by different types of financial institutions. Many insurance companies seem to have been motivated by the expected advantages of broadening their own activities as a means of gaining new customers. Some have probably also seen product initiatives as an appropriate answer to the penetration of their markets by banks.

Far from all cross-border initiatives succeed. The experiences are mixed. Customers are not necessarily interested in buying packages of integrated financial services, and joint marketing arrangements therefore do not always function well. There may also be problems of harmonizing corporate culture and image. It is therefore not surprising that the authorities of the individual countries have introduced regulations on ownership linkages between banks and insurance companies that differ considerably (OECD 1991d). Italy, Luxembourg, Spain and the UK seem to have the most liberal attitude to the establishment of groups of companies comprising both banks and insurance companies.

5.6 Derivative Markets

Since 1980, European financial markets have been transformed by the development of new financial instruments. The term is used here to

Table 5.11   Derivative financial instruments traded on organized exchanges worldwide

	Annual turnover of contracts (million)	Open interest positions at end 1990 (ECU billion)
Futures on short-term interest rate instruments	75.7	1003.9
Futures on long-term interest rate instruments	142.6	150.4
Currency futures	29.7	11.8
Interest rate options and options on interest rate futures	51.3	466.0
Currency options and options on currency futures	18.9	43.5
Total	318.2	1675.6

Source: Annual Report 1990/91, Basle: Bank for International Settlements, 141

describe financial futures, options, swaps, forward rate agreements and several other instruments. A *financial futures contract* is a binding agreement to buy or sell a financial instrument at a specified time in the future. The contracts are traded on regulated exchanges; they are highly standardized; underlying securities are delivered through a clearing system; and the clearing house guarantees the fulfilment of contracts entered into by clearing members (Fitzgerald 1983: 1). A *financial option contract* is the right to buy or sell an underlying financial instrument. The statistics in table 5.11 refer to traded options. Such contracts are traded on regulated exchanges; they are highly standardized; and fulfilment of contracts is guaranteed by a margining and marking to market system operated by a centralized clearing house (Fitzgerald 1987: 2). A *swap* is a financial transaction in which two counterparties agree to exchange streams of payments over time. The term 'currency swap' generally refers to a transaction in which two counterparties exchange specific amounts of two different currencies at the outset, and repay over time according to a predetermined rule which reflects both interest payments and amortization of principal. In an 'interest rate swap', no actual principal is exchanged either initially or at maturity, but interest payment streams of differing character are exchanged according to predetermined rules and based on an underlying notional principal amount (BIS 1986: 37). The International Swap

Dealers Association (ISDA) has produced a standard agreement concerning interest rate and currency exchange, and has published a manual with definitions of transactions, the parties, different types of payments and calculation of rates and prices (ISDA 1991). A *forward rate agreement* is a contract in which two parties agree on the interest to be paid on a notional deposit of specified maturity at a specified future settlement date. The period for which the interest is to be paid starts at a later date than the date at which the FRA contract is signed: 'three against six months' would indicate for example the interest rate for a three-month period commencing in three months' time (BIS 1986: 121).

The innovation process started in the United States, but the forms of trading in derivative financial instruments has shifted towards Europe (BIS 1991a: 140). Table 5.11 shows the worldwide turnover of contracts during 1990 and the open interest positions at the end of 1990. BIS has collected the data for table 5.11 from the Futures Industry Association. The amounts comprise trade on the Chicago Mercantile Exchange–International Monetary Market (CME-IMM), the Singapore Mercantile Exchange (SIMEX), the London International Financial Futures Exchange (LIFFE), the Tokyo International Financial Futures Exchange (TIFFE), the Sydney Futures Exchange (SFE) and several other exchanges. The table accordingly presents a picture of global activity in the derivative markets. The European share of the open interest positions was only approximately 25 per cent at the end of 1990. The different American exchanges accounted for more than 50 per cent of the turnover and the open interest positions. The biggest turnover among the different types of contract is in futures on long-term interest rate instruments. The unit of trading depends on the underlying instrument. On LIFFE, for example, the unit of trading for ECU bond futures is ECU 200,000, for long gilt futures GBP 50,000, for Bund futures DEM 250,000, for US Treasury bond futures USD 100,000, and for Japanese government bond futures JPY 100,000,000. The turnover of 142.6 million contracts represents therefore a very high turnover in terms of ECUs or other currency units.

The open interest positions in table 5.11 are much higher for futures on short-term interest rate instruments than on long-term instruments. This may reflect that the market participants are more willing to carry open positions in short-term instruments with a limited interest rate risk. The turnovers in currency futures and currency options represent only about 15 per cent of the number of traded contracts.

BIS also produces semi-annual and year-end surveys of the markets for interest rate swaps and currency swaps. The data are collected from members of the ISDA. The notional principal of outstanding

Table 5.12   European options and futures exchanges and their contracts in 1991

Country	Exchange	Number of futures contracts	Number of options contracts
Belgium	BELFOX	1	7
Denmark	FUTOP	3	9
France	MATIF	8	3[a]
	MONEP	0	27
Germany	DTB	2	15
Ireland	IFOX	4	0
Netherlands	EOE	0	40
	FTA	3	0
	ATA	4	0
Spain	MEFF	6	0
	MOFEX	0	3
UK	LIFFE	11	6[a]
	LTOM	0	70
	IPE	5	2
	OML	9	9
Total		56	191

[a] Including ECU contracts.
Source: ECOFEX Directory 1991

interest rate swaps was ECU 1147.5 billion at the end of December 1990, while the notional principal of currency swaps was ECU 345.8 billion. The distribution according to location of end user shows that European end users were partners in 40 per cent of the interest rate swaps and 45 per cent of the currency swaps (BIS 1991b: 86–7).

The number of options and futures exchanges in Europe grew during the 1980s. In 1988, the Committee of European Options and Futures Exchanges (ECOFEX) was established. In May 1991, ECOFEX membership included 15 full members and 2 associate members (ECOFEX 1991). The exchanges are active in 8 of the 12 EC member countries. Table 5.12 gives an overview of the number of contracts traded on European options and futures exchanges in the spring of 1991; the totals were 56 futures contracts and 191 options contracts. It is remarkable that 70 options were traded on the London Traded Options Market (LTOM). According to a merger plan, LTOM will be merged with LIFFE, which is the largest exchange in the futures markets. From a European financial management perspective, it is interesting to observe that LIFFE and the Marché à Terme International de France

(MATIF) have both introduced ECU bond futures (Fourt 1991). Both exchanges work with a qualification list for bonds, which have the characteristics necessary to be used for delivery. On LIFFE, the ECU bond must have the following characteristics: be issued by a national government or a supranational entity; have an aggregate amount in issue of not less than ECU 1 billion; have a Standard and Poor's or Moody's credit rating of AAA/Aaa; have a remaining maturity on the delivery day of not less than six years and not more than ten years; have a single redemption date; be non-callable; bear no investor put; pay interest at a single fixed rate semi-annually or annually, solely in ECU; be fully paid and eligible for trading in the secondary market; be deliverable through Euroclear and CEDEL; not be subject to withholding tax; and be listed or quoted on a stock exchange. Futures contracts based on such underlying assets can be used to cover ECU interest rate risk (LIFFE 1991: 6). To some extent, the exchanges compete with one another in order to attract business in the derivative markets. In early 1991, the UK and French governments issued deliverable ECU securities, probably in mutual understanding with their respective exchanges (BIS 1991a: 142).

On LIFFE, the ECU bond future has an underlying asset of an ECU 200,000 notional ECU bond with 9 per cent annual coupon and with March, June, September and December as delivery months. On MATIF, the ECU bond future has a highly rated ECU bond with a 10 per cent coupon as underlying instrument; the unit of trading in Paris is ECU 100,000. On LIFFE, there is also a three-month ECU interest rate future based on the British Bankers' Association interest settlement rate for three-month ECU deposits. The unit of trading is ECU 1,000,000.

5.7 Investment Management and Information Services

Management of portfolios of individual stocks and bonds takes time. The manager must have a thorough knowledge of the securities in the relevant markets and of their risk and return characteristics. He must also follow the current stream of market information in order to buy and sell securities at the appropriate times. Many European investors prefer to purchase shares of investment companies or certificates issued by mutual funds because they feel that they do not themselves have the knowledge and time needed for portfolio management. Such a fund is often called an 'undertaking for collective investment in transferable securities' (UCITS); in French the term is 'organisme de placement collectif en valeurs mobilières' (OPCVM).

In 1985, the EC Council adopted a directive on UCITSs (85/611/

EEC)[12] under which a UCITS which is authorized in one member state can market its certificates throughout the Community, without obtaining further authorizations. The activities of the undertaking are supervised by its home state authorities.

Indirect investment through such undertakings and funds that belong to group 65.23 'Other financial intermediation NEC' in the NACE classification in table 5.1 involves both costs and benefits. The companies and funds must build up an administration. Professional portfolio managers are in general paid well, and there are costs related to collection and analysis of market information and handling of portfolios. On the benefits side, there are economies of scale and diversification effects which cannot be obtained by most indvidual investors.

Many UCITSs are listed on European stock exchanges. There is of course a close relationship between the market value of the individual securities in the portfolio of a UCITS and the quoted market price of its certificates. The difference between the market value of the securities and the liabilities of the UCITS is called the 'net asset value' (Sharpe and Alexander 1990: 634). Investors can choose between open-end and closed-end investment funds. Open-end funds stand ready at all times to purchase their own certificates (shares) at or near the net asset value. Closed-end funds are not obliged to do that.

UCITSs play a significant role in many European countries (Andersen 1990b). Most listed European companies can realistically assume that UCITSs belong to their biggest stockholders. The European Federation of Investment Funds and Companies publishes statistics on the assets of UCITSs; table 5.13 is based on this source. The net assets of all 4396 European UCITSs was ECU 527.8 billion at the end of June 1991. Approximately 43 per cent of the net assets were owned by French funds. The French net asset figure is strongly influenced by money market funds. The relative role of UCITSs can be measured by the ratio between total net assets and GDP, as in the last column of table 5.13. This shows that Luxembourg has an outstanding position: total net assets represent approximately 13 times the GDP. An important explanation is that Luxembourg is a financial centre which offers certain tax advantages to non-resident investors. In a number of cases, UCITSs from other EC countries as well as UCITSs from the United States and Japan have established entities in Luxembourg which sell certificates and shares to investors in their home country. In 1988, Luxembourg passed a law which took into account the relevant EC directives that allow cross-border marketing of certificates (Bourse de Luxembourg 1990a: 6). A number of the UCITSs listed in Luxembourg have recently changed their structure to become umbrella funds and thus offer a wide range of investment opportunities within a single legal entity (Bourse de Luxembourg 1990b: 22).

Table 5.13 Number and net assets of UCITSs in ten EC countries[a] at end of June 1991

	Number of funds	Of which equity	bond	Total net assets (ECU billion)	Total net assets/GDP (%)
Belgium	43	—	—	3.7	2.5
Denmark	112	68	32	3.0	3.0
France	929	151	285	226.8	24.5
Germany	311	114	162	59.6	5.1
Ireland	178	136	42	6.0	18.2
Italy	210	131	79	35.3	4.1
Luxembourg	853	—	—	85.8	1300.0
Netherlands	86	56	30	17.8	8.1
Spain	268	206	62	8.9	2.3
United Kingdom	1406	1215	99	80.9	10.4
Total EC	4396	2077	791	527.8	11.2

[a] The total net assets of UCITSs in Portugal was ECU 2.1 billion at the end of 1990 according to *Rapport Annuel 1991*, Paris: Association des Sociétés et Fonds Francais d'Investissements, 40
Source: *Quarterly Statistics June 1991*, Brussels: European Federation of Investment Funds and Companies

Foreign securities represent a varying share of the European UCITS assets. The foreign shares are very small in Ireland, Italy and Spain, and high in Denmark, Germany and the United Kingdom. German UCITSs seem to be very active in markets for foreign bonds, while British UCITSs have a large part of their portfolio in foreign shares.

Some institutions do not deal in securities markets on their own account. If securities brokers or portfolio management companies etc. exclusively deal on behalf of others, they belong to group 67.12 in the NACE classification in table 5.1. The Commission published in 1990 a *Proposal for a Council Directive on Investment Services in the Securities Field*.[13] At the time of writing, the proposal is still subject to complicated negotiations. According to the proposal, investment service firms will obtain authorization in their home member state before commencing to provide investment services. A firm will have sufficient initial capital in accordance with rules which reflect the so-called position risk on the financial instruments.[14] OECD (1991e) reviews a number of the risks which are relevant in connection with the calculation of capital adequacy for investment firms. Member states will draw up prudential rules to be observed on a continuing basis by investment firms authorized by their competent authorities. Supervision of prudential rules will be within the exclusive competence of the home member state's competent authorities. Article 13 of the proposal obliges host member states to ensure that investment firms which are authorized to provide broking, dealing or market making services by the competent authorities of their home member state can have access, either directly or indirectly, to membership of stock exchanges and organized securities markets of host member states where similar services are provided, and also to membership of clearing and settlement systems there which are available to members of such exchanges and markets. The intended cross-border integration of the market for stockbroking and other investment services is reflected very clearly in a proposed rule according to which investment firms may become members of a national stock exchange without having any establishment in the host member state. Similar provisions are proposed in connection with membership of financial futures and options exchanges.

Stock exchanges are classified in NACE group 67.11 'Administration of financial markets'. Stock exchanges sell information. Listed companies pay quotation fees, because they want to have publicity and contact with as many investors as possible. In addition to quotation fees, stock exchanges earn an income through sale of information to financial institutions and institutional investors. The European stock exchanges cooperate and compete at the same time. The Federation of Stock Exchanges in the EC has recently discussed projects called Euroquote and Eurolist. *Euroquote* was planned to be an electronic information system for distribution of real-time trade information from the EC stock exchanges. The plan was to connect the national exchanges and to create possibilities for distribution of company and market information. The plan was also to establish trade facilities between the markets. In 1990 a new company, Euroquote SA, was set up in Brussels in order to manage the development of the necessary systems. In 1991 the company suffered serious financial difficulties and the European stock exchanges decided to liquidate it. *Eurolist* is a project under which the 300–400 biggest European companies should be listed on all EC stock exchanges. Admission to listing on one of the exchanges should automatically give access also to the other 11 exchanges. The two projects were seen by the exchanges as a practical way to further the integration of capital markets. The EC Commission has followed a parallel approach which focuses on the promotion of standards to facilitate access. One of the implications of these initiatives is that multiple listing of securities is likely to occur to a significant degree in Europe in the future. The choice of intermarket linkage system will become very important (Amihud and Mendelson 1991).

There are other information providers on the market whose business is based on the market participants' need for transparency. Reuters, Telerate and other companies offer information on terminals. Subscribers can buy different packages at different prices. In general, the more decision support a user wants to get, the higher the price. Some of the biggest users of the information services have recently begun to cooperate in order to increase the transparency of the bills written by the information vendors (Austin 1991).

Notes

1 *Council Directive of 13 June 1983 on the Supervision of Credit Institutions on a Consolidated Basis (83/350/EEC), Official Journal of the European Communities (OJ),* L 193, 18–20.
2 *OJ,* L 293, 24 October 1990, 21–2.
3 *Council Directive (89/646/EEC) of 15 December 1989 on the Coordination of Laws, Regulations and Administrative Provisions Relating to the Taking Up and Pursuit of the Business of Credit Institutions and Amending Directive 77/ 780/EEC, OJ,* L 386, 1–12.
4 *OJ,* L 386, 30 December 1989, 1.
5 *Commission Recommendation (90/109/EEC) on the Transparency of Banking Conditions Relating to Cross-Border Financial Transactions, OJ,* L 67, 15 March 1990.
6 *OJ,* L 124, 5 May 1989, 16.
7 *OJ,* L 386, 30 December 1989, 14.
8 *OJ,* L 33, 4 February 1987, 16.
9 *OJ,* L 63, 13 March 1979, 1; *OJ,* L 330, 29 November 1990, 50.
10 *OJ,* L 172, 4 July 1988, 1; *OJ,* L 330, 29 November 1990, 44.
11 *OJ,* L 185, 4 July 1987, 72.
12 *Council Directive of 20 December 1985 on the Coordination of Laws, Regulations and Administrative Provisions Relating to Undertakings for Collective Investment in Transferable Securities (UCITS) (85/611/EEC), OJ,* L 375, 31 December 1985, 3, as amended by *OJ,* L 100, 19 April 1988, 31.
13 *OJ,* 1990, C 42, 7.
14 *Amended Proposal for a Council Directive on the Solvency of Investment Firms etc.,* COM (92) 13, final edition, SYN 257, Brussels, 27 January 1992.

6

Capital Structure Decisions in a Single European Market

The aim of this chapter is to put corporate capital structure decisions into a European perspective. It is argued that capital structure matters in a realistic European environment. Differences in leverage across the EC countries are illuminated by available statistics.

6.1 The Relevance of Capital Structure

In a realistic international environment, capital structure has several dimensions. Leverage, i.e. the balance between debt and equity, is just one of them. Eurocomp can choose between many types of debt. Liabilities can be denominated in several currencies. There is also a choice to be made between several types of equity capital.

Leverage is perhaps the most popular of all corporate finance issues. Let us follow the established textbook tradition and start with a reference to Modigliani and Miller's classic 1958 article in the *American Economic Review* (MM). The authors showed under what conditions capital structure is irrelevant. Their model assumed that firms can be identified by risk class, that individual borrowing can substitute for firm borrowing, that all market participants have full information about the returns of the firm, and that there are no taxes. Under these assumptions, investors have arbitrage possibilities that allow them either to acquire appropriate combinations of shares and debt instruments from levered and unlevered firms or to combine holdings of shares in unlevered firms with personal borrowing to duplicate the cash flows of the firms (Ross 1988). MM admitted explicitly that they had applied drastically simplifying assumptions in order to arrive at the capital structure irrelevance proposition. In the last sentence in their article, they called upon fellow researchers to relax some of the simplifying assumptions in order to give the analysis greater realism and relevance. It is no exaggeration to say that thousands of finance theorists followed this suggestion for further research over the next 30 years (Harris and Raviv 1991).

Some of the most interesting contributions to the sometimes very intense debate over the relevance of capital structure came from authors who did not feel able to accept the conclusion that a company's capital structure is irrelevant (Stiglitz 1988). Recent theory suggests a number of factors that under more realistic assumptions can make capital structure decisions relevant. Let us briefly discuss agency costs, asymmetric information, taxes and corporate control considerations.

Models based on *agency costs* start with the observation that there may be conflicts of interest between shareholders and managers and between debtholders and equityholders. Such models can according to Jensen and Meckling (1976) contribute to an understanding of both managerial behaviour and corporate ownership structure. Ownership structure is a somewhat broader concept than leverage because the variables to be determined are not just the relative amounts of debt and equity but also the amount of equity held by the manager. The theory is thus also relevant to the relationship between majority and minority shareholders.

With respect to leverage, agency costs can give an explanation of the common simultaneous use in companies of both debt and outside equity. As agency costs can be assumed to increase with leverage, it is possible to explain why debt does not completely dominate capital structures. The costs of bankruptcy and reorganization will be of concern to the firm's creditors and limit their willingness to finance the firm.

MM's irrelevance hypothesis assumes that all market participants have full and equal information about the characteristics of the firms. Managers and directors of companies can in practice be assumed to be better informed about the characteristics of the companies' return streams and investment opportunities than outside investors. It is their job to ask for such information from the employees in the firm, to evaluate the information and to make decisions based on it. *Asymmetric information* is obviously the normal state of affairs. The asymmetry may, in the words of Stephen A. Ross, cause differences between the return stream of the company as perceived by the insiders and the return stream as perceived by the market (Ross 1977).

It is also possible that changes in the financial structure can alter the perception of outside investors. By relaxing the MM assumption of symmetric information, a theory of the determination of the financial structure of the firm can be developed. One approach developed by Leland and Pyle (1977) attaches importance to the entrepreneur's willingness to invest his own money in the company. The larger the proportion of equity owned by the manager, the better impression the external investors will have of the quality of the company's projects. Consequently, it should be expected that the value of the firm increases with the share of the firm held by the entrepreneur. When entrepreneurs exhibit risk aversion and behave according to the theory, firms with riskier returns will have lower debt levels even when there are no bankruptcy costs.

The asymmetric information approach has also been applied to analysis of the stock price reaction to new equity issues. New security issues seem in many cases to be interpreted by the market to indicate bad news. Firms seeking new financing often observe a drop in the price of their stock at the announcement date of the new issue. The price reaction depends of course on the conditions offered. Outside investors may, however, be of the opinion that the insiders will be more interested in selling shares in the market in periods in which they believe that the market has overvalued the shares. So the external market participants infer from the decision to issue new shares that there is such a difference between the insiders' and the outsiders' evaluation. Dybvig and Zender (1991) have suggested that price reactions to capital structure changes and dividend announcements do not necessarily repudiate the irrelevancy proposition.

The capital structure irrelevance proposition was derived by MM for a world with no *taxes*. A large number of articles have therefore introduced taxes and the majority of them have concluded that the value of the firm can be increased by debt financing because the interest payments related to the debt can be deducted from taxable corporate income.

Merton H. Miller has repeatedly challenged this modified version of capital structure theory (Miller 1977; 1988). According to Miller, one needs to look at the combined tax effects at the individual and corporate levels. In equilibrium, the price of debt should reflect the tax rate of the marginal investor owning corporate debt. Under certain simplified equilibrium conditions, it is conceivable that the advantage to the levered corporation of the right to deduct interest payments to bondholders is neutralized by a 'grossing up' of these interest payments by any differential in the taxes that the bondholders will have to pay on their interest income. In Miller's equilibrium, the tax rate of the marginal investor in corporate bonds should be equal to the corporate tax rate and hence the tax advantage of debt due to deductible corporate interest payments is offset by the income tax on interest income at the personal level. Miller's analysis has since been generalized by DeAngelo and Masulis (1980) to encompass personal income tax on equity income.

Miller had basically a one-country world in mind. In the present book, it is of course of great interest to look at the implications for capital structure decisions of the funding of Eurocomp in several countries. Bondholders as well as shareholders may have their residence in different European countries. The analyst has then to cope with differential taxation of corporations and individual investors. Lee and Zechner (1984) have taken a first step and considered Miller's theorem of leverage irrelevance in a two-country world. They conclude that in the presence of barriers to international investment, it is possible to maintain the irrelevance proposition. If the tax regimes differ across countries and if capital markets are perfectly integrated, however, the firms will specialize in their capital structure decisions depending upon their location.

A further generalization of Miller's analysis is to apply it in a world with multiple tax jurisdictions and multiple currencies. Hodder and Senbet (1990) assume that there are symmetrical tax codes in all countries and that government restrictions are absent. It is, under these assumptions, still possible to derive Miller equilibrium conditions. The authors assume that corporations are ready to employ all conceivable mechanisms to arbitrage tax rate differences across countries. In their model corporations thus play a critical role in bringing about international capital structure equilibrium. In such an equilibrium, the marginal investor tax rate in world markets should be equal to the highest of the various corporate tax rates among different nations.

As we shall see in chapter 10, there are numerous differences in tax codes across countries that may cause deviations from international capital structure equilibrium. This does not make the equilibrium analysis irrelevant. If there are reasons to believe – at least at the European level – that the tax systems will gradually become more similar, one can imagine a development from the present almost incomprehensible disequilibrium, in which the capital structure decisions of Eurocomp are definitely relevant, in the direction of an equilibrium. There is a very long way to go, however.

Corporate control considerations are related to the probability of a takeover. Debt plays a decisive role in most takeovers (Jensen 1988). Debt creation enables managers to bond their promise to pay out future cash flows. When debt is issued in exchange for stock, managers give shareholder recipients of the debt the right to take the firm into bankruptcy if they become unable to service the debt. Capital structure can affect the outcome of control contests because it determines the balance between voting equity and non-voting debt. Higher debt levels can result in a lower profitability for the acquirer and, therefore, in a lower probability of acquisition (Israel 1991). In chapter 9, takeovers are discussed in a broader European context.

6.2 European Capital Structure Patterns

The long-standing debate on capital structure has been dominated by American researchers and by empirical evidence from American companies. Since there seem to be considerable differences between countries in observed capital structures, a broader basis for the debate is desirable. Once a year, the Directorate for Financial, Fiscal and Enterprise Affairs of the OECD publishes *Non-Financial Enterprises Financial Statements*. This brings together balance sheets, statements of income and change in net worth, and sources and uses of funds, from manufacturing and other non-financial companies in the member countries. The coverage of the material differs from country to country: in some countries, data are taken from only a small sample of companies. The Directorate accordingly warns readers that international comparisons based on the publication are difficult owing to the vast differences in both volume and quality of the basic material available and in the methods employed for calculation and valuation.

With these warnings in mind, let us take a look at table 6.1. There the liability structure of non-financial companies in nine countries is illuminated by means of percentages. Such percentages, in some cases calculated from the balance sheets of several hundred companies, may of course conceal a considerable intercompany variation in liability structures.

The first observation to make in table 6.1 is that the United States and Japan represent the two opposite extreme cases. The American companies included have the highest equity proportion at 56.7 per cent in the balance sheet, while the Japanese companies with 19.2 per cent have the lowest proportion. The second observation is that, within the group of EC countries, the variation in equity proportions is modest. The British companies have the highest proportion at 47.5 per cent, while the Italian companies have the lowest at 32.2 per cent. The composition of the equity capital varies, however, considerably among the EC countries. Reserves and provisions dominate in the British and French companies, while share capital dominates in Belgian and Dutch companies.

The American and Japanese companies are also extreme cases with respect to short-term liabilities. The detailed tables in the OECD publication reveal that the Japanese companies rely heavily on financing by means of short-term bills and bonds, short-term loans from financial institutions and trade credits received. The relative importance of these financing sources is much smaller in the US.

The percentages are based on book values of debt and equity. Ratios based on market values would have been preferable from a theoretical

Table 6.1 Liability structure of non-financial enterprises in 1988 (per cent)

	BEF	DKK	DEM	FRF	ITL	NLG	GBP	USD	JPY
					Country by ISO currency code				
Equity	36.6	42.0	39.7	37.4	32.2	39.8	47.5	56.7	19.2
of which: Share captial	21.1	12.6	13.7	8.7	10.0	23.6	7.9	—	4.6
Reserves and provisions	15.5	29.4	26.0	28.7	22.2	16.2	39.6	—	14.6
Short-term liabilities	42.1	40.7	43.0	47.3	44.6	37.4	36.7	15.5	54.8
Long-term liabilities	21.3	17.3	17.3	15.3	23.2	22.8	15.8	27.8	26.0
Total liabilities	100.0	100.0	100.0	100.0	100.0	100.0	100.0	100.0	100.0

For ISO currency codes see appendix A.
Source: Non-Financial Enterprises Financial Statements, OECD Financial Statistics Part 3, Paris: OECD, 1990

point of view, but let us accept the book values as surrogates for the market values. Most of the figures are based on 1988 accounting data. The exception is the Italian figures, which are from 1983. The pattern observed in table 6.1 is affected by variations in accounting standards and practices. The extent to which balance sheet entries represent historic costs, written-down values or estimates of current value vary. In France and the United Kingdom, there has been a tradition for revaluing of the property portfolio of corporations approximately every five years. In the US, Germany and Japan property has in general been included in the balance sheet at historic cost (Rutterford 1985). In periods with rising property prices, such differences in valuation practices may cause considerable biases in the observed leverage ratios. In the middle of the 1980s, the price trend in the market for industrial property was increasing in most of the OECD countries. Particularly in the case of Japan, this development combined with the use of historic cost accounting must be assumed to have caused a strong underestimation of the equity proportion based on market values. Sekely and Collins (1988) try to explain capital structure differences by means of cultural factors. In his study of leverage in non-financial companies, Borio (1990) finds that the differences between low-leverage countries and high-leverage countries have tended to narrow since the early 1980. Jessen and Frederiksen (1991) have compared the leverage of Danish listed companies within different industries.

The early capital structure literature assumed in general that debt was corporate bonds with fixed interest rates issued in the private capital market. Short-term debt to banks and to suppliers played a very limited role or was in fact omitted. Considering the importance of short-term liabilities in most of the countries in table 6.1, this is a serious omission. Short-term bank financing plays a considerable role in most of the EC countries. European companies to a large extent have preferred to finance themselves through financial intermediaries. The reasons for this may be grouped according to the previously mentioned capital structure relevance arguments, namely agency costs, asymmetric information, taxes and corporate control considerations.

The agency costs of debt can be reduced by the establishment of close relationships between managers and creditors. When companies prefer bank financing rather than public issues of bonds to thousands of investors, negotiations with a few officials from the bank replace disclosure of public information and a formal system for protection of anonymous creditors. In connection with the financing of new investment projects, corporate customers will often seek and get the advice of bank officials. If a company with debt gets into trouble, it is fairly easy for the bank to use its influence on the management, perhaps by appointing new experienced board members. Germany, France and Japan are known for close relationships between banks and non-financial companies. In Germany, bank directors can sit on supervisory boards: this is not allowed in most other EC countries.

Close relationships between banks and their corporate customers can also cause information asymmetries. Banks in France, Germany and Japan can thus be assumed to have information about their client firms which is superior to the information held by the general public. The minimum requirements for the disclosure of information in connection with new public issues apply to financing through the market. It is common practice that banks give their corporate customers advice on the formulation of prospectuses.

Taxation of capital income differs among the countries: this subject is discussed in chapter 10. In studying table 6.1 it should, however, be kept in mind that the observed differences in the corporate liability structures may be affected by the different tax treatment of dividends, capital gains and interest incomes and expenditures.

Corporate control considerations may in this context be looked at as dependent on the closeness of the relationship between banks and corporate customers. Financial intermediation may thus provide a mechanism of commitment in a long-term customer–bank relationship (Hellwig 1991). If Eurocomp finds such a long-term commitment desirable it may prefer to use bank financing because this is seen as an integral part of the contractual relationships with the bank.

There may also be some basic cost considerations behind the choice of financing instrument. It is fairly costly to issue bonds and to sell them directly to private investors. Direct financing of this kind may only be a realistic option for large, well known public companies. As mentioned in chapter 5, it is such companies that have established note issuance facilities in cooperation with their banks. Smaller companies will have to borrow from financial intermediaries which can diversify the risk and transform the claims into forms desired by the individual investors.

6.3 Basis for Debt Financing Decisions

Europe is not a Modigliani-Miller world. In section 6.1 the existence of agency costs, asymmetric information, taxes and corporate control considerations was used to support the relevance of Eurocomp's financial structure. The FM has good reasons to study the characteristics of different financing sources. Different combinations on the liability

Table 6.2   Interest and inflation data for financing decisions in October 1991

Loan currency	Interest rate (% per annum)	12-months forward rate	Inflation rate (% per annum)
BEF	9.43	ECU 0.02382/BEF	2.00
DKK	9.93	ECU 0.12675/DKK	2.01
DEM	9.43	ECU 0.48999/DEM	4.11
GRD	24.12	ECU 0.00388/GRD	17.37
ESP	12.25	ECU 0.00761/ESP	6.03
FRF	9.43	ECU 0.14385/FRF	2.99
IEP	10.62	ECU 1.29455/IEP	3.56
ITL	11.68	ECU 0.00064/ITL	6.04
LUF	9.43	ECU 0.02382/LUK	2.00
NLG	9.43	ECU 0.43485/NLG	4.69
PTE	13.50	ECU 0.00550/PTE	11.44
GBP	10.25	ECU 1.41771/GBP	4.73
USD	5.62	ECU 0.86607/USD	3.76
JPY	6.06	ECU 0.00666/JPY	3.56
	9.87	ECU 1.00000/ECU	

For ISO currency codes see appendix A.
Sources: Eurostatistics 1991 no. 10; Unibank A/S, Copenhagen

side of the balance sheet of debt and equity instruments make a difference to the company. Let us take a look at debt financing. In general, a trade-off has to be made between two objectives: minimizing the expected after-tax cost of financing, and keeping risks to acceptable levels. The job is complicated in a realistic European environment. The FM cannot expect to find an explicit analytical framework for quantifying the trade-off.

Assume that the FM on one particular day has to seek 12-month funding for Eurocomp equivalent to ECU 100,000. Assume further that he has at his disposal the data presented in table 6.2. What currency should the FM choose? If the world has risk neutral investors, floating exchange rates, market determined interest rates, and worldwide symmetric taxation of all types of capital income, then interest rates, spot exchange rates, forward exchange rates and inflation rates are, as explained by Eiteman et al. (1992), related according to a set of international parity conditions (international parity theories are discussed in chapter 8). If all the international parity conditions hold, we have a beautiful model world: let us call it an 'international parity world'. It has certain similarities to the Modigliani-Miller world. One of the similarities is that financing decisions become irrelevant. In an international parity world, Eurocomp should thus be indifferent between debt denominated in different currencies. Considering the range of nominal interest rates in table 6.2, from 5.62 per cent p.a. for USD loans to 24.12 per cent p. a. for GRD loans, this is a striking observation. In the so-called international Fisher equilibrium, the nominal interest rate difference between USD and GRD loans should thus be neutralized by an expected depreciation of the Greek currency.

But Europe is different from an international parity world (Froot and Thaler 1990). Several factors explain the deviations from the idealized model world. First, most market participants seem to be risk averse. They tend to look at the market opportunities from their host country currency point of view and they demand a risk premium in order to expose themselves to foreign exchange risk (Froot and Frankel 1989). Secondly, the European currencies are not floating mutually. Since 1979, the fluctuations of the mutual spot exchange rates between most of the EC currencies have been constrained by the EMS intervention rates. The cooperation between the central banks is described in chapter 3. The market rates have therefore not been free to reflect the portfolio adjustments of private investors and borrowers which form the theoretical basis for the international parity conditions. Neither have the market rates been allowed fully to reflect the adjustments of exporters and importers to changing competitiveness due to different inflation rates between the countries. The purchasing power parity theory is based on such international trade adjustments. When mutual exchange rates among the EMS currencies are managed rather than left to market forces, one may alternatively ask if the adjustments of the bilateral parity exchange rates have attempted to re-establish purchasing power parity. This aspect is included in a study by Edison and Fisher (1991). They conclude that they have found strong evidence that the realignments of the EMS have not served to maintain competitiveness between its member countries. In the sample period 1979–88 Italy, the highest-inflation country in the period of analysis, does seem to have lost competitiveness under the EMS.

There are interest rates in Europe that are not market determined. To some extent, governments have provided for financing at subsidized interest rates. This applies in particular to financing of exports, ship building and agriculture (OECD 1990a). Within the framework of OECD, which has formulated guidelines for officially supported export credits, efforts have been made to reduce the application of subsidized credits. Favourable interest rates on credits for exports are also dealt with in the international trade negotiations that take place in GATT (Snape 1991). The ongoing negotiations will probably result in a reduced level of interest rate subsidies in the European countries, but some subsidies can be expected to remain in operation. Possibilities for financing at rates below the market interest rates represent deviations from an international parity world. Eurocomp should therefore in its debt financing decisions be aware of the arbitrage opportunities.

The international parity world assumes also worldwide symmetric taxation of all types of capital income. The European financial landscape is more complicated than that. The EC member countries do not treat interest expenditures, gains and losses on forward contracts, and gains and losses on uncovered foreign exchange spot positions, in the same way. Differential treatment may be found across different types of capital income, across different categories of economic agents, as well as across countries. As explained in chapter 10, there seems to be a tendency to subject exchange gains and losses to tax rates that are lower than the rates applied to interest expenses. The private agents in the market must be assumed to be interested in the after-tax financing costs. As long as the market participants are subjected to asymmetric tax systems, the rates formed by the international financial markets must be expected to reflect a mixture of different tax induced arbitrage transactions. The observed interest and exchange rate structure will accordingly normally open certain arbitrage opportunities to companies because the observed rate structure is a result of the transactions of different 'tax clients'.

Eiteman et al. (1992) refer to a number of empirical studies. Most interest rate parity studies support the theory, while the results are mixed with respect to purchasing power parity (PPP), the international Fisher effect and the use of the forward rate as a predictor of future spot rates (Pope and Peel 1991). In studies involving European currencies it is not surprising that the results are mixed: the deviations from the international parity world are considerable. The results are, however, also mixed for non-European currencies. Patel (1990) is an example of studies which fail to find support for PPP even in the long run. What might surprise some readers is the fact that interest rate parity studies seem to conclude that combinations of nominal interest differences and forward premiums or forward discounts lie close to equilibrium within narrow arbitrage boundaries primarily determined by transaction costs (Poitras 1988). The FM in Eurocomp could conclude from this evidence that the impact of the covered interest rate arbitrage transactions of banks and other market participants on the forward rates and the money market rates is so powerful that the interest rate parity theory can be given strong empirical support.

7

Stockholder Relations, Investor Information and Dividend Policy

The aim of this chapter is to analyse the information flow from companies to investors, and corporate dividend policy in Europe. Differences in share ownership across countries have implications for the need for disclosure of company information. Not only the EC institutions but also several professional organizations try to improve the comparability of company information. Some accounting researchers support, others oppose the international harmonization of accounting standards. The contents of the EC Insider Trading Directive are discussed. It is finally argued that corporate dividend decisions are relevant, and a number of factors to consider in such decisions are listed.

7.1 Information Flows and Stockholder Relations

Financial markets have an important allocation function. It is essential to the growth of the economy that market participants who save more than they invest in physical assets can use the market to acquire claims on market participants who invest more than they save. It is also essential that the markets allow the investors to readjust their portfolios according to changes in their expectations with respect to yields and risks.

Investors need information in order to form such expectations. When we concentrate on the stock market, the information can be subdivided into financial market information, company information and information provided by financial analysis firms. *Financial market information* illuminates price behaviour for financial instruments in the market. Data are registered by stock exchanges and distributed through information service firms, newspapers and banks. This type of information allows comparative studies of the pricing of financial instruments issued by different companies and of the time series properties of prices and rates etc. *Company information* is produced and disclosed by the companies that issue shares and debt instruments in cooperation with their auditors. The information is distributed through annual reports, interim reports and press releases and is brought to the general public through official gazettes, business newspapers and information services. *Information from financial analysts* is based on the two other types of information. Analysts gather market and company information, make arbitrage calculations and forecasts, and make buy and sell recommendations to their subscribers and other customers.

The appropriateness of the information flows must be evaluated in the light of the relationships between the companies and their shareholders. The majority of the companies resident in the European Community are small and unlisted. The shares are owned by a limited number of investors with residence in the same country as the company's host country, and there are often family relations between the personal investors. The investors own the securities for many years and typically have fairly close contact with the management. Some of the shareholders are employed by the company and/or represented on the board of directors. Unlisted companies are subject to some legal disclosure requirements but these requirements are relatively small compared with the requirements concerning listed companies. The external users of accounting information disclosed by unlisted companies are typically not shareholders but rather banks, large suppliers, customers or other business connections. If the company in question uses bank financing to a considerable extent, the bank will of course possess information about the company which goes beyond the contents of the disclosed annual report.

The framework for information flows is quite different in connection with big listed companies with thousands of shareholders. If some of the shareholders have their residence in other member countries, the information flow must take differences in language and currency into consideration. There are relatively few big listed companies in most of the EC countries but, owing to their size and economic importance, the disclosure practices of these companies have been a matter of political concern for many years. It is in particular in relation to the big listed companies that different groups of participants in the financial markets may take opposing positions on various issues relating to accounting disclosure and measurement (Hakansson 1981). It is costly to produce and disclose company information. Corporate managers must also take into consideration that disclosed information is studied not only by the shareholders and the creditors but also by the competitors. There are therefore limits on the amounts of company information that managers want to disclose. The wish to establish and maintain good relations with actual and potential investors influences corporate disclosure policy in the opposite direction. Verchère (1991) sees the disclosure policy as an essential part of a company's investor relations programme. Financial managers attempting to raise funds from investors with residence in different countries must be able to communicate with readers that reside and operate in socio-economic environments that differ markedly from that of the company (Choi 1989).

Compared with the United States, individual share ownership has been relatively modest in most European countries. There has apparently been a strong tradition for households to put their savings into bank accounts and bonds issued by governments and credit institutions. This tradition is often related to the comparatively dominant position of banks in the financial systems of many European countries (Warren 1990). Individual shareholders have in general no access to private information concerning listed companies. They have to rely on published annual reports and press releases about major corporate financial decisions. More public disclosure will therefore definitely correspond to the needs of small personal investors.

Since the middle of the 1970s, there has been a growing activity in the European securities markets. The number of listed companies has increased, the investments of institutional investors and undertakings for collective investment in transferable securities (UCITSs) have grown, and laws with regulation affording investor protection have been passed by all EC parliaments. Minimum requirements concerning the disclosure of company information have been part of investor protection. The development of the European securities laws has been strongly affected by EC measures (Empel 1990).

7.2   Required Investor Information

In chapter 2, the EC harmonization efforts were surveyed. Of particular interest here is the company law harmonization programme and the measures concerning stock exchanges. The EC measures must be evaluated in the light of the activity of other international organizations. The International Accounting Standards Committee, the International Federation of Accountants, the UN Commission on Transnational Corporations and the Organization for Economic Cooperation and Development are all active in efforts to harmonize accounting standards (Rivera 1989). Among the aims of these organizations are improvements of the comparability of company information from enterprises in different countries, reduction of the costs borne by multinational enterprises which at present have to comply with different national standards, and facilitation of the mutual recognition of prospectuses for multinational securities offerings (IASC 1989).

The relatively slow pace of international accounting harmonization has been disappointing to some proponents of more harmonization. Rivera (1989) explains the limited progress by referring to the lack of a structured theoretical accounting framework underlying the issuance of specific standards, the multiplicity of permitted reporting and recording options included in the current standards, the tendency to address only those issues developed in or related to advanced economic environments where sophisticated markets and information prevail, and the lack of enforceability of the international standards. Choi and Mueller (1978: 23) have a more sceptical attitude towards international harmonization of accounting standards. According to their view, there are such big differences between the socio-economic and cultural conditions in the individual countries that the objectives of accounting systems will always be somewhat different.

The global efforts to harmonize accounting standards can be expected to continue for many years even though the prospects for success remain uncertain. At the time of writing, international accounting diversity remains very important and has profound implications for the decisions of capital market participants (Choi and Levich 1990).

Within the European Communities, accounting diversity has been reduced to some extent by the approximation of the relevant laws. The reason why the harmonization trend seems to be stronger in Europe than elsewhere is probably the enforceability of the EC measures. As briefly mentioned in chapter 2, the Fourth Company Law Directive on the annual accounts of companies (78/660/EEC)[1] obliges the member states to incorporate into their accounting laws and regulations a number of provisions concerning the structure of the balance sheet, the profit and loss account and the notes on the accounts. The Seventh Company Law Directive on consolidated accounts (83/349/EEC)[2] obliges the member states to require parent companies in their jurisdictions to draw up consolidated accounts and a consolidated annual report. Whereas the company and accounting laws of all the member states are today adapted to the Fourth and the Seventh Directives, it should in principle be fairly easy to make comparative studies of the economic performance of companies from different countries in the Community.

As mentioned above, listed companies are subject to tougher information requirements. This is reflected in the following five EC directives: the *Admission Directive* (79/279/EEC as amended by 82/148/EEC), the *Listing Particulars Directive* (80/390/EEC as amended by 82/148/EEC and 89/298/EEC), the *Interim Reports Directive* (82/121/EEC), the *Major Holdings Transactions Directive* (88/627/EEC) and the *Insider Trading Directive* (89/592/EEC).[3]

Table 7.1   Listing Particulars Directive, schedule A: conditions for the admission of shares to official listing on a stock exchange

---

1   *Conditions relating to companies for the shares of which admission to official listing is sought*
   1.1   Legal position of the company
   1.2   Minimum size of the company
   1.3   A company's period of existence
2   *Conditions relating to the shares for which admission to official listing is sought*
   2.1   Legal position of the shares
   2.2   Negotiability of the shares
   2.3   Public issue preceding admission to official listing
   2.4   Distribution of shares
   2.5   Listing of shares of the same class
   2.6   Physical form of shares
   2.7   Shares issued by companies from a non-member state

Source: *Official Journal of the European Communities (OJ)*, L 66, 1979, 21; L 62, 1982, 22; L 334, 1989, 30

It follows from the introductory remarks in these directives that the EC Council wants to put investors in a position to make correct assessments of the risks related to investments in transferable securities. When a company wants to go public or when major financial decisions are being made, for instance in connection with mergers and acquisitions, it is deemed necessary to provide more information to the investors. Thus, an application for stock exchange listing must be accompanied by documentation for fulfilment of a number of minimum conditions. Among the conditions mentioned in the Admission Directive are that the issuer of the securities has a prescribed market capitalization for the shares, that he has published accounts or financial statements for at least three years and that the securities will be freely negotiable.

The Listing Particulars Directive prescribes a number of detailed disclosure requirements that must be fulfilled prior to approval of the listing. Schedule A of the directive reflects the views of the regulators with respect to what they consider to be essential information for investors who contemplate purchases of listed shares. The headings of schedule A are presented in table 7.1. The company seeking official listing will thus have to document that the legal position of the company is in conformity with the laws and regulations to which it is subject (condition 1.1). The foreseeable market capitalization of the shares must be at least ECU 1 million (1.2); however, member states may provide for admission to official listing even when this condition is not fulfilled, provided that the competent authorities are satisfied that there will be an adequate market for the shares concerned. A company must have published or filed its annual accounts in accordance with national law for the three financial years preceding the application for official listing (1.3). The legal position of the shares must be in conformity with laws and regulations (2.1) and the shares must be freely negotiable (2.2). The first listing may be made only after the end of the period during which subscription applications may be submitted (2.3). A sufficient number of shares must be distributed to the public (2.4). The application for admission to official listing must cover all the shares of the same class already issued (2.5). It is necessary and sufficient that the physical form of the shares complies with the standards laid down in the member state in which the issuer has his residence (2.6); if this form does not correspond to the standards in the country where listing is sought, it is the duty of the competent authorities of that country to inform the public. Shares issued by a company with residence in a non-EC country but not listed on the stock exchange of that country can only be admitted to official listing if the competent authorities are satisfied that the lack of listing in the home country does not reflect a need to protect the investors (2.7).

7.3   Inside Information

Insider dealing has been discussed as a regulatory problem at the Community level since 1970, when provisions concerning such dealing were included in the first proposal for a European company statute.[4] In 1977, the Commission issued a formal recommendation to the member states about a European code of conduct relating to transactions in transferable securities.[5] Some, but not all, of the member states took initiatives in the form of formulation of ethical but not legally binding rules for transactions in listed securities. In 1987, the Commission published a draft directive on insider dealing. After a number of modifications, the Insider Trading Directive (89/592/EEC) was adopted by the Council in November 1989.[6] The member states should transform the provisions of the directive into National law by 1 June 1992.

In the directive, inside information is defined as information of a precise nature which has not been made public, but which, if it were made public, would be likely to have a significant effect on the price of the transferable securities in question. The member states are, according to the directive, obliged to prohibit insiders from taking advantage of their knowledge by acquiring or disposing of securities.

Table 7.2 Classification of potential insiders

1 *Primary insiders*
  1.1 Management of the issuing company
  1.2 Members of the supervisory board of the issuing company
  1.3 (Large) shareholders
  1.4 Employees of the issuing company
  1.5 Auditors of the issuing company
  1.6 Attorneys of the issuing company
  1.7 Bankers
  1.8 Suppliers and customers
  1.9 Participants in a planned merger
  1.10 Management of companies with a group affiliation with the issuing company
  1.11 Members of the supervisory board of companies with a group affiliation
  1.12 Employees, auditors, attorneys, bankers and others working for companies with a group affiliation with the issuing company
  1.13 Consultants and advisers
  1.14 Officials of the government, the central bank or Community institutions
  1.15 Members of the press
  1.16 Financial analysts
2 *Secondary insiders*
  2.1 Family members of primary insiders
  2.2 Other persons who get advice and information from primary insiders
  2.3 Members of the same group of companies
  2.4 Other persons who by chance or otherwise get information from primary insiders

The group of insiders is fairly broad. In table 7.2 insiders are classified as primary and secondary insiders (Hopt 1990). *Primary insiders* have in common that they are working close to the origin of inside information. Groups 1.1 and 1.2 consist of decision makers. The management and the supervisory board have among their duties to make investment and financing decisions on behalf of the company. The profitability of such decisions depends in many cases on correct timing in relation to what the competitors are doing. It is therefore essential that groups 1.1 and 1.2 are entitled to keep many kinds of information confidential. It is obvious that they, in their capacity as decision makers, must possess information about company decisions before persons who are not involved in the decision making process.

The preparation of company decisions is normally carried out by group 1.4, the employees of the issuing company. They have therefore access to information at a fairly early stage by virtue of the exercise of their employment. If major corporate investment decisions are to be made, the auditors, attorneys and bankers (groups 1.5, 1.6 and 1.7) will normally also be involved before the final decision is taken. They are therefore included as primary insiders.

Group 1.8, suppliers and customers, can possess inside information, for instance because they are familiar with unusual events or contracts with profound implications for the economy of the issuing company. If merger negotiations are going on or if a takeover proposal is under way, there will be several persons who in the planning stage are external to the issuing company but possess information which could have a strong impact on the security price. Group 1.9 includes the management, board members, employees and other persons working for a potential offeror or offeree as primary insiders.

In listed companies, most shareholders are outsiders in terms of the information they possess. Large shareholders (group 1.3) will in practice often be better informed, but this will in most cases be due to their membership of the supervisory board (group 1.2). If the issuing company is part of a group of companies that work closely together, it becomes natural to include managers, board members and employees of the parent company (groups 1.10, 1.11 and 1.12) as primary insiders. Again, there will often be an overlap with group 1.2.

Consultants and advisers (group 1.13) can be hired by the company, by potential merger partners or by individual shareholders in order to evaluate the implications of big deals. At the moment when they are hired and provided with material, they become primary insiders in the sense of the directive. Under certain circumstances officials of the government, the central bank or Community institutions can become insiders (group 1.14). This may be when the financial performance of the issuing company depends on political decisions concerning the right to exploit natural resources, the allocation of government research or development contracts or access to special project financing arrangements.

Press releases via the stock exchange are not the only way in which the press, financial analysts and the public are informed about company affairs. Inspired by the American tradition, it is becoming more and more common in big European companies that the management meets the press regularly or arranges so-called 'roadshows' during which the information released in annual reports or prospectuses is explained. Questions from journalists (group 1.15) and financial analysts (group 1.16) are answered during such arrangements by spokesmen for the company. Experienced interviewers may occasionally be quite aggressive, and the management and information officers of the company must try to keep in mind the distinction between inside information and information which has been made public.

The *secondary insiders* mentioned in table 7.2 have in common that they are at some distance from the origin of the inside information. Group 2.1, family members of primary insiders, is included because of the close economic ties that normally exist between members of the same family. Group 2.2 covers friends of primary insiders and other persons who are advised by them. Members of the same group of companies (group 2.3) may be at such a distance from the information source that they are classified not in group 1.10 or 1.11 but as secondary insiders. Finally, group 2.4 is a residual group comprising persons who in some way or another get information from primary insiders. The classic example is the taxi driver who listens to a conversation between passengers who are primary insiders.

The insider dealing problem cannot be handled by prohibitions against asymmetric information. Asymmetry of information will always exist because some market participants make the corporate decisions themselves while other market participants have to rely on published company information. The insider dealing problem must be handled by disclosure provisions. Companies must be obliged to disclose price-sensitive information in a way which as far as possible ensures that all investors are given access to new information simultaneously. Article 7 of the directive extends the provisions for timely disclosure from the Admission Directive to all issuers of transferable securities that are admitted to trading on official markets.

7.4 Dividend Policy

In a now classic article, Miller and Modigliani (MM) (1961) demonstrated the so-called 'dividend irrelevance theorem' according to which the value of the firm is independent of its dividend decisions. The theorem was based on a perfect market, no taxes, and full information assumptions. One of the implications of such assumptions is that all external investors have the same information about the firm's earnings prospects as have the company insiders. In section 7.3, asymmetry of access to company information was described as the normal state of affairs. It seems therefore appropriate to select a theory of corporate dividend behaviour which takes account of the fact that company insiders are better informed about the investment and earnings opportunities of the firm than are company outsiders.

Disclosure of company information reduces information asymmetry. Earnings announcements and dividend announcements convey new information to the external investors, and it is well documented in empirical research that such announcements have an impact on stock prices (Beaver 1968; Cornell and Landsman 1989). Corporate managers who care for the wealth of the shareholders must accordingly take the likely price effect of their dividend decisions into consideration. Dividend becomes relevant, but the core of the MM reasoning does not disappear because information asymmetry is introduced. All companies operate under constraints on the sources and uses of funds. A company which pays out part of its current earnings in the form of dividends to the shareholders has to find alternative financing for its investment projects. Money raised from outsiders to provide this financing implies a new burden on the company which reduces the value of the company by an amount more or less corresponding to the value of the disbursed dividend.

It is thus, according to MM, the earnings prospects of the company that really count when investors decide what price they are prepared to pay for the shares. When a dividend announcement effect on share prices is observed, it may be interpreted as an indirect way to convey information about the company's future earnings prospects (Miller and Rock 1985). In particular, if the company tends to have a relatively stable payout ratio, it is fairly simple to estimate the underlying earnings.

The frequency of dividend announcements varies from country to country. Some of the American contributions to the theory of dividend behaviour reflect the common practice of US companies of paying dividends on a quarterly basis. Under this practice, it becomes relevant for financial analysts to try to estimate corporate earnings on the basis of announced dividends. In Europe, it seems to be more common for companies to pay dividends annually. The implication of the European practice is that earnings figures and dividend figures tend to be disclosed by the companies simultaneously. It is therefore in general not possible for analysts to decompose the share price reaction into an earnings announcement effect and a dividend announcement effect.

Brennan (1991) has pointed out some interesting tendencies in the division of labour between financial economists and accounting researchers. His findings have implications for which type of journal readers with an interest in stock price reactions to dividend announcements should look for. According to Brennan, financial researchers have in recent years moved away from trying to relate stock prices to company information and towards the use of close substitutes to price financial assets and contracts. The study of share price reactions to new company information has been largely taken over by accounting researchers.

One of the difficulties these empirical researchers have to cope with is that the accounting income data which can be gathered from published company accounts do not correspond to the theoretical economic concept of income applied by MM. It will in general be impossible for external analysts to get hold of the additional company information, for instance on future investment opportunities, which would be necessary if the flow of earnings is to be adjusted according to the theoretical requirements.

Shareholders will normally have to pay taxes on their dividend income. They may also be taxed on their capital gains in some cases. The company management must therefore take into consideration how the dividend decision is likely to affect the distribution of the shareholders' return on dividend payments and capital gains. If reinvestment of corporate earnings implies capital gains to the shareholders which are taxed moderately or not at all, there is a strong case for keeping the dividend payments at a low level (Miller and Scholes 1978).

In chapter 10, a survey is given of the tax systems in the EC member countries. The taxation of shareholders is not harmonized. Different types of shareholders are subject to different combinations of dividend taxation and capital gains taxation even within the same tax jurisdiction (IBFD 1992). There seem to be several examples of rules in the tax laws of the EC member countries that provide for a certain discrimination in the taxation of dividend income in favour of dividends from domestic companies. The discrimination may have the form of exemptions that apply only to dividends from resident companies or lower income tax rates on such dividends. Accordingly, for companies with a Community-wide shareholder base it is an almost impossible task to formulate a dividend policy which aims at a high after-tax shareholder return.

The evidence shows that most companies do pay dividends in practice (Barclay and Smith 1988) and that cash dividends are the most common form in which companies distribute value to their shareholders (Shefrin and Statman 1984). It seems also to be the case that most boards of directors regard the dividend decision as an important one. It might therefore be helpful for the FM to have a list of questions which can support dividend decisions in Eurocomp. Table 7.3 contains such a list.

In most European tax systems, dividend income is taxed at a higher rate than capital gains. There is therefore a considerable number of companies, in particular companies owned by high-income shareholders, that answer question 1 in table 7.3 with a no. They prefer to

Table 7.3   Practical questions concerning Eurocomp's dividend decision

---

1   Does the company want to pay dividends regularly or to accumulate earnings?
2   If regular dividends are preferred, does the company want a stable payout ratio in relation to accounting income or stability in dividends per share?
3   Are there provisions in company law that constrain the dividend decision?
4   Are there provisions in the company statutes that constrain the dividend decision?
5   What is Eurocomp's current accounting income and how should negative deviations from the expected income (or deficits) affect the dividend?
6   How will a decision to pay dividends affect the need for external financing in the future?
7   What dividends are different groups of shareholders expecting and how are they taxed on dividend income and capital gains?
8   Are there industry standards with respect to dividend decisions?
9   Do we have to take the reactions of the bank or other creditors into consideration?

---

accumulate the current corporate income and postpone the realization of their capital gains for some years. The following questions in the table have relevance for companies that want to pay dividends currently.

Many investors seem to have a preference for stability (Brennan and Thakor 1990). In relation to dividend policy, stability may be interpreted in several ways (question 2). It is the impression of the author that many European companies, in particular companies that are listed on a stock exchange, want to show the investing community a certain stability in dividends per share. If the accounting income is volatile, stability in dividends per share implies variations in the payout ratio.

In chapter 2, the Second Company Law Directive (77/91/EEC) was mentioned. Article 15, which is incorporated in all company laws in the Community, constrains the funds that can be distributed to the shareholders. Question 3 must therefore in general be answered in the affirmative. It is probably also very common that company statutes provide for the building up of statutory reserves so that dividend payments must respect retainings for such reserves (question 4).

The board of directors and the shareholder meeting will almost always attach some importance to the level of the recent accounting income in connection with dividend decisions. Question 5 will, however, be most difficult to answer if the accounts of the company show a deficit. It is not uncommon that European companies with a deficit pay out dividends. When that happens, the board demonstrates a strong preference for stability in dividends per share and accepts a negative sign for the payout ratio.

Dividend payments reduce the amount of funds that are available in the company. With a given investment policy and capital structure, an increase in dividends must be funded with new equity. It is accordingly appropriate for the FM to evaluate the need for external financing in connection with dividend decisions (question 6).

The attitude of the shareholders to dividend payments can be expected to depend strongly on the tax regime (question 7). The shares of Eurocomp may at the same time be owned by shareholders who pay high income taxes on dividend income and by tax-free shareholders. There may also be considerable differences with respect to capital gains taxation. It seems therefore to be appropriate prior to the board meeting in which the dividend decision is discussed to produce an overview of the distribution of the shareholders according to their tax status. The board cannot expect, however, to satisfy all groups of shareholders.

Some companies compare their financing policies with colleagues or competitors in the same industry. When that is the case, it might be appropriate to ask to what extent the dividend decision should be affected by the behaviour of competitors (question 8). Finally, company managers may want to evaluate the reaction of their creditors to dividend decisions (question 9). Transfer of values to the shareholders implies of course a reduction of the company's equity capital and therefore also a reduction of the buffer against future possible losses. Concern for creditor reactions will probably be most important for boards of companies in difficulties.

Notes

1   *Official Journal of the European Communities (OJ)*, L 222, 1978, 11.
2   *OJ*, L 193, 1983, 1.
3   For *OJ* references see chapter 2, notes 24–28.
4   *Proposal for a Statute of the European Company, OJ*, C 124, 1970, 1.
5   *OJ*, L 212, 1977, 37.
6   *OJ*, L 334, 1989, 30.

8

Volatilities and Exposures in Markets for Stocks, Bonds and Foreign Exchange

The aim of this chapter is to present aspects of the volatility patterns in the financial markets in which European companies operate. Volatility causes exposure because our understanding of the movements in the markets for shares, bonds and foreign exchange is incomplete. Arbitrage relationships from financial theory can be of some help to the financial manager. A few important parity conditions derived from such relationships are therefore presented. Brief sections on measurement and management of exposure conclude the chapter.

8.1 The Many Market Participants

Price movements in global financial markets reflect the combined transactions of millions of market participants. The agents may be exporters, importers, multinational groups of companies, personal investors, private banks, institutional investors, central banks or international organizations. Market participants differ with respect to size, objectives and analytical capability. Most of the private agents can realistically be assumed to have profit or wealth maximization motives and to be too small to exert an influence on market prices. They buy information concerning market development and prospects and base their decisions on that information, but there are budget limitations on costs of information and analysis. National and international monetary authorities operate according to obligations in international treaties and provisions in national laws and follow political objectives. Central banks operate in markets for bank deposits, treasury bills and bonds but only under exceptional circumstances in stock markets. When they act together, they have the power to influence exchange rates, money market rates and bond market prices. The official institutions can in general be assumed to belong to the best informed group of market participants with broad access to market data and analysis of global trends. This does not of course imply that central bankers are always able to understand market forces or to predict market development.

How should the management of a private European company orient itself in such a complicated financial landscape? It would of course be nice if it was possible to integrate the behaviour of the most important market participants in a single model. This is evidently not possible. Nevertheless, Eurocomp has to manoeuvre in the environment described.

It is suggested here that the FM should try to find answers to the following questions: what influence can the monetary cooperation in Europe and the increasing integration of European financial markets be expected to have on the volatilities that are relevant to the company? What guidance can be obtained from the theory on the functioning of international financial markets? To what extent can the understanding of the markets be supported by other models from financial theory? In the following sections we will try to provide preliminary answers to these questions.

8.2 Volatility and European Monetary Cooperation and Integration

Eurocomp has to cope with a very complex volatility pattern in the financial markets. The main factors behind the observed volatilities are global market forces that are poorly understood. Meese (1990) has given a particularly pessimistic evaluation of the ability of current models to explain the exchange rate patterns observed since the early 1970s. In his view, the proportion of the exchange rate changes that current models can explain is essentially zero.

Some of the relevant market price volatilities are, however, directly constrained by central bank intervention. The obligations that a considerable number of the world's monetary authorities have to intervene are typically defined in terms of fluctuation bands on spot exchange rates.

Table 8.1 illuminates the exchange rate practices of central banks globally. The International Monetary Fund has classified the 155 member countries into six groups according to the way in which their central banks intervene in the foreign exchange market. The table provides an instantaneous picture of the politically determined framework for exchange rate volatility. The IMF source is updated monthly and it is therefore fairly easy for the FM to use it to rank the currencies according to expected volatility. As Eurocomp is assumed

Table 8.1 Exchange rate arrangements at third quarter 1991

		Number	*Important members of the group*
1	Currency pegged to another currency or composite		
	1.1 USD	25	Afghanistan, Argentina, Iraq
	1.2 FRF	14	Chad, Congo, Senegal
	1.3 Other currency	5	Bhutan, Swaziland
	1.4 SDR	6	Iran, Libya
	1.5 Other composite	33	Hungary, Norway, Poland, Sweden, Kenya, Tanzania, Uganda
	Total group 1	83	
2	Flexibility limited *vis-à-vis* a single currency	4	Bahrain, Saudi Arabia
3	Cooperative arrangements	10	EMS countries in EC[a]
4	Adjusted according to a set of indicators	5	Chile, Colombia, Zambia
5	Managed floating	23	China, Egypt, Greece, India, Indonesia, Mexico, Turkey
6	Independently floating	29	Australia, Brazil, Canada, Japan, Nigeria, Philippines, Romania, United States, Venezuela
	Total	155[b]	

[a] Portugal entered the EMS intervention arrangement on 6 April 1992. It moved accordingly from group 5 to group 3. On 17 September 1992 the UK government suspended the GBP's participation.
[b] One member country (Cambodia) had not notified the Fund of its Exchange rate arrangement.
Source: International Financial Statistics, January 1992, International Monetary Fund

to have its residence in a country participating in the EMS, the currencies in group 3 can be classified as currencies with a low expected volatility against the domestic currency or against the ECU. At the time of writing, the ESP has a ±6 per cent fluctuation band while the normal band applying to the other EMS currencies is ±2.25 per cent. The currencies in group 1.2 are pegged to the French franc. The central banks in the so-called 'franc zone' maintain fixed exchange rates with the FRF and hold their international reserves mainly in the form of

FRFs (Europa 1991: 156). As the FRF belongs to the EMS currencies, there are indirect politically determined constraints on the exchange rate volatility between the group 1.2 currencies and the other EMS currencies. Hungary, Norway and Sweden belong to group 1.5. They have recently chosen the ECU as the currency composite to which they peg their currencies and Eurocomp can therefore expect their exchange rate policy to reduce the relevant exchange rate volatility. Greece is a member of the EC but does not at the moment participate in the EMS. The IMF has placed the country in group 5, the managed floating countries. For political reasons and because of European trade patterns, it seems likely that the central bank of Greece to some extent will try to stabilize the GRD against the other EC currencies.

The rest of the groups in table 8.1 comprise currencies with a potentially high exchange rate volatility against Eurocomp's domestic currency and the ECU. Considering the size of the countries and their participation in international trade and investments, it is of special importance that the USD and the JPY belong to group 6, the independently floating currencies. If the FM finds it appropriate to use the politically determined framework to rank the currencies according to expected volatility from Eurocomp's point of view, the currencies in groups 6, 5, 4, 2, 1.3 and 1.1 should probably be classified as high-volatility currencies.

Table 8.1 was characterized as an instantaneous picture. It follows that the FM should expect the picture to change. When Spain decides to go from the ±6 per cent band to the ±2.25 per cent band, the intra-Community exchange rate volatility can be expected to go down. When new member countries enter the EC and become members of the EMS or the EMU, they will move to group 3 with the lowest expected volatility. If a single EC currency is adopted and replaces the individual currencies, the number of exchange rates relevant to Eurocomp will fall.

As described above, group 3 consists of the low-volatility currencies from the point of view of Eurocomp. Some of the technical aspects of the mutual intervention among the EMS currencies are described in chapter 3 of this book. The convergence effects of the EMS are also dealt with in that chapter. In order to participate on a permanent basis in a system of joint floating against the USD, the JPY and other third currencies, it is necessary for the EMS countries to have similar inflation rates. This implies in turn that differences in nominal interest rates become relatively small. The EMS system has therefore an indirect effect on observed interest rate volatilities across currencies.

The similarity of European interest rate volatility patterns is enforced by the removal of restrictions on international capital movements.

In the 1990s, European portfolio managers will probably look at bonds denominated in different European currencies as close substitutes. Small differences in expected yields of bonds with similar credit risk characteristics can therefore be assumed to be sufficient to trigger large adjustments of the currency composition of bond portfolios. The combined behaviour of central banks and private portfolio managers accordingly produces strong cross-border correlations between bond prices.

The cross-border intercorrelation among stock market prices seems to be much lower. Roll (1992) has provided evidence for and explanations of this. His study is based on data from April 1988 to March 1991. Because of the huge amounts of price data on listed companies, it is customary to measure the correlation by means of stock market indices. National stock market indices differ with respect to the number of stocks included and with respect to industrial diversification. The variation pattern of national stock markets reflects to a considerable extent the country's industrial structure. The implication is that the stock market indices from two countries with similar industrial structures tend to be more highly correlated. An illustrative example is the fairly high correlation among the stock market indices from Norway and the Netherlands which to some extent reflects the high proportion of shares issued by companies in the energy sector in both countries. Roll's evidence also demonstrates that an investment portfolio consisting of a country's stock market index is more volatile when it is less well diversified. Among the European countries in the study, the observed stock market volatilities were relatively high in Austria, Denmark, Norway and Sweden.

The stock markets in the Western European countries have higher cross-border correlations than most other national stock markets in Roll's study. This observation should be evaluated in connection with the high level of intra-Community trade described in chapter 4 and the low intra-Community exchange rate volatility due to the EMS.

8.3   Parity Conditions as Road Signs

Arbitrage relationships have played a central role in the theory of financial markets for many years. Some of the best known international parity conditions can be traced back to the writings of John Maynard Keynes, Gustav Cassel and Irving Fisher. Other parity conditions are the products of capital market theory from the 1960s and option pricing theory from the 1970s and 1980s.

Parity conditions are derived from the assumed behaviour of private market participants. Central bank intervention is normally ignored. For illustration we will therefore use the floating exchange rate between the American dollar and the ECU, i.e. $E_{ECU/USD}$. Expected variables are denoted by *. The time of decision is indicated by t. The time at which loans and forward contracts mature is indicate by $t+n$, where n is the maturity in months.

It may be misleading to study arbitrage relationships separately. Accordingly, there have been several attempts to combine them in an integrated framework (Giddy 1976; Solnik 1978).

8.3.1 Purchasing Power Parity

Purchasing power parity (PPP) is in its relative version a theory relating expected changes in spot exchange rates E to expected changes in commodity prices P. PPP is expressed by the equation:

$$(E^*_{ECU/USD,t+n} - E^*_{ECU/USD,t})/E_{ECU/USD,t} = [(P^*_{ECU,t+n}/P^*_{USD,t+n}) - (P_{ECU,t}/P_{USD,t})]/(P_{ECU,t}/P_{USD,t})$$

(8.1)

On the left hand side of equation 8.1, we have the expected relative change in the spot price of USD in terms of ECU from time t to time $t+n$. On the right hand side, we have the expected relative inflation rate difference between an ECU-based price index and a USD-based price index. If P_{ECU} is expected to increase faster than P_{USD} from t to $t+n$, the right hand side becomes positive. The implication of the equation is then that the price of USD in terms of ECU will increase. This is equivalent to an expected depreciation of the ECU.

In verbal terms, PPP implies expectations among the market participants according to which exchange rate movements tend to cancel out changes in the foreign commodity price level relative to the domestic price level. If PPP holds, real exchange rates should remain unchanged.

There are a number of problems associated with empirical PPP tests (Officer 1976). The methods of calculation of commodity price indices differ from country to country. It is very difficult to establish if the base-period exchange rate is an equilibrium rate as required by the model. In the real world, international trade is multilateral so that bilateral exchange rates are unable to adjust to the overall changes in international competitiveness that influence trade flows. Finally, the exchange rates are in practice influenced not only by trade transactions but also by capital movements, most of which may be independent of changes in the relative competitiveness of exporters and importers. Thus Adler and Lehmann (1983) have suggested that the PPP hypothesis, which is based on interdependencies among commodity markets and national price levels, should be replaced by a theory based on low-cost financial arbitrage among bond markets.

Against this background, it is not surprising that calculated real effective exchange rates tend to move considerably through time. Real effective exchange rates for some of the most important currencies in the world can be studied in the statistical appendix of *World Financial Markets* (Morgan bimonthly). Huang (1987) has found that expected nominal exchange rate changes deviate systematically from expected inflation rate differences under floating exchange rates. Some researchers find recent evidence damaging to PPP theory (Meese 1990: 119).

8.3.2   Interest Rate Parity

Interest rate parity (IRP) is a theory on relationships between spot exchange rates E, forward exchange rates F and interest rates I. IRP is based on covered interest arbitrage which is defined as international transfer of spot funds motivated by interest rate differences and covered by simultaneous forward transactions of the same amount in the opposite direction.

IRP equilibrium is defined by the equation:

$$(F_{ECU/USD,t,t+n}/E_{ECU/USD,t})(1 + I_{USD,t,t+n}) = 1 + I_{ECU,t,t+n} \qquad (8.2)$$

Note that there is no asterisk in the equation, i.e. IRP is not an expectations theory.

Let us explain equation 8.2 by means of the observed rates from October 1991 given in table 6.2. Suppose Eurocomp owns an ECU deposit in a London bank of the amount ECU 100,000 and considers a short-term change to a 12-month USD deposit in New York. Suppose further that the company wants to cover the USD deposit in the forward market. The contemplated arbitrage transaction will then involve the following steps:

1   Eurocomp at time t buys USD for ECU 100,000 at the current spot rate $E_{ECU/USD,t}$ = ECU 0.83257/USD, i.e. it buys (100,000/0.83257) = USD 120,110.
2   Eurocomp at time t invests the proceeds in a 12-month USD bank deposit in New York at an interest rate $I_{USD,t,t+n}$ = 5.62 per cent p.a. The interest income earned in the 12-month period is USD 120,110 × 0.0562 = USD 6750.
3   Eurocomp at time t sells USD (120,110 + 6750) 12 months forward against ECU at the forward rate $F_{ECU/USD,t,t+n}$ = ECU 0.86607/USD. The ECU amount in the forward contract is 126,860 × 0.86607 = ECU 109,870.

4   At the maturity date $(t+n)$ 12 months later, Eurocomp fulfils its
    forward contract commitment to deliver USD 126,860 by drawing
    on the USD deposit account and receives ECU 109,870 in return.

If the company had acquired a 12-month ECU deposit instead it would
have earned an interest rate of 9.87 per cent p.a., i.e. the principal plus
interest would have amounted to ECU 100,000 × 1.0987 = ECU 109,870.
In IRP equilibrium, an investor is thus indifferent between short-term
investments in the domestic money market and investments abroad
covered by forward exchange contracts. IRP implies that the currency
of the country with a higher interest rate tends to be quoted at a
discount in the forward exchange market. In the example with data
from October 1991, $I_{USD,t,t+n}$ is lower than $I_{ECU,t,t+n}$. We observe therefore
that the USD is sold at a premium in the forward market in terms of
ECU.

IRP does not hold exactly in practice. There are different kinds of
interest rates; there may be credit risks or political risks; and there are
transaction costs that may explain deviations from IRP. Some studies
show that transaction costs tend to be higher in turbulent periods in
the foreign exchange markets than in calm periods (Frenkel and Levich
1977). In earlier studies, IRP deviations were often explained by capital
restrictions and government intervention on the forward exchange
market. Tsiang (1959) has written a classic article on this subject. In a
critical survey of the empirical exchange market literature, Kohlhagen
(1978) concluded that IRP studies generally show that the covered
interest rate differential is zero in the long run while transaction costs
and non-comparability of assets adequately explain any observed
deviations.

In today's fully liberalized foreign exchange markets, IRP deviations
tend to be very small, and the FM can safely consider the IRP parity
condition as one of the most reliable road signs in the financial landscape.

8.3.3   International Fisher Effect

The international Fisher effect (IFE) or uncovered interest rate parity
combines observed nominal interest rates and spot exchange rate
expectations:

$$(E^{*}_{ECU/USD,t+n} - E_{ECU/USD,t})/E_{ECU/USD,t} = (1 + I_{ECU,t,t+n})/(1 + I_{USD,t,t+n}) - 1$$

$$(8.3)$$

Note that there is only one expected variable in the equation, namely
the expected spot rate n months later. All the other variables are
observed in the market at time t.

The equation implies that currencies with floating exchange rates and with high nominal interest rates are expected to depreciate while those with low nominal interest are expected to appreciate. When the observed $I_{ECU,t,t+n}$ is higher than $I_{USD,t,t+n}$ the right hand side of equation 8.3 becomes positive, and IFE-based expectations will predict an increase in $E_{ECU/USD}$, i.e. an expected appreciation of USD in relation to ECU. The IFE theory is based on assumptions concerning bond investor behaviour. According to efficient market theory, expected returns from holding bonds denominated in different currencies should in the long run be the same. The observed interest rate differentials can therefore be interpreted as the outcome of the weighted spot exchange rate expectations of the market participants.

Many authors have found that IFE does not hold or that the evidence must be interpreted from a risk premium point of view (Geweke and Feige 1979; Cumby and Obstfeld 1981; Cumby 1988).

8.3.4 *Forward Rate Based Estimation*

According to the efficient markets hypothesis, the expected rate of return to speculation in the forward exchange market conditioned on available information should be zero. In its pure form, the hypothesis assumes that the market participants are risk neutral, that transactions costs are zero, and that information is used rationally. The forward rate based estimation (FRE) condition is then:

$$(E^*_{ECU/USD,t+n} - E_{ECU/USD,t})/E_{ECU/USD,t} = (F_{ECU/USD,t,t+n} - E_{ECU/USD,t})/E_{ECU/USD,t}$$
(8.4)

The reasoning behind FRE is as follows. Market participants who believe that the forward rate which can be observed in the market is above their prediction of the future spot rate will sell USD in the forward market, thus bidding down $F_{ECU/USD,t,t+n}$ until equation 8.4 is fulfilled. Those who believe that the USD is undervalued in the forward market will buy dollars forward, bidding $F_{ECU/USD,t,t+n}$ up until it reaches the expected future spot rate. Under rational expectations, $F_{ECU/USD,t,t+n}$ must therefore correspond to the market's expectations if the expected return to forward speculation is to be zero.

FRE has been subjected to empirical studies by Hansen and Hodrick (1980), Agmon and Amihud (1981), Froot and Frankel (1989) and Pope and Peel (1991). Almost all studies cast doubts on the usefulness of the forward rate as a predictor of the actual future spot rate. Many of the studies try to interpret observed deviations as the result of risk premiums. Froot and Thaler (1990) find no positive evidence that the forward rate's poor performance as a basis for spot rate forecasts is due to risk. In their view, it is more likely that the poor performance is attributable to expectational errors than to risk.

In an evaluation of empirical studies of the international parity conditions one should not forget the intervention practice of the central banks. The parity conditions are derived from the assumed behaviour of exporters and importers (PPP), private banks (IRP) and private investors with international bond portfolios (IFE), but these market participants are not alone in the financial markets. With the exception of interest rate parity, which is a fairly reliable road sign in the financial landscape, Eurocomp should be prepared to observe considerable deviations from the parity conditions.

8.4   Some Important Financial Models

8.4.1   *Portfolio Theory and Capital Asset Pricing*

It is important to distinguish between theories of portfolio selection and theories of price determination in the stock market. Harry M. Markowitz and James Tobin developed the mean-variance portfolio selection theory (MVPT) in which portfolio risk is measured as the variance or standard deviation of the portfolio return. Building on MVPT, John Lintner, Jan Mossin and William F. Sharpe developed the capital asset pricing model (CAPM), a model of the factors that determine the prices of risky securities in the stock market. MVPT is thus a normative theory which is constructed with the aim of guiding the individual investor in his choice of an appropriate combination of securities. Sharpe (1970: 3) suggests that the term *portfolio theory* should be used to denote the normative MVPT approach, while the term *capital market theory* should be used to denote the positive CAPM approach.

Both MVPT and CAPM are built on simplifying assumptions. The fundamental MVPT assumption is that an investor only needs the expected returns and the variances of the feasible portfolios in order to select the optimal portfolio. All other information about the securities is redundant. Considering the number of securities in the market, MVPT is, in spite of this limitation of investor relevant information, quite demanding with respect to estimation and calculation. In order to compute the standard deviation of the portfolio return, the investor needs a covariance matrix for all available securities. The so-called index models were later developed in order to simplify the formula for portfolio variance. The index models assume that the returns of the individual securities are only correlated because they are influenced by an index which is usually understood as the return of the market portfolio (Haugen 1990: 153). The sensitivity of individual stocks to changes in a stock market index can be estimated empirically: it is called *beta*. In many countries, stockbrokers and investment advisers use regression analysis to estimate betas as an information service to their customers. If a customer decides to apply such betas in his portfolio selection he should make it clear to himself that he accepts the betas as a reasonable measure of the stocks' sensitivities towards a market index. He should also remember that empirically determined betas tend to be unstable and that they are conceptually different from CAPM betas.

Given the level of risk, investors are in MVPT assumed to prefer portfolios with a higher expected rate of return. Given the level of expected return, they prefer security combinations with lower risk. The so-called efficient set is defined as the portfolios that have the highest attainable expected rate of return given a particular level of standard deviation.

CAPM is based on the behaviour of investors that choose their portfolios according to the MVPT assumptions. In addition to these assumptions, CAPM assumes that all market participants have homogeneous expectations, i.e. that they are looking at the same efficient set. CAPM also assumes that there are no transaction costs and no taxes and that there exists a risk-free asset. Sharpe and Alexander (1990: chapter 8) provide a thorough discussion of the CAPM assumptions and implications.

The CAPM was first developed for a single-currency world. In perfect financial markets in which investors have homogeneous expectations and can lend and borrow at a riskless interest rate, an equilibrium can be determined in which all market participants hold a combination of the market portfolio and the riskless asset. The asset pricing equation has the following form:

$$S_j^* = I_f + (S_m^* - I_f) \beta_j \qquad (8.5)$$

where S_j^* is the expected rate of return on stock j, I_f is the risk-free interest rate, S_m^* is the expected rate of return on the market portfolio, and β_j is the slope of a characteristic line which relates the return of stock j to the return of the market portfolio. All investors will thus demand a risk premium of β_j multiplied by $(S_m^* - I_f)$ in order to hold stock j.

Let us now consider international portfolio diversification. It is of course necessary to take this further step in order to establish a theoretical relationship between spot exchange rates, interest rates and stock price indices. Several attempts have been made to apply the MVPT and CAPM on international stock markets (Solnik 1977; Chiang 1991). The immediate effect of moving to an international environment is that the individual investor faces a much broader menu of securities. His efficient set moves so that he can build up a portfolio with a better performance (Biger 1979; Eaker et al. 1991). In order to preserve CAPM equilibrium, the assumptions must be extended to the variation patterns in the foreign exchange market. It is no longer sufficient for the investors to be in agreement with respect to the covariance matrix for the stock prices. They must also be in agreement with respect to the covariance matrix between the exchange rates. Investors form their expectations on the basis of data from the financial markets. It is fairly obvious that there is asymmetric information across investors in different countries and across different kinds of investors within the individual country. It is therefore hard to accept that they should be in agreement with respect to the efficient set of portfolios if they look at different market data.

A number of authors apply a very empirical approach to the linkages among national stock markets. Some of them try to test CAPM while others with a strong emphasis on the statistical properties of covariance matrices concentrate on the development of market imperfections (Giovannini and Jorion 1989; Raymond and Weil 1989; Eun and Shim 1989; Koch and Koch 1991; Hamao et al. 1990). The empirical performance of international asset pricing models is generally poor. Rates of return on international financial assets tend to be highly volatile and largely unpredictable. Cochrane (1991) refuses to interpret volatility tests as rejections of efficient market theory. In his strong words, there is no need for a paradigm shift in which the basic efficient market structure is replaced by a model in which fads, fashion and the psychology of crowds are the driving forces behind price changes, constrained only by riskless arbitrage. Volatility tests have a splendid history but their future is limited. Statistically reliable estimates of exchange rate and asset price movements are, however, difficult to find. The instability may be considered a symptom of our poor understanding of the international markets. In spite of these pessimistic conclusions, most authors seem to be interested in the performance of international stock portfolios. Measures of portfolio performance have a currency dimension. This applies also to the Sharpe index

$$Shi = (S_p^* - I_f)/(\text{standard deviation of portfolio return})$$

where S_p^* indicates the expected portfolio return. *Shi* may be used to rank portfolios from the point of view of an investor who wants to maximize the excess return per unit of portfolio risk. It is, however, not certain that investors from different countries will rank portfolios in the same way. The expected foreign exchange rate affects both S_p^* and the standard deviation and it is therefore likely that investors that look at the portfolios from the perspective of different currencies will disagree about the ranking (Eun and Resnick 1988).

Furthermore, it is not obvious what a risk-free interest rate is in an international environment. Usually, the short-term interest rate of government bonds is selected as I_f. The investor in a realistic European environment has access to government bonds denominated in different currencies. If risk is derived from real consumption opportunities, assumptions will have to be made concerning consumption baskets in different countries. Grauer et al. (1976) assume that investors in different countries have identical tastes. They also assume away international capital market segmentation. The latter assumption has, owing to liberalizations of capital movements, become more realistic since the publication of their article. On the whole, however, asset pricing models are still built on assumptions that are far removed from the institutional environment facing international investors (Jacque 1981: 82).

Finally, the stability through time of the relevant covariance matrices is open to question. The matrices must be determined on historical data, and if the variation pattern changes then portfolio decisions may be affected. Engel and Rodrigues (1989) and Harvey (1991) have performed tests of international CAPM with covariances that are changing over time. Their approaches relax the CAPM assumptions somewhat but they conclude, as do many researchers before them, that the restrictions placed by CAPM on more general asset demand equations cannot be accepted.

8.4.2   Term Structure Models

There is a comprehensive financial literature devoted to the measurement and management of the interest rate risk of securities. Most of the contributions to this literature assume a single-currency world. Eurocomp's environment is a multicurrency world. The arbitrage conditions derived from term structure modelling (TSM) theory must therefore be adapted to a plurality of currencies (Kaufold and Smirlock 1986).

The concept of duration D plays a key role in TSM (Bierwag et al. 1983). D is recommended as a measure of the extent of the cash flow associated with a security which is superior to the concept of maturity. The price volatility of bonds tends to be inversely proportional to their duration. An investor can therefore measure his exposure to interest rate risk by the D of his expected cash flows.

In D, the times to the individual payments are weighted according to their present value. The formula looks like this:

$$D = \left[\sum_{t=1}^{n}(tC_t)/(1+R)^t\right] \Big/ \left[\sum_{t=1}^{n}C_t/(1+R)^t\right] \qquad (8.6)$$

where C_t is the cash flow at time t, t is the time to the cash flow, n is the time to final maturity, and R is the yield to maturity.

Suppose that Eurocomp expects a series of USD payments $C^*_{USD,t}$ in the next n periods. Suppose further that R_{USD} is the appropriate USD discount rate and that the yield curves are flat. We can then express the net present value in terms of ECUs as:

$$NPV_t = E_{ECU/USD,t}[\Sigma\ C^*_{USD,t}/(1+R_{USD})^t] \qquad (8.7)$$

If we consider this series of future USD payments as a set of zero-coupon bonds with maturities ranging from 1 to n periods, the percentage change in the value of equation 8.7 will be:

$$dNPV_t/NPV_t = (dE_{ECU/USD,t}/E_{ECU/USD,t}) - D_{USD}\ d(1+R_{USD})/(1+R_{USD}) \qquad (8.8)$$

where D_{USD} is the duration of the stream of USD cash flows. In a single-currency world, D can be used in immunization strategies. From a USD perspective, Eurocomp is exposed to future changes in the USD interest rate. By decreasing the USD duration, Eurocomp can reduce its exposure to USD interest risk. The company is, however, assumed to be interested in risk from an ECU point of view. Equation 8.8 demonstrates that the relative reaction of NPV_t depends on the possible relation between changes in the USD interest rate and the exchange rate between USD and ECU. Some of the empirical tests referred to in the earlier sections on IRP and IFE can illuminate the interest and foreign exchange rate relationships.

TSM theory assumes flat interest rate structures and parallel shifts in yield to maturity curves. In practice, yield curves have positive and occasionally negative slopes and the shifts need not be parallel. Immunization based on TSM can therefore not be complete. TSM theory assumes also in most cases that bonds are non-callable. A call provision gives the issuer an option to buy back the security at a specified price before maturity. Such a provision means therefore that the expected cash flows to the bondholder depend on the future interest rate development. Option pricing theory can be used to evaluate the impact of a call provision on bond prices (Dunetz and Mahoney 1988; Jakobsen and Jørgensen 1991).

8.4.3   Black-Scholes Model

The Black-Scholes Model (BSM) is probably the most frequently used option pricing model in the financial industry. The model explains a relationship between interest rates, stock prices and option prices (premiums). It is derived under a set of simplifying assumptions and on the basis of the behaviour of a representative market participant who takes a hedged position, consisting of a long position in the stock and a short position in call options on that stock (Black and Scholes 1973). The idea is that the impact of changes in the stock price is neutralized by changes in the value of the option. The number of call options sold short must be adapted through time according to changes in the price of the underlying asset in order to ensure that the combined position is not exposed to stock price risk.

With the notation applied here, the Black-Scholes formula is:

$$Y = S\, N(d) - Xe^{-I_{ECU,f}T})\, N(d - \sigma\sqrt{T})$$

$$d = \{[\ln(S/X) + r\, T]/\sigma\sqrt{T}\} + (1/2)\sigma\sqrt{T} \qquad (8.9)$$

where Y is the call option price (premium), S is the current price of the underlying asset (stock), X is the exercise price, T is the time to expiration, $I_{ECU,f}$ is the riskless ECU interest rate, $N(\ )$ is the cumulative normal distribution function, ln is the natural logarithm, and σ is the instantaneous standard deviation of the price of the underlying asset (volatility).

The formula looks complicated. It has, however, the big advantage that it is fairly easy to provide most of the data needed for the calculation of Y. The FM can find the current stock price S and the yield ($I_{ECU,f}$) of treasury bills with a maturity date corresponding to the expiration date in a business newspaper. The exercise price X and the time to expiration T are specified in the option contract. Only the volatility σ has to be estimated. Most market participants probably apply the variation of the daily rate of return of the underlying asset as an estimate of σ. It is in fact possible to buy hand-held calculators with routines based on the BSM.

8.4.4   Garman-Kohlhagen Model

The Garman-Kohlhagen model (GKM) is a modified version of the Black-Scholes model. The GKM is a formula for the pricing of currency options (Garman and Kohlhagen 1983). Spot exchange rate changes are assumed to be log-normal. As usual, we assume that USD is the representative foreign currency while ECU is the domestic currency:

$$Q = E_{\text{ECU/USD}}\ e^{-I_{\text{USD},f}{}^T}N(d) - X_{\text{ECU/USD}}\ e^{-I_{\text{USD},f}{}^T}N(d - \sigma\sqrt{T})$$

$$d = \{[\ln(E_{\text{ECU/USD}}/X_{\text{ECU/USD}}) + (I_{\text{ECU},f} - I_{\text{USD},f})T]/\sigma\sqrt{T}\} + (1/2)\sigma\sqrt{T}$$

(8.10)

where $X_{\text{ECU/USD}}$ is the exercise price at which the holder of the currency option has the right to buy USD for ECU. The premium Q of a currency option is seen to increase with the current spot rate of the USD in terms of ECU, with the domestic interest rate $I_{\text{ECU},f}$, with the maturity of the option contract T and with the volatility of the exchange rate σ. Q decreases when the exercise price $X_{\text{ECU/USD}}$ increases and when the foreign interest rate $I_{\text{USD},f}$ increases.

8.5 Exposure Measurement and Management

8.5.1 *Questions Concerning Exposure*

To be exposed is to be subject to an influence one does not control. According to this general definition, all market participants are exposed. Individual investors and companies have decision making power but the outcome of their decisions depends on external factors such as price developments in the market and the ability or willingness of business partners to fulfil their obligations. Some external factors can be predicted with a certain probability while others are essentially unpredictable. The more sceptical a decision maker is with respect to the reliability of forecasts, the more he will be interested in buying protection against the negative impacts from the external factors in question.

Most investors and company managers are risk averse. However, if they want to do business, they cannot avoid risk completely. What they can do is to operate in such a way that they keep the exposures within acceptable limits. Those limits must be decided by the board in cooperation with the management. Risk reducing activities involve costs, and the top management must make it clear how to balance these costs against the benefits of risk reduction (Shapiro and Titman 1985).

Before an appropriate exposure management system can be selected, an exposure analysis must be carried out. The first question for an FM to pose in a company exposure analysis is: *what company performance variable is it we want to protect?* There are several possible answers. If the board of directors of Eurocomp measures the performance of the company management by means of the time pattern of current reported income, it is likely that the management will want to protect the company's accounting income against external impacts. The company can then be expected to select an accounting approach to measuring exposure (Srinivasulu 1983). If, on the other hand, the board of directors is more cash flow oriented and concerned with the market value of the company, it is likely that the management will want to protect the net present value of the company's future cash flows. The company will then prefer a transaction or economic approach to measuring exposure. Rodriguez (1979) has strongly recommended that companies should measure their exposure by means of the net present value of future cash flows.

The second question to pose is: *what kind of external factors* are so important that they should be included in the company's exposure management system? The answer depends on how serious the potential threats to the company's performance are considered to be. If Eurocomp has a few very large customers, it will be essential to include a current credit risk evaluation of these customers in the exposure management system. If Eurocomp has large USD-denominated sales contracts, accounts receivable or other debt obligations, the likely range for fluctuations in the USD exchange rate in terms of Eurocomp's reference currency becomes essential. If Eurocomp to a considerable extent has financed itself with floating rate ECU-denominated loans, the interbank ECU interest rate should be included in the exposure management system.

The third question is: *how can we measure the impact* of the external factors on the company performance variable? The relative popularity in practice of accounting approaches to exposure measurement may be partly explained by the fact that it is fairly straightforward to compute the impact of, for instance, fluctuations in the ECU/USD exchange rate on reported company income when the accounting rules and conventions have been selected. It is much more difficult to estimate the impact of variations in external factors on the market value of the company. The sensitivity of future cash flows and the net present value of such flows to changes in external factors cannot be estimated before a long list of assumptions has been made. The necessary assumptions include demand and supply elasticities on product and factor markets and the future reactions of foreign competitors. European managers will rarely deny the theoretical relevance of the economic approach to exposure measurement, but they may be concerned about the possibilities of a sufficiently reliable measurement.

Flood and Lessard (1986) prefer the term 'operating exposure' instead of 'economic exposure'. They explain how the exposed items, namely the company's future revenues, costs and profits, are responsive to exchange rate changes through both a competitive effect and a conversion effect. Adler and Dumas (1984) challenge the view that exposure should be measured in terms of the impact of unexpected exchange rate changes on the present value of the company's future cash flows. They prefer to measure exposures as regression coefficients resulting from regressing the value of assets in terms of the reference currency against exchange rates.

The fourth question is: *in terms of what currency should exposure be measured?* The management of Eurocomp has to select a currency of reference. By far the largest share of European companies use the currency of the company headquarters residence country for exposure measurement. In spite of the integration process, most of the company interested parties (CIPs: see chapter 1) prefer to receive company information in terms of the residence currency. Owing to provisions in the national accounting laws that are derived from EC directives, listed companies also disclose main accounting data in terms of ECU. At the time of writing, however, ECU-denominated company data must mainly be considered as supplementary information for the benefit of foreign investors and business connections. So long as the majority of the shareholders evaluate company performance in terms of local currency, it is natural for the management to apply this currency in exposure measurement. An adoption of the ECU as a single European currency will of course change this company practice.

The fifth question is: *should the external factors be included separately or combined* in the exposure management system? Many authors discuss foreign exchange exposure management on a currency-by-currency basis (Wentz 1979; Madura 1992: 313ff.). Wentz recommends that the FM applies a three-stage procedure in foreign exchange exposure management. In the first stage, estimates are made of each of the company's exposures in the most important foreign currencies. The estimates are presented in exposure sheets that give an overview of the size and date of future transactions. In the second stage, the currencies are grouped according to perceived volatility and exchange rate forecasts are made. In the third stage, the FM decides, after having evaluated the costs and risks, what exposures to reduce or to remove.

Portfolio theory leads to a fundamentally different approach (Makin 1978; Soenen 1979). The movements of the relevant external factors are never perfectly correlated. The FM will therefore obtain an exaggerated impression of the company's risk level if he ignores the mixed variation pattern of the relevant variables. Exposure management based on a portfolio approach must rely on regular re-estimation of correlations. The FM cannot expect the correlation patterns to be stable through time, but he can probably reckon with a certain inertia in the patterns so that he can have an updated view of the diversification benefits to the company. Jorion (1992) incorporates the effects of measurement error on international portfolio diversification. Madura and Tucker (1992) explain that the effects on portfolio performance of hedging by means of forward exchange contracts depend on the covariance structure between exchange rate and stock price movements.

8.5.2 Exposure Management

For some years it has been debated whether or not corporations should establish exposure management systems (Eckl and Robinson 1990). The international parity conditions have played an important role in the argument. If PPP holds, there is no foreign exchange rate exposure. If IFE holds, companies should be indifferent to the combined interest rate and exchange rate risk. However, as described earlier, the evidence suggests that neither PPP nor IFE can be trusted to hold, which implies that companies are exposed to foreign exchange rate and interest rate risk. They will meet unexpected exchange rate and interest rate changes in the market.

Given that companies are exposed, it is problematical whether company managers should hedge the exposures or leave hedging to the shareholders. The CAPM suggests that a publicly traded corporation should not hedge (Logue and Oldfield 1977). If all the external factors are unsystematic, they can be diversified away by the investors as they build up their portfolios. If the company management uses hedging instruments to reduce or eliminate earnings variability, this must be characterized as pure accounting gimmickry that should not fool well informed investors. Giddy (1977) and Dufey and Srinivasulu (1983) have attacked the CAPM-based reasoning and explained the need for corporate exposure management systems. Managers should, according to these authors, hedge if they are concerned about the total variability of cash flows and the cost of financial distress. They also question the ability of the individual investor to plan and achieve efficient diversification because of his limited knowledge about the level and timing of foreign exchange exposure for the companies whose shares are represented in the portfolio.

It is also the view of the author of this book that there is a strong case for establishing a corporate exposure management system. The FM of Eurocomp should ask the board of the company to make it clear how the five exposure questions above should be answered and subsequently try to evaluate the costs and benefits of the foreign exchange exposure management instruments listed in table 8.2 (inspired by Eiteman et al. 1992 and Martinovits 1985). In connection with the discussion of the instruments in the table, it is assumed that Eurocomp is a company without subsidiaries or branches abroad.

Table 8.2 Foreign exchange exposure management instruments

1 *Managed through internal guidelines or instructions*
   1.1   Choice of currency in contracts
   1.2   Payments and credit conditions in contracts
   1.3   Currency clauses
   1.4   Timing of contracts
2 *Managed through financial market transactions*
   2.1   Leads and lags of payments
   2.2   Bank deposit level and structure
   2.3   Debt level and structure
   2.4   Negotiable instruments
   2.5   Forfaiting and factoring
   2.6   Forward exchange contracts
   2.7   Price conditional orders on foreign exchange
   2.8   Currency futures contracts
   2.9   Currency options contracts
   2.10 Swaps and forward rate agreements

Instruments 1.1 to 1.4 are managed by means of guidelines or instructions from the FM to the sales and purchase departments of Eurocomp. In order to maintain an overview of the foreign exchange risk implications of new contracts, it seems to be appropriate to constrain the number of foreign currencies that officials of the two departments are allowed to use in new contracts. The officials should also be obliged to report the signing of new contracts to the finance department without delay, so that the FM can have an updated record of all contracts involving exchange exposure to the company. In some industries there are strong traditions in the use of particular currencies, so that instrument 1.1 is limited for instance to USD, DEM, GBP and JPY. With a view to the ranking of currencies according to expected volatility which was discussed in section 8.2 it might in Eurocomp be appropriate to recommend the use of EMS currencies or currencies pegged to the ECU in connection with signing of new trade contracts.

In a going concern with stable sales and purchases through time, the size of receivables and payables depends on the length of the credit periods. It follows that the exposure of Eurocomp in connection with trade credit items denominated in foreign currency can be influenced through the company's credit policy. The use of instrument 1.2 must of course be evaluated in the light of the competitive situation and the likely reactions of the customers.

A currency clause normally stipulates that a contract price must be adjusted if a particular exchange rate changes so that it moves across a certain threshold. A currency clause is therefore an exposure management instrument (1.3) which can be used to move foreign exchange risk from one party to another.

The signing of trade contracts denominated in foreign currency can be advanced or postponed. Since the contracts affect the exposure of the company, the FM can use timing instructions to the officials of the sales and purchase departments as an exposure management instrument (1.4). In a going concern which is dependent on regular supplies of raw materials and components and has customers who want stable deliveries, there are of course strong practical limitations to the use of instrument 1.4.

The rest of the instruments in table 8.2 are managed through transactions in financial markets. Such transactions are normally carried out by officials in the finance department or perhaps by the FM himself. Payments to foreign suppliers can be advanced and in some cases postponed. By use of instrument 2.1, the FM can accordingly adjust the structure of the company's exposure sheet. Decisions to lead or lag payments must be based on an analysis of the interest cost implications. Prepayments normally imply reductions in Eurocomp's bank deposits or increases in bank debt. If foreign customers are asked to accelerate their payments to Eurocomp, it may be necessary for the FM to offer a discount. The application of instrument 2.1 is not without cost.

In most Western European countries, companies are allowed to have bank deposits denominated in foreign currencies. They can therefore adjust the current level and currency structure of their bank deposits according to their future need for funds and the structure of their other exposures (instrument 2.2). If Eurocomp regularly has large cash inflows and outflows in the same foreign currency, the company can save considerable transaction costs by avoiding changing amounts, for instance from USD to DEM and later in the opposite direction from DEM to USD. The interest rates earned on bank deposits will normally depend on the interbank rates for the currencies in question. It seems to be customary that the European banks pay interest rates approximately 1 per cent below the relevant LIBOR rate for the same maturity.

Eurocomp can borrow in foreign currencies. By adjusting the level and currency structure of the company's debt, it can revise the exposures. The interest rates charged by the banks will normally be calculated as LIBOR for the currency in question plus a margin which depends on the credit standing of the borrowing company. In the management of instrument 2.3, the FM may find it convenient to ask the bank to establish a credit line which can be used for some months or years according to the changing needs of the company.

The FM can change the current level and composition of the company's holdings of treasury bills or other negotiable instruments that are denominated in foreign currency. A considerable share of the available short-term instruments are zero-coupon bonds or notes. Some of the instruments that are available in the market are issued by well known industrial companies under so-called note issuance facilities (NIFs). It depends on the tax regime whether zero-coupon bonds bought at a price below the par value are attractive in connection with instrument 2.4 in comparison with interest bearing paper or bank deposits.

Forfaiting is defined as the purchase by a finance company of bills or promissory notes without recourse to the original holder. If Eurocomp exports goods to a customer in Eastern Europe and the customer issues promissory notes in favour of Eurocomp, it might be possible for Eurocomp to sell the notes, without recourse, for instance to a Swiss finance company. As an exporter, Eurocomp receives the face value of the notes minus a discount and a fee, and the finance company assumes the exchange rate risk, the credit risk on the importer plus responsibility for the collection of payments. The obligations of the importer will often be supported by a guarantee from his bank, perhaps in the form of a letter of credit. Thus, by applying instrument 2.5, Eurocomp can remove credit risk, political risk and foreign exchange risk on export transactions.

A forward contract is defined as a contract in which there is a specified period between the date at which it is signed and the settlement date. According to the normal conventions in the international bank market, there must be at least two business days between the contract day and the delivery day. The forward exchange contract is one of the most important foreign exchange exposure management instruments (2.6). The biggest turnover seems to be in forward contracts with maturities of one, two, three or six months. All Western European currencies are traded in forward markets. Eurocomp can cover the exchange risk on accounts receivable in a foreign currency by selling that currency forward to the bank. The company can similarly cover the exchange risk on accounts payable or other types of debt by buying the relevant foreign currency forward from the bank. The forward exchange rates quoted by banks depend on the maturities of the forward contracts. There is a margin between the banks' bid and offer rates in the forward market as well as in the spot market, because the banks want to earn a trading profit on foreign exchange dealing. Cooper and Mello (1990) have analysed the pricing of forward contracts with emphasis on the bid–ask spread. In their view, the spread compensates the bank offering the forward contract for default risk. The forward exchange rates are related to the interest rates on the money markets for the currencies concerned. The rationale for this relation was explained earlier in connection with the interest rate parity theory. When the nominal interest rates converge due to European monetary cooperation, there can also be observed a reduction in the premiums and discounts on forward contracts between the EMS currencies. The need for forward cover goes down because of the reduced mutual exchange rate volatility in Europe, and at the same time the price of forward cover goes down because of the narrowing of the interest rate differences. Forward exchange contracts are over-the-counter (OTC) contracts, in contrast to futures contracts which are traded on organized exchanges.

In the stock market, it has been customary for many years for customers to instruct their brokers to buy a given stock if the stock price moves below a certain threshold level or alternatively to sell the stock if the price moves above another level. It is in most cases possible to make a similar price conditioned trade agreement with the bank concerning foreign exchange. Especially in connection with transactions in high-volatility currencies, it will be possible for Eurocomp by using instrument 2.7 to obtain on the average better exchange rates.

Currency futures contracts are similar to forward exchange contracts in some respects. Thus, there is a specified period between the day on which the contract is entered into and the day (or days) on which settlement takes place. Eurocomp can therefore use instrument 2.8 to manage foreign exchange exposure in almost the same way as it can use forward contracts. Futures contracts are, however, traded on organized exchanges which implies that they must be standardized in a number of respects. This applies in particular to the size of the contracts and the delivery dates. There is also an important difference between forwards and futures with respect to the cash flow effects in the maturity period. Forward exchange contracts have no liquidity effect before the settlement date, while futures contracts involve an initial margin deposit plus daily settlements to the market price. Madura (1992: chapter 5) gives a particularly clear description of currency futures contracts and their uses. Block and Gallagher (1986) have described how financial futures can be used to manage interest rate risk.

A currency call option contract gives the holder the right but not the obligation to buy a certain amount of one currency against another currency at a specific price within a specific period. Conversely, a currency put option gives the holder the right to sell one currency against another currency. An option that can only be exercised at maturity is known as a European option. If the instrument can be exercised by the holder at any time between the date of writing and the expiration date it is known as an American option. The pricing of currency options and the variables connected with such options were described in section 8.4. The FM of Eurocomp can use instrument 2.9 to hedge the company's foreign exchange exposures (Lombard and Marteau 1990). Currency options are traded on organized exchanges as well as in OTC markets (Shah 1989). Some of the European exchanges on which derivative instruments are traded are mentioned in chapter 5 of this book.

Currency swaps (instrument 2.10) are transactions in which two counterparties exchange specific amounts of two different currencies at the outset and repay over time according to a predetermined rule which reflects both interest payments and amortization of principal (BIS 1986: 37ff.). In interest swaps there is no exchange of principal, but interest payment streams of differing character are exchanged according to predetermined rules and based on an underlying notional principal amount. The value of a swap depends on the interest rates in the market. Smith et al. (1988) have explained how the net present value of cash flows associated with interest rate swaps can be compared with the net present value of bonds with fixed or floating interest rates and forward and futures contracts. A forward rate agreement (FRA) is a contract between two parties in which is fixed an interest rate for a specified period from a specified future settlement date based on an agreed principal amount. No commitment is made by either party to lend or borrow the principal amount. Their exposure is only the interest difference between the agreed and actual rates at settlement. Swaps and FRAs have become very popular instruments for the management of interest rate and foreign exchange exposures (Brown and Smith 1988)

According to what criteria should the FM choose exposure management instruments? The answer depends on how the board of Eurocomp has answered the five questions concerning the definition and measurement of company exposure (section 8.5.1). The criteria must of course be derived from the measure of company performance which is preferred by the board. Having said that, it will in general be relevant for the FM to consider the costs involved in hedging operations. Before it is decided to use one of the 14 instruments in table 8.2, the FM must estimate the net interest cost, fees, premiums and other cost items that are related to the instrument in question. He must also compare the costs with those that are associated with other instruments that could provide almost the same kind of protection against unexpected impacts of the external factors. Other relevant considerations can be flexibility in the sense that decisions to hedge can be revised later, the time required for implementation, the achievable correspondence between the length of the exposure and the maturity of the instrument, and the potential reactions from customers, suppliers and the bank. Brealey and Kaplanis (1991) compare different exchange rate hedging strategies. One of their conclusions is that simple policies of selling foreign exchange forward on a rolling basis are potentially very inefficient. Yet such policies seem to be widely used. Company managers should devote much attention to the choice of hedging strategy.

Hedging decisions should not necessarily be formulated as a choice between no hedge or a complete hedge. Kwok (1987) has explained that partial hedges in many cases will be superior to full hedges. This will particularly be the case in companies that have several cash in-flows and outflows of the same foreign currency arriving at different times over the financial year. Kaufold and Smirlock (1986) recommend that financial managers should deal simultaneously with exchange and interest rate risk. In agreement with Kwok, they find it imprac-tical for multinational corporations to eliminate entirely their net foreign exposures.

8.6   An Illustrative International Portfolio of Shares

In order to illustrate the implications of international portfolio diver-sification from a European investor's point of view, let us take a sim-plified portfolio example. We suppose that the investor is interested in portfolio performance in terms of ECUs. He does not invest in indi-vidual shares but buys fractions of ten national share price indices. Accordingly, the portfolio decision problem is reduced to the choice of the weights by which these indices will be represented in the port-folio. The indices are Morgan Stanley Capital International stock market indices in local currency from eight EC countries, from the US and from Japan.

The portfolio is exposed to a combination of share price volatility and foreign exchange rate volatility. In the statistical analysis that follows, the combined effects of these volatilities are illuminated by correlation analysis.[1] The data period starts in January 1981 and ends in December 1991. Correlations are calculated on the basis of monthly changes in indices and exchange rates. The currency codes are given in appendix A.

Table 8.3 shows correlations between share price index changes and exchange rate changes. It can be observed that there have been signifi-cant positive correlations between the share price index changes in Japan, the UK and Italy on the one hand and the exchange rate changes of JPY, GBP and ITL in terms of ECU on the other. The remaining correlations are insignificant. Only one has a negative sign, namely the correlation between the Dutch share price index S_{NLG} and $E_{ECU/NLG}$.

Table 8.3 Correlations between stock index changes and exchange rate changes in terms of ECU, 1981–1991

	S_{USD}	S_{JPY}	S_{GBP}	S_{DEM}	S_{FRF}	S_{NLG}	S_{ESP}	S_{BEF}	S_{DKK}	S_{ITL}
E_{USD}	0.06									
E_{JPY}		0.29								
E_{GBP}			0.17							
E_{DEM}				0.03						
E_{FRF}					0.04					
E_{NLG}						−0.02				
E_{ESP}							0.03			
E_{BEF}								0.05		
E_{DKK}									0.02	
E_{ITL}										0.24

Source: data from Morgan Stanley Capital International

Table 8.4 Correlations between exchange rate changes in terms of ECU, 1981–1991

	E_{USD}	E_{JPY}	E_{GBP}	E_{DEM}	E_{FRF}	E_{NLG}	E_{ESP}	E_{BEF}	E_{DKK}	E_{ITL}
E_{USD}	1	0.40	0.33	0.24	0.27	0.32	0.44	0.22	0.32	0.16
E_{JPY}		1	0.27	0.24	0.23	0.21	0.24	0.18	0.29	0.05
E_{GBP}			1	0.18	0.20	0.28	0.50	0.20	0.18	−0.04
E_{DEM}				1	0.57	0.94	0.36	0.32	0.75	0.10
E_{FRF}					1	0.59	0.43	0.45	0.65	−0.04
E_{NLG}						1	0.40	0.35	0.72	0.07
E_{ESP}							1	0.22	0.38	0.06
E_{BEF}								1	0.52	0.14
E_{DKK}									1	0.16
E_{ITL}										1

Source: data from Morgan Stanley Capital International

Table 8.4 presents observed correlations between exchange rate changes from an ECU point of view. In the data period, there were high correlations between the following pairs of exchange rates: DEM and NLG, DEM and DKK, NLG and DKK, FRF and DKK, and DEM and FRF. Owing to the EMS intervention arrangement which has been in operation during the whole data period, the mutual exchange rate changes among the EC currencies have been fairly small. Larger changes are only observed in the months in which exchange rate alignments have taken place. The correlation pattern reflects that DEM

Table 8.5 Correlations between exchange rate adjusted stock index returns, 1981–1991

	A_{USD}	A_{JPY}	A_{GBP}	A_{DEM}	A_{FRF}	A_{NLG}	A_{ESP}	A_{BEF}	A_{DKK}	A_{ITL}
A_{USD}	1	0.37	0.61	0.40	0.44	0.69	0.40	0.48	0.42	0.34
A_{JPY}		1	0.41	0.31	0.38	0.41	0.45	0.43	0.30	0.41
A_{GBP}			1	0.40	0.43	0.65	0.43	0.46	0.33	0.36
A_{DEM}				1	0.58	0.58	0.32	0.53	0.39	0.42
A_{FRF}					1	0.49	0.40	0.60	0.32	0.47
A_{NLG}						1	0.37	0.54	0.40	0.45
A_{ESP}							1	0.35	0.22	0.45
A_{BEF}								1	0.34	0.44
A_{DKK}									1	0.29
A_{ITL}										1

Source: data from Morgan Stanley Capital International

Table 8.6 Decomposition of variance in exchange rate adjusted stock index returns, 1981–1991

	(1) var A	*(2)* var S	*(3)* var E	*(4)* var S + var E	*(5)* cov
USD	0.00368	0.00218	0.00131	0.00349	0.0001
JPY	0.00521	0.00342	0.00075	0.00417	0.00046
GBP	0.00417	0.003	0.00067	0.00367	0.00024
DEM	0.0039	0.00374	0.000076	0.003816	0.000018
FRF	0.00429	0.0041	0.000126	0.004226	0.000029
NLG	0.00296	0.00286	0.000085	0.002945	−0.00009
ESP	0.0049	0.00454	0.000276	0.004816	0.00003
BEF	0.00382	0.00352	0.000194	0.003714	0.000042
DKK	0.00297	0.00289	0.000048	0.002938	0.000007
ITL	0.00582	0.00531	0.000119	0.005429	0.00019

Source: data from Morgan Stanley Capital International

and NLG have been adjusted in the same direction in connection with EMS central rate alignments. The relatively low correlation coefficients for ITL and GBP should be evaluated in the light of the broader band for the ITL until January 1990 and the fact that GBP did not participate in the exchange rate mechanism until October 1990.

Table 8.5 shows correlations between exchange rate adjusted share price indices. Here the changes in the share price indices have been adjusted for changes in the exchange rate between local currency and the ECU. The correlation pattern is thus directly relevant to an investor who prefers portfolio performance measurement in terms of ECUs. If he is interested in diversification benefits, he should consider combinations in the portfolio of fractions of the share indices with relatively low correlations.

In table 8.6, the variances on the exchange rate adjusted share price indices are decomposed. Column 1 presents the total variance of each of the ten indices. According to this measure, stock market volatility has been relatively high in Italy and Japan and relatively low in the Netherlands, Denmark and Germany. Column 2 shows the part of the total monthly variance which can be attributed to share price index volatility, while column 3 illuminates the contribution of exchange rate volatility. The effect of the European monetary cooperation is reflected in the observation that the total volatility is almost exclusively explained by stock market volatility. Exchange rate volatility contributes only significantly to the total variance of the American and Japanese share price indices.

In table 8.7, the covariance structure between the changes in the share price indices and in the exchange rates are described in detail.

Table 8.7 Covariance structure between stock index returns and exchange rates, 1981–1991

		cov	*cov S*	*cov E*	*cov S (%)*	*cov E(%)*
USD	JPY	0.00162	0.00103	0.0004	0.635802	0.246913
USD	GBP	0.0024	0.0018	0.00031	0.75	0.129166
USD	DEM	0.00153	0.00126	0.000077	0.823529	0.050326
USD	FRF	0.00175	0.00154	0.00011	0.88	0.062857
USD	NLG	0.00227	0.00155	0.000077	0.682819	0.033920
USD	ESP	0.00169	0.00121	0.00026	0.715976	0.153846
USD	BEF	0.0018	0.00125	0.00011	0.694444	0.061111
USD	DKK	0.00138	0.00103	0.00008	0.746376	0.057971
JPY	GBP	0.00191	0.00137	0.00019	0.717277	0.099476
JPY	DEM	0.0014	0.00123	0.000056	0.878571	0.04
JPY	FRF	0.00178	0.00152	0.000069	0.853932	0.038764
JPY	NLG	0.00162	0.00121	0.000052	0.746913	0.032098
JPY	ESP	0.0023	0.00185	0.00107	0.804347	0.046521
JPY	BEF	0.00192	0.00149	0.000069	0.776041	0.035937
JPY	DKK	0.00118	0.00099	0.000055	0.838983	0.046610
GBP	DEM	0.0016	0.00159	0.000039	0.99375	0.024375
GBP	FRF	0.00183	0.00172	0.000057	0.939890	0.031147
GBP	NLG	0.00228	0.00205	0.000065	0.899122	0.028508

Table 8.7   (Cont.)

		cov	cov S	cov E	cov S (%)	cov E(%)
GBP	ESP	0.00193	0.0016	0.00022	0.829015	0.113989
GBP	BEF	0.00184	0.00163	0.000072	0.885869	0.039130
GBP	DKK	0.00115	0.00101	0.000033	0.878260	0.028695
DEM	FRF	0.00236	0.00228	0.000056	0.966101	0.023728
DEM	NLG	0.00198	0.0019	0.000075	0.959595	0.037878
DEM	ESP	0.00141	0.00139	0.000052	0.985815	0.036879
DEM	BEF	0.00205	0.00193	0.000039	0.941463	0.019024
DEM	DKK	0.00133	0.00125	0.000046	0.939849	0.034586
FRF	NLG	0.00175	0.00168	0.00006	0.96	0.034285
FRF	ESP	0.00183	0.00169	0.00008	0.923497	0.043715
FRF	BEF	0.00242	0.00234	0.000071	0.966942	0.029338
FRF	DKK	0.00116	0.00114	0.000051	0.982758	0.043965
NLG	ESP	0.00141	0.00135	0.000061	0.957446	0.043262
NLG	BEF	0.00181	0.00172	0.000045	0.950276	0.024861
NLG	DKK	0.00118	0.00111	0.000046	0.940677	0.038983
ESP	BEF	0.00154	0.00137	0.000052	0.889610	0.033766
ESP	DKK	0.00084	0.00084	0.000044	1	0.052380
BEF	DKK	0.00115	0.00109	0.00005	0.947826	0.043478
ITL	USD	0.00156	0.00109	0.00063	0.698717	0.403846
ITL	JPY	0.00224	0.00174	0.000014	0.776785	0.00625
ITL	GBP	0.00175	0.00162	−0.00001	0.925714	−0.00571
ITL	DEM	0.00198	0.0019	0.000009	0.959595	0.004545
ITL	FRF	0.00234	0.00231	−0.000005	0.987179	−0.00213
ITL	NLG	0.00186	0.00175	0.000007	0.940860	0.003763
ITL	ESP	0.00238	0.00212	0.000011	0.890756	0.004621
ITL	BEF	0.00206	0.00195	0.00002	0.946601	0.009708
ITL	DKK	0.00122	0.00109	0.00001	0.893442	0.008196

Source: data from Morgan Stanley Capital International

Column 4 confirms the observation that it is share price index covariation which dominates the overall covariance pattern as far as the EC countries are concerned. Exchange rate volatility plays a significant role in the covariance pattern only in cases in which American and Japanese data are involved.

Note

1   My colleague at the Aarhus Business School, Hans Jørn Juhl, has carried out the statistical analysis.

9

Mergers and Acquisitions in a Single European Market

The aim of this chapter is to put mergers and acquisitions (M&A) into a European perspective. EC competition policy has implications for M&A activity. So has the internal market programme. There are many types of barriers to takeovers and their relative importance varies from country to country. Some recent reports on such barriers are surveyed. The contents of the EC regulation on large-scale mergers and of the proposed EC directive on the regulation of takeover bids are discussed.

9.1 Takeover Types and Motives

Ownership and control of European companies are subject to changes all the time. Stocks issued by listed companies are traded regularly on the stock exchanges but such transactions in general do not affect the influence of the controlling shareholders. There are of course current changes in the composition of managements and supervisory boards as a reflection of normal recruitments, appointments and retirements.

In the present chapter, the focus is on mergers and acquisitions transactions or takeover transactions. Ownership and control can change according to agreement between the parties involved in takeover transactions and without significant changes in the company structure. The public is always informed about such changes but most of them do not make headlines in the newspapers. In contrast, there is in general much publicity when changes in corporate ownership and control are the results of unfriendly tender offers or when important restructurings of companies take place.

There is in the Anglo-Saxon world a long tradition in connection with takeovers and reorganizations to use the term 'the market for corporate control'. Recent contributions are Franks and Mayer (1990), Nyborg (1991) and Thadden (1990). The authors in the field see the market as a market for the right to control the management of corporate resources. Alternative management teams compete for the right to manage the firms, and the outcome of that competition has far-reaching consequences for the efficiency of the corporate sector.

There are several types of M&A transactions that imply transfer of corporate control from one group of managers to another. In the following, the company which is approached in a takeover attempt is called company T – the target company. The company which wants to acquire company T is called company A. The shareholders of the two companies are called respectively the T-shareholders and the A-shareholders, and the managements are called the T-management and the A-management.

Mergers are generally carried out in relative secrecy at the initial stages through private negotiations (Berkovitch and Khanna 1991). In most cases in practice, the T-management negotiates the deal on behalf of the T-shareholders. The general public is not informed until the parties have agreed upon a merger proposal to present to the shareholder meeting. It is therefore important for the T-shareholders to ensure that the managers' contracts give them the incentives to deal with the A-management in accordance with their interests as shareholders. As described in chapter 2, the merger agreement must according to European company laws subsequently be approved by the shareholders.

In a *tender offer*, company A makes an offer directly to the T-shareholders to buy some or all of the T-shares. If company T is a listed company, the tender offer must be made through a public bid. There is accordingly an important difference in the information flow between mergers and tender offers. In some cases, company A will have to compete with other bidders that are interested in the control of company T.

Tender offers can be friendly or hostile. A *friendly tender offer* is an offer which is supported by the T-management. It is most likely that such support is given in cases in which the incumbent T-management has been promised by the A-management that it will not be replaced after the deal. It is also likely that targets of friendly tender offers (and mergers) in most cases are well managed companies with attractive growth prospects.

A *hostile tender offer* is opposed by the T-management. Supporters of free access to hostile or contested takeovers (Jensen 1988; Jarrell et al. 1988) state that incumbent managers often have trouble abandoning strategies which they have devised themselves but which are no longer profitable to company T. A new management team can more easily carry out a major restructuring of corporate assets and improve company T's future performance. They argue also that the mere threat of hostile takeovers may have beneficial effects because it forces incumbent managements to be more efficient.

The fight for corporate control in a stockholder meeting can take the form of a *proxy contest*. In such a contest, a group of shareholders related to company A attempts to obtain control of the board of directors of company T. If they succeed, they get the power to fire the T-management.

Takeovers can finally take the form of *leveraged buyouts* (LBOs) or *management buyouts*. The incumbent management will in most cases play a decisive role in this kind of takeover and in many cases the company goes private since the shares are placed in the hands of relatively few people and institutional investors. We can still refer to the new owners as the A-shareholders but in buyout cases there will in general not be a company A. In the literature, there has been a debate about the probable longevity of LBO organizations. Some authors consider buyouts as 'shock therapy' for companies which relatively quickly have to return to public ownership in order to have access to outside investors, while others expect the companies to remain private for a longer period. According to a recent empirical study, the median life of US LBO organizations exceeded six years (Kaplan 1991).

Acquisition motives differ from case to case. In the present book, attempts to classify the motives of international acquisitions seem to be particularly interesting. Cooke (1988) has collected evidence from studies of 16 countries including five EC member countries. The evidence shows that important stated strategic reasons for M&A activity are to diversify regionally and politically; to protect profit margins by acquiring market share; to protect margins by acquiring competitors; to obtain economies of scale; to compete better internationally; to provide access to needed technology; to acquire undervalued companies; to integrate forwards and backwards; to obtain knowhow, patents and trademarks; and to acquire management or technical personnel.

9.2   An Illustrative Merger Analysis

Let us use the merger as the illustrative type of takeover. The analysis can subsequently be adapted to other takeover types. In order to clarify the costs and benefits of mergers, we will follow the textbook tradition and assume that the primary goal of the managers is to maximize shareholder wealth. The reader who is interested in a more detailed analysis is referred to the merger chapters in leading textbooks in corporate finance such as Brealey and Myers (1991: chapter 33) and Ross et al. (1990: chapter 28).

Assuming rational decision makers, mergers are only carried out if a majority of the parties involved expect that the benefits will exceed the costs. In terms of shareholder wealth, there can only be benefits if the value of the companies A and T combined is expected to be greater than the sum of the values of the two companies as separate entities. This can be expressed as:

$$MS_{A+T} = V_{A+T} - V_A - V_T \qquad (9.1)$$

where MS_{A+T} represents the merger synergy, and the three Vs represent respectively the present values of the merged company A+T and the separate companies A and T.

How can a positive MS_{A+T} be explained? Economies of scale are one possible cause of synergy. In a European context, it is likely that the removal of border controls in connection with the establishment of the internal market makes it possible to achieve new economies of scale in several industries. If there are economies of scale, the average cost of production decreases while the level of production increases.

The synergy effect depends on the type of merger. A distinction can be drawn between horizontal mergers, vertical mergers and conglomerate mergers. In a *horizontal merger*, companies A and T belong to the same industry and have similar product lines or trade with products that can substitute each other. The companies are actual or potential competitors. A merger between the companies can give them benefits due to both economies of scale and a reduction of the competition. If the firms are large, however, the transaction may be of concern to the anti-trust authorities (Jacquemin et al. 1989). In a *vertical merger*, companies A and T may have a supplier–customer relationship prior to the deal. A combination of the two companies can result in cost savings due to easier coordination of their activities. In a *conglomerate merger*, companies A and T produce goods which, from the point of view of demand, are neither substitutes nor inputs for one another.

Mergers can also give synergy if companies A and T have complementary resources. There are numerous cases in which a firm has been established in order to develop, produce and sell a new product but where the owner later merges the firm with a bigger company because he lacks the necessary capital base and engineering and sales organization. The two firms are thus worth more together than apart, and the two groups of owners share the value which is created through the merger.

If the management of company T has lost its energy and its ability to develop the organization and product lines according to the needs created by changes in technological and market conditions, a merger implying a replacement of the management may give rise to synergy.

If the T-shareholders realize that the management of their company has become inefficient and makes an increasing number of mistakes, they can of course try to replace it through the stockholder meeting and the board. It does not have to happen through a merger.

Finally, a merger can be motivated by the expectation that the cost of capital in company A+T will be lower than the cost of capital in the companies separately. The costs of issuing debt and equity are thus relatively lower for larger issues than for smaller issues.

The *cost* of a merger is usually defined from the point of view of the A-shareholders. In order to specify the cost, it is necessary to distinguish between cash mergers and share exchange mergers.

In a *cash merger*, the T-shareholders receive their compensation in cash. The merger cost can in this case be expressed as:

$$MC_{A+T} = C_T - V_T \tag{9.2}$$

where C_T is the cash payment to the T-shareholders. Still from the point of view of the A-shareholders, the net gain of the merger is:

$$\begin{aligned} NG_{A+T} &= MS_{A+T} - MC_{A+T} \\ &= V_{A+T} - V_A - V_T - (C_T - V_T) \\ &= V_{A+T} - V_A - C_T \end{aligned} \tag{9.3}$$

The A-Shareholders will only benefit from the merger if $NG_{A+T} > 0$. From the point of view of the T-shareholders, $C_T - V_T$ represents their part of the merger gain or the premium which they receive over the value of their company as a separate entity. The two groups of shareholders obviously have opposite interests in the level of C_T.

In a *share exchange merger*, the T-shareholders receive their compensation in the form of A-shares. In contrast to the cash merger case, their reward now depends on the success of the merger. Their wealth is affected by the future development of company A+T. The merger cost can be written:

$$MC_{A+T} = \alpha V_{A+T} - V_T \tag{9.4}$$

where α is the proportion of the combined company A+T owned by the former T-shareholders after the merger.

The EC Mergers Tax Directive of 1990 is discussed in chapter 10. In order to qualify for favourable treatment according to the directive, the T-shareholders must primarily be paid in the form of A-shares. It is therefore likely that the great majority of future mergers in Europe will be share exchange mergers.

Let us accordingly explain the merger costs and benefits by means of a simplified numerical example of a share exchange merger. Both company A and company T are assumed to be all-equity firms. The share prices in the example are assumed to be determined by Gordon's constant growth formula $P_0 = D_1/(k - g)$, where P_0 is the present value of a dividend stream which is expected to grow at a constant rate for ever, D_1 is the dividend in period 1, k is the discount rate and g is the anticipated growth rate (Brealey and Myers 1991: 52). Assume a share exchange ratio of four A-shares for five T-shares. This ratio implies, as indicated in table 9.1, that the T-shareholders receive 400,000 (4/5) = 320,000 new A-shares in compensation for their T-shares. The number of shares in the merged company A+T becomes 1,120,000. Assume further that the expected perpetual dividend stream from company A+T will start at the level determined by the ECU amount from the two hitherto separate companies:

$$ECU \ (4.00 \times 800,000 + 3.00 \times 400,000) = ECU \ 4.4 \ million$$

Other things being equal, the after-merger share price becomes ECU 4.40 / (0.12 – 0.08) = ECU 110. In the example, V_{A+T} becomes ECU 110 × 1,120,000 = ECU 123.2 million. The proportion of the merged company owned by the former T-shareholders becomes α = (320,000/ 1,120,000) = 0.2857. The cost of the merger can according to expression 9.4 be calculated as:

$$
\begin{aligned}
MC_{A+T} &= 0.2857 \times ECU \ 123.2 \ million - ECU \ 24.0 \ million \\
&= ECU \ 11.2 \ million
\end{aligned}
$$

Gordon's constant growth formula assumes that the share prices are determined as the present value of perpetual future dividend flows. This assumption facilitates the discussion considerably but it is of course unrealistic. In practice, the parties involved in takeovers must estimate the future cash flows and they may also have difficulties in selecting appropriate discount rates. It is therefore common to use other valuation methods in connection with takeover negotiations and in planning takeover bids. Alternative valuation methods may be based on book values, market values or prices established for tax purposes.

9.3   European Takeover Trends

Mergers and acquisitions tend to come in waves. In the 1980s, the volume of takeover transactions was growing both in the US and in Europe (Jarrell et al. 1988: 49; Walter and Smith 1990). An increasing number of mergers and acquisitions took place within single European countries, between European countries, and between European and non-European companies.

Every year, the EC Commission publishes a *Report on Competition*

Table 9.1 Hypothetical merger cost–benefit analysis (share exchange ratio 4A: 5T)

Variable	Company A	Company T	Company A+T
Expected dividend per share D_1	ECU 4.00	ECU 3.00	ECU 4.40
Discount rate k	0.12	0.10	0.12
Growth rate g	0.08	0.05	0.08
Share price $P_0 = D_1/(k - g)$	ECU 100	ECU 60	ECU 110
Number of shares outstanding N	800,000	400,000	1,120,000
Total market value $V = P_0N$	ECU 80 million	ECU 24 million	ECU 123.2 million

Table 9.2 EC mergers and acquisitions of majority holdings in 1989/90

Sector	National (same EC country)	EC (different EC countries)	International (EC + non-EC)	Total
Industry	241	257	124	622
Distribution	31	17	4	52
Banking	65	23	25	113
Insurance	16	18	12	46
Total 1989/90	353	315	165	833
Total 1985/86	145	52	30	227
Annual increase 1985/86–1989/90	25%	57%	53%	38%

Sources: *Twentieth Report on Competition Policy*, 1991, Brussels: Commission of the European Communities; *European Economy*, 1989, no. 40, Brussels: Commission of the European Communities

Policy in the Community (Commission of the EC 1991). The report presents statistics on mergers and other 'concentrations' involving firms in the Community. It is thus a primary source of information on trends in the European acquisitions market. Table 9.2 is based on this source. The Commission collects reports in the business press on mergers and acquisitions of majority stakes involving at least one of the top 1000 largest manufacturing firms in the Community according to turnover, the 500 largest firms in the world, plus the largest firms in service, distribution, banking and insurance. The material thus comprises only very big companies, and probably also for other reasons it must be considered to be incomplete. The trends and patterns are, however, so significant that a few observations are appropriate. The expansion of the acquisitions involving big companies in the EC is reflected in an annual growth rate of approximately 38 per cent of the total number of acquisitions. In 1989/90, 75 per cent of the deals involved manufacturing firms while 14 per cent involved banking firms. More than 40 per cent of the deals were national transactions in the sense that only companies within the same EC country were involved. The growth rate is, however, much higher for international mergers and acquisitions and for M&A transactions between companies located in different EC countries. Annual growth rates of more than 50 per cent are impressive by any standard.

The report also presents an analysis of the main motives for mergers and acquisitions. Among the factors stimulating M&A activity in Europe are special motivations associated with the internal market programme. Many Japanese and American companies have invested in European companies in order to take advantage of the expected growth of the integrated markets. Improved access to customers in other EC member countries has undoubtedly triggered some takeovers initiated by EC-based companies, and the liberalizations of the capital markets have facilitated the financing of such transactions. In the most recent *Report on Competition Policy*, the main motives pointed out are strengthening of market position, expansion and rationalization and restructuring. According to Walter and Smith (1990), the development has also been accelerated by the transfer to Europe of much of the M&A know-how that accumulated in the US during the 1980s. It seems, however, to be the view of other experienced takeover researchers (Ward et al. 1991) that companies and financial institutions in continental Europe have a good deal to learn before they can reach the level of sophistication of the Anglo-Saxon market participants.

It is not at all certain that an aggressive takeover approach similar to that often observed in the US acquisitions market will prove successful in continental Europe. In most of the European business communities, the attitude to hostile merger deals seems to be quite sceptical. It is therefore possible that the European takeover market will be characterized by deals of a generally amicable nature (Morland and Zenic 1991). Only a comparatively small percentage of the companies in the continental European countries have so far participated in contested M&A transactions. A disproportionately large share of the European M&A activity in the 1980s seems to have involved UK companies. In contrast to the majority of continental EC countries, the UK has a long tradition of an active market for corporate control that resembles the tradition in the US (Wright et al. 1991).

The differences in the use of regulatory and other barriers to take-over activity in the European countries seem to be a very important feature of the financial landscape. They are the subject of the following section.

9.4 Barriers to Takeovers in Europe

In 1989, the British government commissioned the accounting and consulting firm Coopers and Lybrand to produce a report on barriers to takeovers in the EC countries (DTI 1989). Table 9.3 indicates how the authors of the report classified the barriers they found. Through-out the report, the authors try to look at the barriers from the point of view of a company management contemplating an acquisition in another EC country. Eurocomp can potentially be in the position of either company A or company T. In the first case table 9.3 can be considered as a checklist of possible barriers to overcome. In the second case, group 2 in the table is a list of potential barriers to use.

The information collected is summarized in matrices that indicate whether or not the individual barriers are found in each of the ten EC member states in the study. Ireland and the UK are not covered. The authors warn that the matrices should not be considered as a definite assessment of the presence of the barriers but rather as a guide to the more detailed country surveys.

The classification in table 9.3 uses three levels. At the highest level, the barriers are classified in three groups: (1) regulatory and legisla-tive barriers, (2) company imposed barriers, (3) general corporate environment. In group 1, the report provides a list of all the relevant measures adopted by parliaments and supervisory and regulatory bodies. In group 2 is given a list of defensive measures typically initiated by the incumbent managements. Finally, in group 3, economic, insti-tutional and cultural factors relevant to takeover are surveyed.

The British report on takeover barriers is the main source here. There are of course other important sources with information on the appli-cation of takeover barriers in Europe. In the following, we will supple-ment observations from the British report with observations from a Dutch/Belgian report edited by Maeijer and Geens (1990), from a French report (Booz Allen 1990) and from a Danish dissertation (Christensen 1991). The Dutch/Belgian report is a collection of papers written by lawyers and professors of law in 11 EC countries: only Luxembourg is missing. The authors have answered the same detailed questionaire so that comparative takeover barrier studies are facilitated.

It is of course not possible to summarize in a few pages the wealth of information in these comprehensive reports. We will limit ourselves

Table 9.3 Types of barriers to takeovers

1 *Regulatory and legislative barriers*
   1.1 *Employee rights*
      1.1.1 Supervisory boards
      1.1.2 Union power
      1.1.3 Workers' councils
      1.1.4 Redundancy rights
      1.1.5 Transfer of business rights
   1.2 *Shareholder rights*
      1.2.1 Equality of treatment
      1.2.2 Free transfer of shares
      1.2.3 Voting rights
      1.2.4 Power to elect management
      1.2.5 Partial bids and control blocks
      1.2.6 Acquisition of residual minority
   1.3 *Availability of information*
      1.3.1 General economic and market information
      1.3.2 Shareholder register information
      1.3.3 Financial information
      1.3.4 Financial market information
   1.4 *Taxation policies*
      1.4.1 Stimuli for bids
      1.4.2 Degree of disclosure
   1.5 *Quasi-legal/regulatory bodies*
      1.5.1 Stock exchange regulations
      1.5.2 Professional bodies
      1.5.3 Cartel offices
      1.5.4 Foreign investment review bodies
2 *Company imposed barriers*
   2.1 *Management rights and powers*
      2.1.1 Entrenchment powers
      2.1.2 Fiduciary responsibilities
      2.1.3 Investment powers
   2.2 *Shareholder rights*
      2.2.1 Voting rights
      2.2.2 Election of directors
      2.2.3 Notification of major transactions
      2.2.4 Shareholding disclosure
      2.2.5 Pre-emption rights on new issue
      2.2.6 Pre-emption rights on share transfers
   2.3 *Accounting practices*
      2.3.1 Stimuli for bids
      2.3.2 Compliance and standardization
      2.3.3 Quality of published information

Table 9.3 (Cont.)

---

3 *General corporate environment*
  3.1 Economics
    3.1.1 Growth of the economy
    3.1.2 Liquidity of finance sector
    3.1.3 Degree of state support
    3.1.4 Attitude to foreign investment
    3.1.5 Strength and sophistication of stock exchange
    3.1.6 Ability to secure advisory support
  3.2 Institutional powers
    3.2.1 Degree of equity ownership
    3.2.2 Attitude to cross-shareholding
    3.2.3 Use of influence
    3.2.4 Investment return criteria
    3.2.5 Degree of disclosure to shareholders or customers
    3.2.6 Strength and sophistication of stock exchange
  3.3 Cultural
    3.3.1 Attitude to family ownership
    3.3.2 Attitude to foreign investment
    3.3.3 Shareholder value
    3.3.4 Language barriers
    3.3.5 Risk orientation
    3.3.6 Protectionism
    3.3.7 Power of media
    3.3.8 Willingness to disclose information
    3.3.9 Attitude to honest reporting

Source: Barriers to Takeovers in the European Community, 1989, Department of Trade and
Industry, London: HMSO, vol. 1, appendix C (reproduced by permission of the
Controller of Her Majesty's Stationery Office)

to a few observations and refer readers in need of more detailed information to the three reports.

9.4.1 Regulatory and Legislative Barriers

In table 9.3, category 1.1 is called employee rights. The questions raised here are whether the employees in the country under study have the right to be represented on supervisory boards and to prevent unwelcome bids through the influence of trade unions, and whether there are legal restrictions on making employees redundant. According to the British report, employees have some kind of redundancy rights in all ten EC countries. They have, however, the right to be represented on supervisory boards only in Denmark, Germany, Luxembourg and the Netherlands.

In category 1.2, the questions studied are for instance whether small shareholders have the same rights as large shareholders, whether shares are freely transferable, whether certain classes of shares may be limited in their voting rights, and whether the acquirer of a qualified majority has the right to buy all the shares held by residual minority shareholders. There seem to be very few takeover barriers of this type in Luxembourg and Spain, while they seem to be relatively important in the Netherlands. In Belgium, the principle of 'one share, one vote' is upheld as a main rule. The Commission has supported the view that listed companies should be required to have a one-share, one-vote security structure. Politicians from continental member countries other than Belgium tend to regard this view with suspicion (Grossman and Hart 1988). In most of the other European countries, it is the rule that different kinds of shares can have different voting rights. In France, company law allows the creation of shares with double voting rights. The option of creating such shares must be laid down in the statutes of the company. Under certain conditions it is also allowed in France to issue shares with no voting rights. In Greece, preference shares with or without voting rights are permitted. In Italy, the main rule in company law is that shares must confer equal rights on their holders, but under certain conditions classes of shares with different rights may be issued. Spanish company law allows public limited companies to issue shares with no voting rights if the sum of their nominal values does not represent more than half of the paid-up capital. British company law does not prohibit that different classes of shares carry different voting rights.

In the proposed Fifth Company Law Directive which was mentioned in chapter 2, article 33 states the main principle that the shareholder's right to vote is to be proportional to the fraction of the subscribed capital which the shares represent. The proposed provisions allow, however, the laws of the member states to authorize company statutes with restrictions on or exclusion of the right to vote. Such exceptions are acceptable in connection with shares which carry special advantages provided that the restriction applies to all shareholders of the same class.

In category 1.3, it is considered whether would-be investors have access to relevant information on industry sectors, shareholders in target companies, accounts of target companies and financial market information. According to the British report, there is relatively free access to general economic and market information and financial market information in all the continental EC countries. Difficulties in the gathering of shareholder register information are, however, indicated as potential takeover barriers in all the countries.

In category 1.4, the authors ask to what extent tax regulations penalize or assist foreign acquirers. They find a certain discrimination against foreign acquirers in the tax laws of Belgium, Denmark, Germany, Greece, Portugal and Spain.

In category 1.5, the authors investigate regulations set by the stock exchange on the acquisition and disclosure of significant shareholdings, on shareholders' rights of subscription, to dividends, to information and of voting. They try to answer the questions: what are the requirements in connection with the takeover process? Are there special regulatory bodies or cartel offices that issue regulations on mergers, acquisitions and partial shareholdings? The most important type of takeover barrier found within category 1.5 is restrictions resulting from the regulation of cartel offices. In the UK, there are virtually no statutory or common law rules regulating takeover and merger procedures. Companies preparing acquisitions in the UK must, however, take the procedures covered by the 'City code on takeovers and mergers' into account. The code is administered by the Panel on Takeovers and Mergers (Roberts and Wiseman 1990: 213). The panel has a policy of discouraging the accumulation of cross-shareholdings as a measure of takeover defence.

In 1977, the EC Commission issued a recommendation concerning ethical rules for trade procedures for securities listed on a stock exchange.[1] Several national stock exchanges have subsequently adopted ethical rules based upon the recommendation. One of the recommended provisions is that it should be the main rule that bidders for large blocks of listed securities should give equal treatment to minority and majority shareholders. In Denmark, for instance, the adherence to the ethical rules is subject to supervision by the Stock Exchange Board in cooperation with the Danish Supervisory Authority for Financial Affairs (Gomard 1990).

9.4.2 Company Imposed Barriers

Category 2.1 in table 9.3 refers to management rights and powers. The authors of the British report here try to find out whether the incumbent management can entrench their position so that it becomes very difficult for outside acquirers or ordinary shareholders to change management, whether directors are under a legal duty to put shareholders' interests first in preference to their own view of the company's interests, and whether the management is able to invest company funds in defensive shareholding without shareholder approval. One of the observations of the British report is that German managers seem to have strong rights and powers while the opposite seems to be the case for managers in Luxembourg and Denmark.

In category 2.2, it is studied whether voting rights can be concentrated in certain shareholdings or withheld from others, how easy it is for the shareholders in the country to elect and dismiss directors, how easy it is for shareholders to ascertain who their fellow shareholders are, and whether shareholders have the right of first refusal over new share issues or pre-emption rights in connection with share transfers. It seems to be common in European company law that shareholder meetings can decide to withdraw pre-emption rights under certain conditions. Increasing capital without giving pre-emption rights is thus a possible defensive measure against hostile takeovers. According to the British report, the possibility of concentrating voting rights in certain shareholdings is indeed an important takeover barrier in almost all continental EC countries. The Dutch/Belgian report provides details on a Dutch practice according to which so-called administration offices receive shares in return for certificates. The administration offices can exercise the voting rights arising from the shares in the interests of the companies while the certificate owners retain only the proprietary right. In Luxembourg and Spain, the barriers under category 2.2 seem to be of minor importance. In the majority of the EC countries, pre-emption rights are not considered to be used regularly as barriers. It is quite common in Europe to include a ceiling to the number of votes which one shareholder can exercise at the shareholder meeting. Such ceilings are for instance allowed in the company laws of Denmark, Germany and the Netherlands and used in the statutes in several large listed companies.

Accounting practices in category 2.3 in general do not function as takeover barriers. In Greece, Portugal and Spain, however, the low degree of compliance with international accounting standards may cause difficulties to deals.

9.4.3   *General Corporate Environment*

Under the heading 3.1, economics, the authors try to answer questions such as: are companies able to finance their own expansion or is overseas capital welcome? Would state support be lost if a company were acquired by an overseas investor? What is the attitude to foreign investment? Is the relative number of companies listed on the stock exchange and the liquidity of the markets conducive to agreed and contested takeovers? After studying the environment in the ten countries, the authors seem to be sceptical with respect to the capability of most of the continental stock exchanges to contribute in a significant way to the financing of takeovers. The stock exchanges of Paris, Luxembourg and Amsterdam are named as exceptions. The attitude to foreign investment is found to be so positive in all countries that it does not function as a barrier.

In connection with 3.2, institutional powers, the British report investigates possible restrictions on the portfolio composition of institutional investors such as pension funds, life insurance companies and mutual funds. The authors ask to what extent institutional investors seek to be involved in management through board representation, what their investment criteria are, to what extent the institutional investors are required to disclose their own investment return performance to the ultimate beneficiaries etc. In some of the continental EC countries, banks seem to have so strong an influence on their corporate customers that it may provide effective protection against unwanted takeover attempts. In a relatively large number of cases, the authors were unable to answer the questions posed because relevant information was unavailable. Only for Germany do they conclude that many of the institutional powers are used as takeover barriers. The German company situation is characterized by relatively few listed companies and a modest amount of blocks of shares that are in dispersed ownership. In the Dutch/Belgian report it is further pointed out that it is common practice for small shareholders in Germany to hand over their voting rights to banks in the form of so-called *Depotstimmrecht* (Lutter and Lammers 1990: 113).

The term 'cultural' is used in the British report in a very broad sense. Thus the cultural barriers under category 3.3 include the attitude of proprietors of companies with respect to retaining family control, the acceptance of shareholder value maximization as the primary objective of a business, the attitude to debt financing and risk, the degree of protection of key industries from foreign acquisition on the grounds of national strategic interest, and the attitude among proprietors to disclosure of information. Most of these questions are generally regarded as belonging to the field of finance.

Belgium, Germany, Greece, Italy and Portugal are mentioned as countries in which relatively many companies are still in family hands. The desire to maintain family control is evidenced by the relatively frequent use of non-voting shares or shares with a low voting power in connection with first-time issues of shares on the stock exchanges.

Shareholder value maximization is, according to the report, not the primary concern of most managements in Belgium, Denmark, France, Germany, Italy, the Netherlands and Spain. In these countries, the management's first duty is rather to act in the long-term interest of the business. The degree of risk aversion seems to vary from country to country. Managements in Denmark, Italy and the Netherlands are characterized as relatively conservative, while managers in Greece and Spain seem to be more willing to take risks.

Most of the countries protect some of their key industries for strategic reasons. In France, for instance, foreign investment in the defence and public health industries is subject to barriers. A certain unwillingness to disclose information may be found in companies in Belgium, Greece, Italy, Luxembourg, Portugal and Spain.

9.4.4 Contrasting Traditions

A distinction can be drawn between the Anglo-Saxon tradition and the continental tradition in the takeover markets. In the US and the UK, emphasis is traditionally placed on the functioning of the capital market and on shareholder value. The performance of corporate managers is primarily evaluated in terms of its compliance with the interest of the shareholders. In Germany, the Netherlands and other continental EC countries, there is a tradition of viewing the company as an important institution in the society and to talk about the 'interests of the company' as a phenomenon more or less independent of the interests of the shareholders. Franks and Mayer (1990) have compared takeover activity in France, Germany and the UK. They find that the main difference is the higher occurrence of contested takeovers in the UK than in the continental countries.

Company imposed barriers can be evaluated very differently by observers belonging to the two different traditions. Anglo-Saxon observers tend to see such barriers as harmful to the interests of the shareholders. Resistance from the incumbent management can reduce the gains to the shareholders, and it has therefore been proposed that the T-management should follow a 'passivity rule' instead of trying to impose barriers (Baron 1983). Takeover barriers make the position of the incumbent management too secure, with negative implications for the efficiency of the corporate sector.

Continental observers, on the other hand, find that the short-term interests of the shareholders should not be allowed to determine the fate of the company. The constant threat of hostile takeovers may undermine the contractual relations between the managers and the shareholders and be harmful to the motivation of the managers with respect to long-term investment and research projects. It is accordingly to some extent acceptable that the company builds up defences to protect itself from hostile takeover attempts. Tichy (1990) is a very outspoken representative of the continental approach.

In the long term, a gradual integration of the two traditions may result in a 'European tradition', but at present it is very difficult to predict what an integrated tradition will look like.

9.5 Valuation Problems and Market Efficiency

When takeover bids are made for a listed company T, the T-shares already have an observable market price. Many of the informed investors in the stock market have probably followed the information flow from company T over a long period and have made a record of the performance of the T-management. Based on this investor information, the portfolio managers have decided whether or not to include T-shares in their portfolios. According to efficient market theory, the market price of the T-shares should reflect all the relevant information available to the general public.

If the management of company A decides to make a takeover bid, it will always offer a price to the T-shareholders above the current market price. As the T-shareholders always have the option to sell their shares at the market price, a bid below that price is out of the question. How can a bid above the current market price be justified? Can it be rational for the A-management to offer a price which is different from the price which reflects the combined evaluation of perhaps thousands of investors?

Most corporate managers have only a few opportunities to make takeover offers during their career. Very few managers can claim that they have experience from a long series of takeovers. They will probably, partly for that reason, in most cases seek the assistance of investment bankers and consultants with experience from similar deals. Unfortunately, even the best and most experienced advisers make mistakes from time to time. A decision to launch a takeover bid at a price above the current market price must in fact reflect a conviction of the A-management that potential synergies are not reflected in the market price. The share is underpriced by the market and it is therefore justified to pay a premium to the T-shareholders. To assume that bidders believe they can evaluate the shares more accurately than the market has been called the 'hubris hypothesis of corporate takeovers' (Roll 1986).

9.6 Trends in Takeover and Merger Regulation

A number of EC measures and initiatives relevant to corporate finance were surveyed in chapter 2. Two groups of measures and initiatives are in particular relevant to the acquisitions market: measures concerning company law and competition policy.

All the 'old' company law directives that were adopted between 1968 and 1984 have been incorporated into the national legislation of the member countries for many years and provide today a general legal background for European companies involved in acquisitions as either acquirers or targets. The provisions concerning the voting rights of shareholders in the Second Company Law Directive are one important example. In the following, we will focus on the Community measures that aim directly at M&A transactions.

The competition rules in the EEC Treaty (articles 85–90) establish a framework within which the firms can operate. The conduct of the firms is at the same time evaluated from an efficiency and a competition point of view. George and Jacquemin (1992) give a good explanation of the trade-off which often has to be made by the competition authorities between efficiency and competition. Some acquisitions can improve efficiency without any reduction of competition: such acquisitions should not give the competition authorities cause for concern. Other acquisitions can be harmful to competition, and the possible positive effect on efficiency must therefore be weighted against the negative implications of the reduction of the competition. Within the Commission, the trade-off requires cooperation between officials charged with responsibilities for company law (DG XV) and officials concerned with competition policy (DG IV). Afonso (1992) has compared the authorities' attitude to mergers in Europe and the US.

Many Commission initiatives have the aim of removing takeover barriers. Such initiatives can enhance competition first in the acquisitions market and subsequently in the markets for goods and services. They may also in some cases lead to replacement of inefficient managements. On the other hand, takeovers may result in the creation of dominant positions. In such cases, the authorities are in a trade-off position.

The Thirteenth Company Law Directive on the regulation of takeover bids was proposed by the Commission in 1988.[2] The aim of the proposal is to harmonize takeover regulation in the member countries. The proposal reflects many of the ideas in the Anglo-Saxon tradition. It thus contains limitations on the defensive measures that can be undertaken by the T-management after a tender offer has been launched. The target company should for instance be prevented from the issuing of voting securities or from engaging in other transactions outside the usual course of business without shareholder approval. The directive should only cover bids for target companies whose securities are listed on a stock exchange. The proposal has met strong resistance from governments in continental EC countries. At the time of writing, it does not seem likely that the directive will be adopted in the near future. The proposal has also met resistance in the United Kingdom. Bittner (1992) has summarized British concerns over the threats from the takeover bid proposal to the well functioning self-regulating system in London.

The *Major Shareholdings Directive* (88/627/EEC) was adopted by the Council in 1988.[3] The directive requires the shareholders to disclose information on their holding and voting rights in listed companies.

In December 1989, the EC Council adopted a *regulation* (4064/89/ EEC) *on the control of large-scale mergers* etc.[4] The regulation provides for the prior notification and control of mergers, acquisitions and certain joint ventures that have a 'community dimension'. Smith and Farquharson (1990) describe the practical steps to be taken by the companies which by virtue of their size are covered by the notification procedure. At the outset, the threshold is set at concentrations involving undertakings whose aggregate turnover exceeds ECU 5 billion worldwide or ECU 250 million in the EC (Alexander 1990). Mergers which on account of the small market share of the firms concerned are unlikely to impede effective competition may be presumed to be compatible with the common market. Such a presumption exists in particular when the merging firms do not have a market share of over 25 per cent in the Community as a whole or in any substantial part of it. Even large mergers are not considered to have a community dimension where each of the firms concerned has more than two-thirds of its total sales within the Community in one and the same member state.

As mentioned in chapter 2, there is a current debate about the level of the threshold that separates deals with a Community dimension and deals below that level. The debate can be expected to continue for many years. A member of the Commission has expressed confidence that within a few years the Council will be persuaded that the thresholds must come down (Brittan 1990). Adjustment of the rules must be expected and they will have implications for the division of labour between the Commission and the national competition authorities. The present high level of the thresholds means that most European mergers, acquisitions and joint ventures are beyond the scope of merger control at the Community level (Venit 1990; Ommeslaghe 1991).

In 1985, the Commission proposed a *Tenth Company Law Directive on cross-border mergers*.[5] The Commission wanted to reduce existing regulatory barriers to cross-border mergers. One of the difficult subjects discussed in the negotiations about the directive is employee rights.

Member countries in which employees are represented on supervisory boards have insisted that they should be allowed to condition approval of interstate mergers on continued compliance with employee participation rules. Such views have, on the other hand, been opposed vigorously by the British and other governments which do not accept employee representation. At the time of writing, approval of the Tenth Directive seems unlikely.

Finally, the reader is referred to chapter 5, in which the directives concerning stock exchanges are discussed in more detail. It can obviously be very important in a takeover process what the rules are for admission, disclosure, prospectuses and insider dealing.

Notes

1   *Official Journal of the European Communities (OJ)*, 1977, 212/37.
2   *Commission Proposal for a Thirteenth Council Directive on Company Law Concerning Takeover and Other General Bids*, OJ, 1989, C 64, 8.
3   *Council Directive on the Information to be Published When a Major Holding in a Listed Company is Acquired or Disposed Of*, OJ, 1988, L 348, 62.
4   *OJ*, 1990, L 257.
5   *Proposal for a Tenth Directive Based on Article 54,3,g of the Treaty Concerning Cross-Border Mergers of Public Limited Companies*, OJ, 1985, C 23, 11.

10

Tax Laws, Tax Treaties and Tax Management

The aim of this chapter is to demonstrate some corporate finance implications of the fact that there are 12 different tax regimes in the EC.
Cross-country differences in tax structures, tax rates and tax bases are
illuminated. Features of tax treaties are described and references are
given to a number of important European tax information sources.

10.1 Neutrality and Principles in European Taxation

Theoretically, tax neutrality is the property of a tax system under
which firms, investors and households can be assumed to take the
same decisions as they would have taken in a tax-free world. Such a
tax system does not exist in practice. All existing national tax systems
distort the market participants' investment and financing decisions to
some extent. All systems contain certain elements of non-neutrality.

In the EC, there are at present 12 tax territories, each with its own
tax system. The tax bases and the tax rates differ, and so – by implication – do the tax structures. The national variations in tax systems
multiply the distortions of the investment and financing decisions. For
decades, the Commission of the European Communities and the
member countries have been making efforts to reduce the inefficien-
cies following from the lack of tax neutrality. Until 1990, the results in
terms of successful initiatives at the Community level were modest. In
July 1990, two Council directives were adopted dealing with cross-
border dividends within EC groups of companies and with cross-
border reorganizations. In addition, a convention providing for arbitration in cases of transfer pricing adjustment was published (Muray
1991). At the beginning of 1991, the Commission proposed two further
directives on withholding taxes on royalties and interest and on cross-
border loss relief. At the time of writing these two directives are not
yet adopted (Hamaekers 1992).

The political breakthrough in 1990–2 which is bound to exert a strong
influence on the tax planning strategies of European companies in the

1990s probably reflects an increasing understanding of the significance of the problem. The economic importance of distortions due to non-neutrality in the tax systems is increasing. Capital and certain categories of labour are becoming more geographically mobile as the European economies become more integrated, and most trade barriers have already been removed. Member state governments increasingly feel that they cannot maintain tax systems that are significantly out of line with those of their major competitors and trading partners (OECD 1990b: 15).

From a corporate point of view, the presence of differences between national tax systems and non-neutrality means opportunities for tax savings. The management of a European company cannot afford to ignore the tax implications of cross-border investment and financing decisions. The management should, however, realize that the necessary comparative tax law studies can be very complicated and that assistance from external tax lawyers and consultants will be needed in most cases.

Corporate financial managers cannot be expected to be concerned about the welfare conditions for efficiency in the allocation of investments and in the international capital market. Politicians and officials of national governments and Community institutions, on the other hand, should be concerned about the welfare and the standard of living of the population in Europe. Isard (1990) emphasizes the negative effects of tax induced shifts of production facilities between different countries.

From a Community point of view, it would therefore seem logical to try to establish a Community tax regime or to harmonize the national tax systems in order to come closer to tax neutrality. Order, standardization and administrative tidiness tend to be important ideals for bureaucrats (Chown 1992). At the time of writing the expenses of the Community institutions are financed primarily through contributions from the member states. Under the present institutional arrangements in Europe, taxes are levied first of all to meet financial needs at the state or local government level. The EC institutions do not have the legal power or the institutional base for the collection of taxes. It seems likely that this situation will continue for many years (Kuile 1991). What can realistically be expected in the years ahead is therefore not the establishment of a Community tax regime but rather a continued gradual process of tax harmonization or coordination of the national tax laws (as proposed in Commission of the EC 1962). Tax harmonization proposals, however, traditionally meet strong resistance from member countries which typically want to retain as much as possible of their fiscal autonomy. The right to raise revenue is seen as being close to the very essence of sovereignty (Devereux and Pearson

1989: 13). In addition, harmonization of direct taxes has to be based on article 100 of the EEC Treaty, according to which the Council must act unanimously on proposals from the Commission (Thömmes 1990). It follows that one single member country can stop such harmonization proposals. Harmonization of direct taxes was therefore not on the agenda of the internal market programme. The Commission decided to concentrate on harmonization of indirect taxes (Falthauser 1991).

In the spring of 1992, the main conclusions and recommendations of the Ruding Committee were published (European Taxation 1992). The committee, which was set up in December 1990, was given the task of evaluating the importance of taxation for business decisions with respect to the location of investment and the international allocation of profits between enterprises in the Community. According to the report, there are major differences in the corporate tax systems operated by each member state. The evidence suggests that tax differences distort the foreign location decisions of companies. Some convergence of the tax regimes can be observed but wide differences remain.

The distorting effects of the lack of international tax neutrality have been remedied to some extent by bilateral double taxation agreements. In the Commission's view, such agreements are far from providing a satisfactory answer to the requirements of the internal market (Commission of the EC 1990c: 3). Indeed, bilateral double taxation agreements still do not exist between all member states: Greece and Portugal, in particular, lack agreements with several other member states.

The majority of the double taxation agreements between the EC countries follow the structure of the OECD draft convention (OECD 1977). The stated purpose of such agreements is to promote cross-border exchanges of goods and services and international movements of capital and persons by eliminating international double taxation. This formulation corresponds well with the aim of article 220 in the EEC Treaty. The EC member states, according to that provision, are to enter into negotiations with each other, for the benefit of their nationals, to secure the abolition of double taxation within the Community. The recent EC convention on the elimination of double taxation in the case of profit adjustments between associated businesses is based on article 220.[1] The OECD draft convention contains articles on business profits, dividends, interest and other types of income. In the following, we will limit the exposition to the types of income that are most closely related to corporate financial management, i.e. corporate income, dividends and interest income.

Border-crossing income flows can be taxed according to the source principle or the residence principle. Under the *source principle*, taxation takes place in the country in which the income is earned. Under the *residence principle*, the income is taxed in the country where it is received. In Europe, interest income is in most cases taxed according to the residence principle. Article 11 in the OECD draft convention allows the source country the right to impose a withholding tax of up to 10 per cent, but the withheld tax can often be deducted from the income tax in the residence country (Sinn 1987: 197). Some European double taxation agreements waive the withholding tax completely.

10.2   Tax Structure Differences

The tax mix varies among the EC member countries. In most of them, income taxes and social security contributions provide the bulk of revenues (Bannock 1990: 17). Table 10.1 presents data for the tax level in the member countries and for measures that can illuminate the relative role of taxes on corporate income.

The tax burden can be measured both in absolute terms and in relative terms. Total tax revenue in the OECD statistics includes personal income taxes, other income and profit taxes, labour market contributions, taxes on wealth and real estate, general sales taxes, customs duties, duties on specific goods and services, etc. As a percentage of gross domestic product in market prices, the total tax revenue in the Community varies from 33.2 per cent in Greece to 49.9 per cent in Denmark. The shares of GDP in the big member countries lie in a rather narrow interval between 36 per cent and 44 per cent. It is also interesting to observe that the tax burdens in the United States and Japan according to this measure are very similar and are significantly lower than in Europe. Adjusted for government budget deficits, the figures reflect the relative size of the public sector in the individual countries.

Taxes on corporate income play a relatively large role in the financing of the public sector in Japan, Luxembourg and the United Kingdom. The opposite is the case in the taxation systems of Ireland, Portugal, Denmark and Greece. The aggregate corporate tax burden in the individual countries is probably not a good indicator of the attractiveness from a direct investment point of view. Companies differ with respect to their dependence on the public sector. In locating a new entity, it is by no means certain that Eurocomp should look for the host country with the lowest corporate tax burden. If the company is dependent on a high level of services provided by government institutions, or if it has considerable sales to such institutions, the best localization decision could be to choose a high-tax country.

Labour market contributions represent a considerable part of the tax burden in the Netherlands, France, Belgium and Germany. Indirect

Table 10.1 Tax levels and tax structures in the EC in 1989

	Tax revenue (ECU/capita)	Tax revenue (% of GDP)	Taxes on corporate income (% of GDP)	Taxes on corporate income (% of total taxation)
Belgium	5667	44.3	3.0	6.7
Denmark	8579	49.9	2.1	4.2
Germany	6075	38.1	2.1	5.5
Greece	1493	33.2	1.5	4.6
Spain	2781	34.4	3.0	8.6
France	6241	43.8	2.4	5.5
Ireland	3019	37.6	1.3	3.4
Italy	4755	37.8	3.8	10.1
Luxembourg	7500	42.2	7.5	17.7
Netherlands	5769	46.0	3.5	7.7
Portugal	1351	35.1	1.4	3.9
UK	4449	36.5	4.5	12.3
US	5090	30.1	2.6	8.5
Japan	6039	30.6	7.5	24.4

Source: Revenue Statistics of OECD Member Countries 1965–90, 1991, Paris: OECD

taxes play a relatively significant role in Denmark, Ireland and Greece. The different types of taxes vary according to their redistributive effects. Personal income taxes are normally progressive on comprehensive income. The relationship between personal income and the amount of indirect taxes paid by households depends on the composition of the consumption at different income levels. Indirect taxes and social security contributions are generally proportional to or regressive on personal income. Differences in tax structures across countries accordingly reflect to some extent the differences in political attitudes to income redistribution or equity in taxation.

The revenue of a given tax is a product of the tax base and the tax rate. The tax structure of a country in a given year therefore reflects its current mix of tax bases and tax rates. This mix changes over time. In recent years, the mix in the European countries has been strongly influenced by the liberalization of capital movements and other factor movements. Firms, investors and households can to some extent move the bases on which they are taxed to other tax jurisdictions. The implication from a tax policy point of view is that it becomes relevant to rank the different tax bases according to their degree of international mobility. The more mobile a tax base is, the stronger the tax competition among the member countries can be expected to be. Bank deposits, bond portfolio investments and stockholdings are highly mobile. Labour has a relative low mobility owing to language differences and differences in education and training. Real estate is immobile (Sørensen 1990). National tax authorities are under pressure to harmonize not only politically but also from market forces. The pressure from market forces is strongest in relation to the most mobile tax bases.

10.3   Tax Rate Differences

Table 10.2 provides a very rough picture of the pattern of corporate tax rates and withholding tax rates in the EC. The picture is rough in the sense that a lot of details, modifications and exceptions in the tax laws and tax treaties are ignored. Readers who wish to study matrices of withholding tax rates applicable to interest and dividend income flowing between residents and non-residents are referred to Commission of the EC (1990: appendixes 2 and 4). The matrices summarize the provisions in the intra-EC network of double taxation treaties.

Table 10.2 is also an instant picture. The different rates were in force or passed by parliaments at the end of 1991 according to the International Bureau of Fiscal Documentation. The FM should keep in mind, however, that adjustments of some of the rates are made virtually

Table 10.2 Statutory corporate tax rates and ranges for withholding rates in the EC in 1991

Source country	Normal rate (%)	Range for withholding rate on dividends[u] (%)	Range for withholding rate on interest (%)
Belgium	39	5–25	5–10[a]
Denmark	38	0–30	0–15
Germany	50/36[b]	0–25	0–10[c]
Greece	35–46[d]	25–42	0–46[e]
Spain	35[f]	10–20	10–25
France	34[g]	0–25[h]	10–45[i]
Ireland	40[j]	0	0–30[j]
Italy	36[k]	0–32.4[l]	0–30[m]
Luxembourg	33[n]	5–25[o]	0[o]
Netherlands	35–40	0–25[p]	0[p]
Portugal	36	5–25[q]	10–25[q]
UK	33[r]	0[s]	0–25[t]

[a] In special cases 25%.
[b] Split rate system: 36% applies to distributions, 50% to undistributed amounts. Rates do not include local government tax.

Table 10.2 (Cont.)

c In the first half of 1989, a withholding tax of 10% was applied on certain bonds and dividends from shares in investment funds.
d The rate varies according to industry. Industrial companies quoted on the stock exchange 35%.
e 25% for residents, corporate rate for non-resident companies.
f Lower rate for rural savings banks, cooperative institutions and quoted investment institutions.
g Standard corporate income tax rate 34%. Additional tax of distributions from income taxed at 34% will raise the rate to 42%, effectively on distributed corporate income.
h 0% for domestic shareholders, 25% for foreign shareholders.
i Income from fixed income securities qualifies for a special withholding tax that individuals may elect to pay instead of income tax at regular progressive rates. Once this withholding tax is paid, the taxpayer can exclude the related income from his income tax base. It is mandatory for foreign persons, subject to certain exceptions. The normal rate is 45%.
j Rules about franked investment income favour dividends from Irish resident companies. In Irish tax treaties with other EC countries, the withholding tax rates are zero.
k Plus 16.2% local tax.
l 32.4% withholding tax of dividends to non-resident individual shareholders.
m The withholding tax on interest is an advance payment of the corporate income tax for resident corporations, limited liability companies and certain other entities. It is a final withholding tax for individuals and non-resident entities and companies which have no permanent establishment in Italy.
n Plus surcharge 1% for the employment fund.
o Exempt from withholding tax are distributions made by a Luxembourg holding company and distributions to a resident company which owns more than 10% of the capital of the distributing company. There is a withholding rate of 10% on interest payments to French residents.
p Under the majority of the double taxation agreements concluded by the Netherlands, the rate is reduced or waived completely. There is a withholding rate of 10% on interest payments to French residents.
q The rate 20% applies to quoted shares.
r The rate of corporation tax on small profits is 25%. The rate of income tax payable by non-resident companies with UK source income not related to a UK branch, agency or permanent establishment is 25%.
s There is no withholding tax on distributions made by a UK company, except that where a non-resident is entitled to a tax credit on UK dividends by virtue of a double taxation treaty, UK tax at a rate of 5% or 15% is imposed by the treaty on the aggregate of the dividen·'· and the tax credit.
t The normal rate is zero, but ι)n-resident creditors in some countries are subjected to British witholding tax according to double taxation agreement.
u Most countries have reduced withholding rates or exemption rules for intercompany dividends. Reductions or exemptions may be conditioned by a minimum participation in the distributing company. The main rule is that domestic parent companies are exempt from taxes of dividends from domestic subsidiaries.

Source: Guides to European Taxation, 1991, Amsterdam: International Bureau of Fiscal Documentation

every year. A comparison with the situation in 1989 reveals a number of recent changes (Giovannini and Hines 1991). On average, the corporate tax rates in the EC have been reduced. As the highest rates have been reduced the most, the dispersion among the corporate tax rates in Europe has also declined in recent years.

The withholding rates for dividends and interest payments vary among the source countries and within the individual source countries. Ireland, the UK and Luxembourg have zero rates or relatively low rates, while Greece and Italy have high withholding tax rates. The authorities of most of the individual EC countries have to cope with different withholding rates in their tax treaties. The highest rates apply in general to interest and dividend payments to small investors that are residents in countries without a double taxation agreement with the source country.

In recent years, a certain convergence of tax rates has been observed. Further changes are under way. The Parent and Subsidiary Directive (90/435/EEC: see section 10.6) abolishes withholding taxes on dividends remitted cross-border from a subsidiary corporation to its parent corporation within the Community. According to the directive, the member state in which the parent is resident may either exempt such dividends from taxation entirely, or subject the dividends to taxation but allow a foreign tax credit for taxes paid by the subsidiary which are attributable to the dividends received. When all member countries have incorporated the Parent and Subsidiary Directive in their legislation, the *de facto* elimination of double taxation of profits distributed from subsidiaries to parent companies will be extended from purely domestic groups of companies to groups with entities in several member states. The directive also has implications for groups with their parent company outside the Community (Tomsett 1992).

It is likely that the countries with more than one normal corporate tax rate will adjust their tax systems during the 1990s. Greece and Germany have multiple rates. In Germany, discussions of reforms of the corporate tax system have included the introduction of a single tax rate (Herzig 1990). Another indication of the prospects for reform of the corporate tax regime in Germany is the fact that in article 5 of the Parent and Subsidiary Directive that country has been permitted to impose a 5 per cent withholding tax for a transitional period ending 30 June 1996.

10.4   Tax Base Differences

In this section, the tax base is understood to be taxable corporate income or capital income related to companies and their shareholders, debtors and creditors. The rules according to which corporate taxable income and taxable capital income are measured in the EC member countries are described in comprehensive books, articles and guides in looseleaf binders. These texts cover thousands of pages, and it is impossible to summarize the rules in one short chapter on European tax management problems. What can be given within the limited space available here is a short survey of selected features that convey an impression of the multifarious tax environment in which European firms operate, and a few references to tax guides and articles with more detailed and accurate information.

The best European tax guides allow a comparison of the definitions of corporate taxable income in the EC member countries (see especially IBFD various years). The definitions are different but there are also a number of common features. In most countries, the tax laws enumerate the types of income to be included in the tax base. Taxpayers, both persons and companies, are required to file their tax returns to the authorities of the residence country. It is specified to what extent capital gains and losses are included or excluded: the allowed deductions are listed. A common formulation is that the company can deduct business expenses necessary for the purpose of producing income, including wages and salaries paid to employees, goods and services acquired from third parties, interest expenditures, charges for royalties and technical service fees if they are based on contracts, and doubtful debt provisions. It is also a common feature that the tax laws contain rules according to which assets used for business purposes are to be evaluated.

The rules on depreciation represent an important part of each of the 12 national tax systems. They have therefore been selected for a short comparative study here. Table 10.3 contains information on the allowed or mandatory depreciation methods in the Community. The depreciation base is for practical purposes historic cost in all the member countries. The formulation may vary but in most cases the rules mention the acquisition price of the assets or the cost of production if the assets have been manufactured by the taxpayer. The depreciation periods vary also. Most national rules refer, however, to the expected useful life of the assets as the criterion according to which the allowed depreciation periods have been selected. Two countries, Greece and Italy, do not allow depreciation according to the declining balance method. All the other member countries allow both straight line depreciation and declining balance depreciation. The conditions are in general most restrictive for access to declining balance depreciation.

The tax bases in the national tax systems differ in many other respects, for example in the number of years that tax losses can be carried

Table 10.3   Depreciation methods in the EC tax systems in 1991

	Straight line method	*Declining balance method*
Belgium	Allowed for all assets[a]	Allowed but maximum of twice straight line values
Denmark	For buildings	For other fixed assets[b]
Germany	Allowed for all assets[c]	For movable fixed assets
Greece	Normal method[d]	Not available
Spain	Allowed for all assets[e]	For assets subject to fast physical or technical depreciation
France	Normal method[f]	Optional for most assets
Ireland	Normal for buildings	Other fixed assets[g]
Italy	Normal method[h]	Not available
Luxembourg	Allowed for all assets	Allowed for certain tangible assets (not buildings)[i]
Netherlands	Allowed for all assets[j]	Allowed for all assets except buildings (excuding hotels)[k]
Portugal	Allowed for all assets[l]	Allowed for fixed assets other than buildings
UK	Allowed for industrial buildings	Allowed for plant an machinery[m]

[a]   Belgian tax law prescribes that depreciation on establishment costs and on tangible or intangible assets used for business purposes is deductible as a business expense or charge if the costs or assets are necessary for the conduct of a business and correspond to an actual decrease of value during the relevant taxable period.

[b]   Danish depreciation law lists specific categories of tangible business assets which may be depreciated and each category is governed by separate rules. Each category has a normal method of depreciation to cover wear and tear of the asset during its useful life.

[c]   The rates of depreciation for buildings are set out in the German 'Einkommensteuergesetz'. The normal rate is 2% p.a. When the actual life of the building can be shown to be less than 50 years, higher annual rates may be applied.

[d]   Greek tax laws provide for compulsory annual depreciation for fixed, movable and immovable assets which are used for business purposes. No depreciation is allowable on land.

[e]   In Spain, all fixed assets except land are depreciable for tax purposes. Guideline rates are usually contained in orders issued by the Ministry of Economy and Finance. A maximum per annum rate and a maximum number of years is given.

[f]   Straight line depreciation is prescribed for all assets which are excluded from the

Table 10.3   (Cont.)

field of application of the declining balance method of depreciation, and is optional for all other assets.

ᵍ Ireland provides several incentive measures in order to attract business investments. The measures include accelerated depreciation.

ʰ Only the straight line method is permitted in Italy. A table of allowed percentages is issued by the Ministry of Finance. All fixed assets are depreciable. Accelerated depreciation may be claimed in the first three tax periods by increasing up to 2.0 times the amount indicated under ordinary depreciation.

ⁱ The taxpayer may switch from the declining balance method to the straight line method when the depreciation obtained by applying the straight line method to the original depreciation base exceeds the deduction available by the declining balance method. A changeover from the straight line method to the declining balance method is not permitted.

ʲ The depreciation rates differ according to the useful life and salvage value of the asset.

ᵏ Declining balance depreciation only accepted if the utility of the asset declines over time. Combinations of straight line and declining balance depreciation applicable in some cases.

ˡ Specific maximum depreciation rates are specified.

ᵐ Immediate write-off is allowed in the UK for scientific research expenditure, mining works in development areas and in Northern Ireland and for buildings in enterprise zones of the UK.

Source: Giovannini and Hines 1991: 180; *Guides to European Taxation*, 1991, Amsterdam: International Bureau of Fiscal Documentation

forward or back and in the treatment of gains and losses on foreign exchange, inventories and other assets. These aspects are excluded here.

10.5   Income Flows, Tax Systems and Tax Management Recommendations

The management of Eurocomp has a strong influence on the structure of the company's future income and expenditure flows. Changes to-day of the balance between debt and equity capital will to some extent imply changes in the future balance between interest payments and dividend payments. Changes today between domestic funding and funding abroad imply changes in the future balance between domestic and cross-border interest and dividend payments, and so on.

Different types of capital income and expenditures are treated differently by the tax laws and tax treaties. The same applies to domestic versus cross-border income and expenditure flows. The investment and financing decisions of Eurocomp have therefore far-reaching implications for the future tax burden of the company and its shareholders.

What recommendation can we give to an FM who wants to take the

Table 10.4 Income flows and features of two tax systems

	Country R	Country S
Operating profit earned	O_R	O_S
Interest income received	I_{mR}	I_{mS}
Interest expenditure paid	I_{vR}	I_{vS}
Dividends received	D_{mR}	D_{mS}
Dividends paid	D_{vR}	D_{vS}
Taxable income	B_R	B_S
Corporate tax rate	τ_R	τ_S
Withholding tax rate for interest to group external creditors	W_{ieR}	W_{ieS}
Withholding tax rate for interest to group internal creditors	W_{igR}	W_{igS}
Withholding tax rate for dividends to group external shareholders	W_{deR}	W_{deS}
Withholding tax rate for dividends to group internal shareholders	W_{dgR}	W_{dgS}

tax implications of the company's financial decisions into consideration? First of all, he should be warned of the danger of drowning in
details, specific conditions and exceptions in the European tax laws
and tax treaties. The FM's knowledge of the tax environment should
be sufficient for intelligent communication with tax consultants and
tax lawyers, but he should not aim at becoming a tax expert himself.
Secondly, the FM should try to establish a systematic search procedure
which will enable him to identify the most important features of the
relevant tax regimes. In the following, we will try to give an outline
of such a procedure. In order to keep the exposition relatively simple,
we will apply a two-country case. We will assume that Eurocomp is
a resident for tax purposes in EC member country R, and that the
company earns a foreign source income in another member country S.
The central features of the assumed income flows and the tax systems
of the two countries are summarized in table 10.4.

All tax rates concerning personal shareholders are excluded from
table 10.4. If the effect of the company's decisions on different groups
of shareholders and the effect of the type of integration between corporate and personal taxation should be taken into consideration, the
marginal income tax rates and the rates applying to capital gains in
the two countries should be included. Furthermore, there are only two
corporate tax rates in the table. This reflects the assumption that both

countries have a proportional corporate tax regime which does not distinguish between retained and distributed profits.

The information needed for an analysis of the tax implications of financial decisions depends on the way the company organizes itself. So does the administrative burden connected with the obligation to disclose information to the tax authorities. The FM should examine table 10.4 for the income flows that are relevant in connection with Eurocomp's actual or planned organizational structure and payments pattern and concentrate on the tax rules and rates that become effective in relation to those flows.

Let us suppose that the company wants to compare three types of organization of its business activity in country S: cross-border business, business through a foreign branch, and business through a foreign subsidiary (Jacobs 1991: 560ff.). In practice, foreign business can be organized in several other ways, of course. The following factors must be taken into consideration in tax burden comparisons:

1 the corporation tax system in country R
2 the double taxation agreement (DTA) between country R and country S
3 the tax system in country S
4 the profit and loss situation in all entities in the company (group)
5 the legal form and tax status of an entity in country S
6 the capital structure of an entity in country S
7 remittances between the entities in the two countries
8 the domestic entity's degree of participation in the foreign entity.

The three types of organization differ with respect to the obligations to provide the authorities with *tax returns*. A foreign subsidiary must fill in the tax forms of country S because it is a separate legal person which is a resident of country S. The income earned in the subsidiary, that is O_S, I_{mS}, D_{mS} minus I_{vS}, forms part of B_S and is measured according to the tax laws of country S. A branch or permanent establishment can also be subjected to certain tax disclosure requirements in the host country but these requirements are in general smaller than in the subsidiary case (according to OECD 1977, a permanent establishment can be a place of management, an office, a factory, a workshop, a mine or a quarry). If Eurocomp has sales to customers in country S without having any entity there – the cross-border business case – the company does not have to disclose information to the tax authorities in country S.

In the cross-border case, the *profits* earned are only reported to country R and they enter only into the tax base of that country B_R. In the branch case, the principle is that there are attributed to the branch (permanent establishment) 'the profits which it might be expected to make if it were a distinct and separate enterprise engaged in the same or similar activities under the same or similar conditions and dealing wholly independently with the enterprise of which it is a permanent establishment'.[2] The aggregate profits earned by all entities in Eurocomp must therefore in the branch case be divided so that part is included in B_S while the rest is included in B_R (Raad 1991).

Income taxation in country S of earnings received by Eurocomp in connection with sales in that country is, according to article 7 of the OECD draft convention, excluded in the cross-border case. Taxation of O_S only takes place in country S if Eurocomp carries on business through a permanent establishment in that country. Other types of income such as I_{mR} and D_{mR} may, however, be taxed by the source country even if the company does not have an entity there. Interest income and dividends from shares may be subject to limited taxation in the source country. Articles 10 and 11 of the OECD draft convention contain limitations of the withholding tax rates (w_{ieS}, w_{igS}, w_{deS} and w_{dgS}) that the source country can impose on capital income to non-residents. The draft convention applies a lower ceiling (5 per cent) of the gross amount of the dividends if the non-resident shareholder owns more than 25 per cent of the dividend paying company. The EEC Parent and Subsidiary Directive (90/435/EEC) provides for exemption from withholding tax in cases where the parent company in another member country holds a minimum of 25 per cent of the capital of the subsidiary.[3] These provisions refer to w_{dgS} in table 10.4.

Earnings in connection with cross-border business are subject to full *income taxation in country R*. The majority of the EC countries apply the residence principle as the main principle in their tax systems (Giovannini and Hines 1991: 183). $B_R \tau_R$ is therefore a first approximation to the company's tax burden in country R. However, as mentioned above, there are also elements of the source principle in the EC tax systems. A sample of the most important withholding rates in 1991 are shown in table 10.2.

If in table 10.4 all *interest expenditures and dividends* paid in country S are group internal and paid to Eurocomp in country R, the withheld taxes will be $I_{vS} w_{igS}$ and $D_{vS} w_{dgS}$ respectively. As Eurocomp has income in two tax jurisdictions, the applicable system of double taxation relief becomes relevant. The FM must study the relevant articles in the DTA between country R and country S. Most of the DTAs between the EC member countries provide double taxation relief in the form of credit. This implies that taxes paid in country S may be credited against the tax liability in country R. In practice, limitations are often imposed on the amount by which taxes paid in country S can be credited against taxes on foreign income in country R. Such ceilings are normally called 'maximum credit'. A common formulation is that the deduction from the tax liability in country R cannot exceed that part of the income tax, as computed before the deduction is given, which is attributable to the income which has been taxed in country S.

We will come back to the dividend question in relation to the subsidiary case in section 10.6. The Parent and Subsidiary Directive of 1990 has changed the tax implications of cross-border dividend payments between subsidiaries and parent companies in the EC.

Until now we have assumed that the entity in country S shows a positive profit. The picture is somewhat different if the accounts of the foreign entity show a *deficit*. If the entity is a branch, a deficit will automatically reduce B_R. If it is a subsidiary, it will normally have the opportunity to carry losses forward or backward in the later or earlier B_S. It is, however, not very attractive to do this if the losses in the subsidiary are expected to continue for several years. Eurocomp may instead apply for tax consolidation of the accounts of foreign and domestic entities. If tax consolidation is expected to be very important to the group, the management may consider an adaptation of the group structure according to the rules for tax consolidation in country R and country S (Jonas 1991).

Some of the inter-European double taxation treaties provide tax relief in the form of *exemption*. If country R and country S have an exemption agreement, the income of the affiliate is taxed either by country R or by country S but not by both. There will be no overlap between the income flows that are included in B_R and B_S.

10.6   Cross-Border Dividends and Taxes

Dividends from a company to domestic shareholders are taxed as capital income. As the income has been subjected to corporate income tax before the distribution to the shareholders, economic double taxation occurs. There are several systems of capital income taxation which can provide a reduction of economic double taxation. Spain and Portugal have shareholder relief arrangements under which shareholders receive a tax credit amounting to a fixed percentage of the dividends received. Denmark recently introduced a scheme according to which the personal tax rate on dividend income is fixed at a lower level than the normal marginal income tax rate. Greece allows companies to deduct distributed profits (dividends) from B_R, while France, Germany, Ireland, Italy and the UK have imputation systems under which shareholders receive a credit for part or all of the corporation tax underlying the dividends received. It is beyond the scope of this chapter to go deeper into these varying relief systems. The reader is referred to Sinn (1987) and Sørensen (1991).

With respect to cross-border intragroup dividend payments, the European tax environment was changed fundamentally in 1990 by the Parent and Subsidiary Directive.[4] The directive implies obligations for both country S and country R. With effect from January 1992, country S should have abolished any withholding tax on dividends paid by subsidiaries within its tax jurisdiction to parent companies registered in country R. The implication is that $W_{dgS} = 0$. Country R is required to exempt the dividend from corporate taxation (D_{mR} from subsidiaries in the EC excluded from B_R) or to allow indirect tax credit for the corporate tax paid by the subsidiary on the profits out of which the dividends are paid (relief is $B_S \tau_S (D_{mR}/B_S)$).

Article 5 of the Parent and Subsidiary Directive contains exceptions for Germany, Portugal and Greece. In a transitional period, these three countries are allowed to levy withholding taxes on intercompany, inter-EC dividends. If Germany is country S the transitional period may last until 30 June 1996, which should give time for a repeal of the German split rate system. Schonewille (1992) has provided a survey of some juridical questions concerning the Parent and Subsidiary Directive.

10.7   Cross-Border Mergers and Taxes

In July 1990, the EC Council adopted the Mergers Tax Directive.[5] The directive introduces a tax deferral regime for capital gains arising as a result of cross-border reorganization transactions. The transactions covered are listed in article 2. Within our two-country framework we can assume that Eurocomp registered in country R wants to merge with Transfercomp which is registered in country S. The shares of each of the two companies have up to now been owned by shareholders living in the country in which their company is resident. Suppose the managements of the two companies and their boards have signed a merger agreement according to which all assets and liabilities of Transfercomp will be transferred to Eurocomp. In order to qualify for the treatment according to the Mergers Tax Directive, the shareholders of the company to be dissolved – Transfercomp – must primarily be paid in the form of shares in the surviving company – Eurocomp. The merger agreement is expected to contain provisions for the necessary issue of new shares in Eurocomp. A cash payment to the shareholders of Transfercomp is permitted, however, of up to 10 per cent of the nominal value (or accounting par value) of the securities issued.

According to article 8 of the directive, the allotment of new shares in Eurocomp will not give rise to taxation. The new shares will replace the old shares in the stockholders' portfolios and a possible capital gains taxation is postponed until a sale of the Eurocomp shares takes place.

10.8   Transfer Pricing Adjustments

The EC *Convention on the Elimination of Double Taxation in Connection with the Adjustment of Profits of Associated Enterprises* (90/436/EEC) introduces in reality a transfer pricing adjustment procedure. The convention applies both in the branch case and in the subsidiary case. When the entity in country S is a subsidiary, the 'arm's length principle' is to be applied if conditions are made or imposed between the parent company and the subsidiary company 'which differ from those which would be made between independent enterprises'.[6] The convention places pressure on the tax authorities in country R and country S not to attempt to levy tax in a way which discriminates against companies located in or owned in the other country (Muray 1991: 75).

10.9   Value-Added Tax

The indirect tax regimes of the EC member countries are strongly influenced by Community measures. The value-added tax (VAT) is the most important indirect tax in the EC. The EC Council adopted in 1967 and 1977 directives concerning the harmonization of turnover taxes. The directives have been incorporated into the VAT systems for several years. The further harmonization of the VAT systems was given a high priority in the internal market programme (Falthauser 1991: 324).

In connection with indirect taxes, it is appropriate to distinguish between the country of origin and the country of destination. Let us call them respectively country O and country D. We assume that Eurocomp is the exporter of goods subjected to VAT either in country O in which the company is resident or in country D where some of the goods are sold.

Under the present VAT arrangements in the EC, goods that are moving from country O across the border to country D are taxed according to the VAT rules of country D. This so-called 'destination principle' implies that goods supplied by foreign and domestic firms are taxed in the same way. The competition between foreign and domestic goods is not distorted. Another benefit ascribed to the principle is that country D can itself decide on the level of the VAT to be paid by its citizens. If the member countries apply very different VAT rates, however, the destination principle necessitates border controls in order to ensure that goods are subjected to the VAT rate of the importing country. Member countries have based their indirect tax systems on border tax adjustments in order to ensure that exported goods leave country O free of tax and that imports are subject to tax at the rates of country D. No VAT is payable on export sales, so Eurocomp receives a refund for VAT paid to the company's suppliers.

An application of the 'origin principle' would make the VAT burden independent of the rules in the country in which the goods are used. By application of either the destination principle or the origin principle, the taxation of the traded goods will only take place in one country.

During 1991, different proposals for convergence of VAT rates in the Community were discussed. The Commission seemed to support proposals that could put pressure on the national tax authorities. It recommended a gradual repeal of the limitations on the amounts of goods that travellers are allowed to take with them across borders. In December 1991, the Council agreed to introduce a minimum VAT rate of 15 per cent. The member countries with lower rates were obliged to increase their rates to the minimum level before 1 January 1993. Countries with higher VAT rates, however, can continue with the high rates but they will be under pressure from market forces to reduce them (Hauser and Hösli 1991). Residents of high-VAT countries can be expected to travel to neighbouring low-VAT countries in order to take advantage of the price savings on their purchases. High-VAT countries will not be allowed to limit the amounts of goods which can be taken home across the border by their citizens.

10.10   Tax Harmonization Perspectives

Since 1990, there has been a certain convergence of the tax systems in the EC countries. The reduction of the dispersion between the corporate tax rates and other rates contributes to a reduction of the distortions of the investment and financing decisions in the Community. Considerable differences still exist. It is still very profitable to take the remaining tax structure differences into consideration in choices of location and capital structure for new entities.

The question now is whether it is desirable to aim at a complete harmonization of the tax systems in the EC countries. The broad conclusion of most of the existing research is that there is no need for either income taxes or social security contributions to be completely harmonized. VAT rates need not be completely equalized but only brought gently into line (Emerson and Huhne 1991: 96). The probable effects of harmonization of the corporate income tax systems have been analysed by Fuente and Gardner (1990). The authors conclude from their simplified simulation model that a complete harmonization of corporate tax systems would result in an increase of the net domestic product in the total Community of about 2 per cent. Ireland and Luxembourg might lose to some extent because a harmonization of the corporate tax systems would imply stricter rules in those two countries.

At the beginning of this chapter we observed that all tax systems contain certain elements of non-neutrality. This implies that further harmonization of the tax systems in the EC countries will bring us from one level of distortion to another (lower) level. Further harmonization will never remove all distortions. If this evaluation of the potential economic benefits of further harmonization is combined with the political resistance that can be expected, it seems realistic to conclude that Eurocomp should expect to operate in a European tax environment with different bases and rates for many years ahead.

Notes

1 *Convention on the Elimination of Double Taxation in Connection with the Adjustment of Profits of Associated Enterprises* (90/436/EEC), *Official Journal of the Euorpean Communities* (*OJ*), 1990, L 225.
2 Convention on the Elimination of Double Taxation, article 4.
3 Germany, Greece and Portugal have obtained exceptions that are related to the use of multiple corporate tax rates in their tax systems.
4 *Council Directive (90/435/EEC) on a Common System of Taxation Applicable in the Case of Parent Companies and Subsidiaries of Different Member States, OJ,* L 225, 6–9.
5 *Council Directive (90/434/EEC) on a Common System of Taxation Applicable to Mergers, Divisions, Transfers of Assets and Exchanges of Shares Concerning Companies in Different Member States, OJ,* L 225, 1–5.
6 *OJ*, 1990, L 225, 13.

Postscript

It has always been a truism to observe that the world is changing. The observation is, however, more true than ever when we look at the political events in Europe since 1989. Disintegration in Eastern Europe and the former Soviet Union and the reunification of Germany have changed the economic and political climate and environment in several fundamental ways. Nobody can pretend to have a complete understanding of the implications for decision makers in the European business community.

In the present book, an attempt has nevertheless been made to identify some of the factors that have the most signficant impact on the changing financial environment in Europe. An attempt has also been made to outline the kinds of challenges from this environment for which decision makers in the business community should prepare themselves. The reader of the book should keep in mind the difficulties of such an exercise. Readers looking for definitive answers will be disappointed.

The point of view in the book is that of a financial manager in a European company called Eurocomp. It is the FM's job to make or recommend decisions. Such decisions should be based on information which is the best available but in the nature of the case will be incomplete. The FM needs external information in order to evaluate the development of markets and institutions. He also needs company internal information which makes it possible to estimate the likely consequences for Eurocomp.

Studies of the financial environment should give the FM a sense of direction. Such a sense can to a certain extent be supported by studies of the recent past. The book's survey of adopted and proposed EC measures with financial management implications can hopefully contribute to an understanding of the forces at work. The book deals with the completion of the internal market programme, the company law harmonization programme, competition law initiatives, measures concerning stock exchanges and securities markets, liberalization of capital movements, and EC measures in the field of taxation. The time dimension of the political processes can be illustrated by the periods between dates for proposals from the EC Commission, dates for adoption of proposals by the Council, dates for subsequent amendments, and dates for the incorporation of directives into national legislation. The book also refers to the empirical evidence for market integration and convergence of inflation rates in Europe since the beginning of the 1980s. The functioning of the European Monetary System, which has played a central role since its inception in 1979, is explained in some detail.

The EMS should, according to the Maastricht Agreement of December 1991, be replaced as a consequence of the establishment of a European Economic and Monetary Union. It is important for the FM to evaluate whether the agreed timetable will be kept or whether the EMU will be postponed, modified through renegotiations, or even dropped. If the EMU plans are carried out according to the 1991 agreement and if the company's residence country can meet the convergence criteria, Eurocomp will eventually have to adjust to the ECU as a single European currency. If the EMU is postponed or if the country of residence stays out of the single-currency part of the arrangement, Eurocomp must be prepared to apply the currency of the residence country for some years beyond 2000.

Several possible scenarios are conceivable. It might be useful to recall that an EMU in Europe was proposed as early as 1970 in the so-called Werner Plan. The plan failed to get sufficient political support. The EMS, on the other hand, came into operation in 1979 and has been a success: it is still working. Monetary cooperation in Europe has therefore had a mixed history of successes and setbacks. Perhaps it is realistic to assume that the implementation of the EMU in the 1990s will also be a combination of advances and retreats (Thiemann 1992).

The developing legal framework for financial management in Europe reflects a continuing struggle between groups in the Community with different points of view with respect to Europe's political architecture (Hailbronner 1991; Noël 1991). In a very simplified way, three groups can be said to participate in the political debate: the Euro-enthusiasts, the Euro-sceptics and the Euro-pragmatists (Chown 1992). The *Euro-enthusiasts* prefer to see differences in national practices and rules disappear as soon as possible. They use every possible occasion to exert pressure for more integration, more standardization and removal of all barriers to cross-border transactions of every kind. They welcome transfer of political power to institutions at the Community level and some of them see the creation of a European federal state as the final goal (Kohl 1991). At the other end of the political spectrum we have the *Euro-sceptics*, who look with suspicion at every move in the direction of transfer of power to the Community institutions (Eltis 1990).

Somewhere between the Euro-enthusiasts and the Euro-sceptics we have the *Euro-pragmatists*. They are prepared to support a current adaptation of the institutional structures in order to improve trade conditions, investments and macroeconomic performance. They are in favour of European solutions if they see the problems at hand as more European than national or local. Bertrand (1992) sees European integration as a series of cautious steps reflecting a search for new institutional machinery to produce solutions to problems that have become more and more international. Expanding upon this kind of reasoning, the European Union can be considered as an attempt to intensify joint action for a collective response to problems that are of importance to all member countries. According to Brittan (1991), proposals for changing Europe's monetary structures should be judged in a concrete and practical way: do they help to improve our competitiveness, benefit our industry, create new jobs and generally make the market work more efficiently? In his view, most of the questions should be answered with a yes. Some of the Euro-pragmatists are also concerned with a strengthening of democratic control of the bureaucracy in Brussels (Martin 1991).

It is interesting to observe that the Euro-sceptics in the political debate have been able to use quotations from several central bankers who have expressed concerns with respect to different aspects of the EMU plans. The Governor of the Danish Central Bank (Hoffmeyer 1992) has criticized the European Commission for always stretching the arguments in favour of the economic benefits of integration. In his view, the EMU must be considered as a stepping-stone to political integration rather than an instrument to improve economic growth.

Issing (1992), who is a member of the management board of the Deutsche Bundesbank, has criticized the positive reactions to the Maastricht Agreement by ECU bond investors. He points out that the agreement has to go through a ratification procedure in the 12 member states and that it is an error to assume that the ECU as we know it today will become the single European currency with effect from 1 January 1999. Issing's warnings with regard to the ratification procedure were put into perspective when a narrow majority of the Danish people voted against the Treaty of Union in a referendum on 2 June 1992 (Economist 1992). The result of the referendum underlined the need to gain popular support when political leaders agree to intensify economic and political cooperation among democratic nations.

Helmut Schlesinger (1992), the President of the Deutsche Bundesbank, has expressed doubts concerning the ability of several member states to meet the convergence criteria for entering the EMU. Some of the EC member states in southern Europe are very far from meeting the convergence criteria, and it seems unlikely that they will be able to meet them in 1999. Similar concerns have been expressed by Kenen (1992).

There seem therefore to be at least three reasons for an FM to prepare Eurocomp for operations in a Europe with EC member states moving towards further integration at different speeds. The first is *differences in macroeconomic performance*. If stage 3 of the EMU starts in 1999, it seems likely that some of the EC member states will not participate from the beginning. The exchange rates of the currencies in question will probably be managed by the central banks according to an intervention arrangement similar to the EMS.

The second is *differences in political attitude to European Union*. The balance of power between Euro-enthusiasts, Euro-pragmatists and Euro-sceptics varies among the member states. The protocols to the 1991 Maastricht Treaty indicate that the politicians and voters in Denmark, Ireland and the UK have stronger reservations with respect to the transfer of power to the Community institutions than the politicians and voters in the original six member states. One possible development is therefore that political integration will move faster among the six older members and somewhat slower among the new member states.

Formally, Denmark's June 1992 refusal to ratify the Maastricht Treaty made it null and void for the other EC member states. Politically, the situation might be quite different. The majority of the other member states have continued with their ratification procedures. The British government has stressed that a solution of the 'Danish problem' has to be found before the Treaty can enter into force. The Irish referendum in June 1992 resulted in a clear majority of yes votes. The French referendum on 20 September 1992 resulted in a very narrow majority in favour of the Treaty.

The third is the *entry of new member states*. Sweden, Finland, Austria, Switzerland, Cyprus, Malta and Turkey have applied for membership of the EC. Norway and some of the countries in Eastern Europe are expected to apply later. Some of the countries that have applied already have a free trade agreement with the EC as members of the European Economic Area. The applicants are all democracies: this implies that a wide range of political views is represented in their parliaments. Their admission will therefore add to the numbers in all the three groups within the Community: Euro-enthusiasts, Euro-pragmatists and Euro-sceptics.

There seems to be a certain preference among Euro-sceptics and some of the Euro-pragmatists for quick admission to the Community of those of the applicants who can demonstrate a macroeconomic performance similar to that of the member states. The explanation might be that they see a trade-off between a widening and a deepening of the Community. The entry procedure is so demanding that it will be difficult for the Commission to find time for initiatives on deepening.

The political struggle concerning the future architecture of Europe will continue and the number of EC member states will probably grow. The FM must be on the lookout for signals that can be used to the benefit of Eurocomp. Some trends in the financial environment will represent threats to the company; other trends will open new profitable opportunities. There is so much uncertainty in the European situation in the 1990s that it must be considered impossible to rank the scenarios according to probability of occurrence. One prediction can, however, be made with relative certainty: Eurocomp's financial environment will also be characterized by diversity in the twenty-first century. The conditions under which financial institutions and markets operate will probably be further harmonized, but complete harmonization lies many years ahead. New member states will be allowed transitory arrangements that will last for years.

Appendix A: ISO Currency Codes

ISO code	Currency name	Country
ALL	lek	Albania
BEF	Belgian franc	Belgium
BGL	lev	Bulgaria
CAD	Canadian dollar	Canada
CHF	Swiss franc	Switzerland
CSK	koruna	Czechoslovakia
DEM	German mark	Germany
DKK	Danish krone	Denmark, Faeroe Isles and Greenland
ESP	peseta	Spain, Andorra
FIM	Finnish mark	Finland
FRF	French franc	France, Monaco and five other countries
GBP	pound sterling	United Kingdom
GRD	drachma	Greece
HKD	Hong Kong dollar	Hong Kong
HUF	forint	Hungary
IEP	Irish pound	Ireland
ITL	Italian lira	Italy, San Marino
JPY	yen	Japan
LUF	Luxembourg franc	Luxembourg
NLG	Dutch guilder	The Netherlands
NOK	Norwegian krone	Norway
PLZ	zloty	Poland
PTE	escudo	Portugal
ROL	leu	Romania
SEK	Swedish krona	Sweden
SUR	rouble	Russia
USD	US dollar	United States and nine small countries

XAU   gold
XDR   Special Drawing Right (SDR)
XEU   European Currency Unit (ECU)

Source: *International Organization for Standardization*

Appendix B: Central, Bilateral Parity and Intervention Rates for EMS Participants at 17 September 1992

	Copenhagen DKK	Frankfurt DEM	Paris FRF	Brussels BEF	Amsterdam NLG	Rome ITL[a]	Dublin IEP	Madrid ESP	Lisbon PTE
ECU central rate	7.75901	2.03412	6.82216	41.9547	2.29193	1,632.36	0.759300	139.176	176.844
100 DKK		26.810	89.925	553.00	30.21	21,517	10.0087	1,904.6	2,420.1
		26.2162	87.9257	540.723	29.5389	21,038.3	9.78604	1,793.73	2,279.22
		25.630	85.97	528.70	28.8825	20,570	9.5683	1,689.3	2,146.6
100 DEM	390.16		343.05	2,109.50	115.2350	82,068	38.1825	7,262.2	9,233.6
	381.443		335.386	2,062.55	112.673	80,248.8	37.3281	6,842.07	8,693.93
	373.00		327.92	2,016.55	110.1675	78,462	36.4964	6,443.3	8,190.0
100 FRF	116.32	30.495		628.970	34.3600	24,472	11.3830	2,166.1	2,752.4
	113.732	29.8164		614.977	33.5953	23,927.3	11.1299	2,040.06	2,592.21
	111.20	29.150		601.295	32.8475	23,395	10.8825	1,921.3	2,441.3
100 BEF	18.9143	4.959	16.6310		5.5870	3,979.3	1.8510	352.230	447.56
	18.4938	4.84837	16.2608		5.46286	3,890.77	1.80981	331.729	421.513
	18.0831	4.740	15.8990		5.3415	3,804.2	1.7695	312.422	396.98
100 NLG	346.24	90.77	304.44	1,872.15		72,844	33.8868	6,447.7	8,190.0
	338.537	88.7526	297.661	1,830.54		71,222.3	33.1293	6,072.44	7,715.97
	331.02	86.78	291.04	1,789.85		69,638	32.3939	5,719.0	7,267.0

Appendix B (Cont.)

	Copenhagen DKK	Frankfurt DEM	Paris FRF	Brussels BEF	Amsterdam NLG	Rome ITL[a]	Dublin IEP	Madrid ESP	Lisbon PTE
100 ITL*	0.48614	0.12745	0.42744	2.62867	0.14360		0.0475738	9.053	11.503
	0.475325	0.124612	0.417932	2.57018	0.140405		0.0465154	8.52606	10.8337
	0.46475	0.12185	0.40863	2.51300	0.13728		0.0454806	8.029	10.203
100 IEP	1,045.11	274.00	918.90	5,651.15	308.70	219,873		19,462.3	24,729.9
	1,021.86	267.894	898.480	5,525.45	301.848	214,982		18,329.5	23,290.5
	999.13	261.90	878.50	5,402.50	295.10	210,199		17,262.7	21,935.0
100 ESP	5.9196	1.552	5.2048	32.0080	1.74856	1,245.4	0.579284		134.92
	5.57496	1.46155	4.90182	30.1451	1.64679	1,172.87	0.545568		127.065
	5.2504	1.377	4.6165	28.3905	1.55094	1,104.6	0.513816		119.67
100 PTE	4.6586	1.221	4.0961	25.19	1.376	980.1	0.455895	83.563	
	4.38747	1.15023	3.85772	23.7241	1.29601	923.048	0.429360	78.6999	
	4.1321	1.083	3.6332	22.3435	1.221	869.3	0.404371	74.118	

ECU central rates: Athens 250.550 GRD per ECU; London 0.689533 GBP per ECU.
* Temporarily suspended.
Source: Danish Central Bank

Appendix C:
Statistical Offices in the EC

Belgium	Institut National de Statistique, Rue de Louvain 44, B-1000 Bruxelles. Tel. (02) 5139650.
Denmark	Danmarks Statistik, Sejrøgade 11, DK-2100 Copenhagen Ø. Tel. (31) 298222.
France	Institut National de la Statistique et des Études Économique, 18 Boulevard Adolphe Pinard, Paris Cedex 14. Tel. (1) 45401212.
Germany	Statistisches Bundesamt, Gustav Stresemann Ring 11, D-6200 Wiesbaden 1. Tel. (06121) 751.
Greece	National Statistical Service of Greece, 14–16 Lycourgou Street, GR-10166 Athens. Tel (01) 32447846.
Ireland	Central Statistics Office, St Stephen's Green House, Earlsfort Terrrace, Dublin 2. Tel. (01) 682221.
Italy	Istituto Centrale di Statistica, Via Cesare Balbo 16, I-00184 Rome. Tel. (06) 4673 2384.
Luxembourg	Service Central de la Statistique et des Études Économique, Boîte Postale 304, 19–21, Boulevard Royal, L-2013 Luxembourg. Tel. 4794 292.
Netherlands	Centraal Bureau voor de Statistiek, Prinses Beatrixlaan 424, PO Box 959, NL-2270 AZ Voorburg. Tel. (070) 3694341.
Portugal	Instituto Nacional de Estatistica, Avenida Antonio Jose de Almeida, P-1078 Lisbon. Tel. 43719.
Spain	Instituto Nacional de Estadística, Avenida de Generalismo 91, Madrid 16. Tel. 5839100.

United Kingdom	Central Statistical Office, Information Branch, Room 65C/3, Great George Street, London SW1 3AQ. Tel. (071) 270 6363.
European Community	Eurostat, Statistical Office of the EC, Bâtiment Jean Monnet, Rue Alcide de Gasperi, L-2920 Luxembourg. Tel. 352 43011.

References

Adler, Michael and Dumas, Bernard 1984: Exposure to currency risk: definition and measurement, *Financial Management*, 13, 41–50.

Adler, Michael and Lehmann, Bruce 1983: Deviations from purchasing power parity in the long run, *The Journal of Finance*, 38, 1471–87.

Afonso, Margarida 1992: A catalogue of merger defenses under European and United States Antitrust Law, *Harvard International Law Journal*, 33, 1–66.

Agmon, Tamir and Amihud, Yakov 1981: The forward exchange rate and the prediction of the future spot rate, *Journal of Banking and Finance*, 5, 425–37.

Alexander, W. 1990: Le contrôle des concentrations entre entreprises. Une affaire communautaire, *Cahiers de droit Européen*, 26, 529–73.

Amihud, Yakov and Mendelson, Haim 1991: How (not) to integrate the European capital markets, in Giovannini, Alberto and Mayer, Colin (eds), *European Financial Integration,* Cambridge: Cambridge University Press, 73–111.

Arthur Andersen & Co. 1978: *An Analysis of the Fourth Company Law Directive of the European Communities on the Annual Accounts of Companies,* London: Arthur Andersen.

Arthur Andersen & Co. 1983: *The Seventh Directive on Consolidated Accounts: an analysis of contents and implications,* London: Arthur Andersen.

Arthur Andersen & Co. 1990a: *Insurance in a Changing Europe 1990–95,* London: Arthur Andersen and The Economist Publications.

Arthur Andersen & Co. 1990b: *UCITS – a view across Europe,* special supplement, *Euromoney,* London: Arthur Andersen.

Andersen, Torben M. and Sørensen, Jan Rose 1991: *Exchange Rate Risks, Interest Rates and European Monetary Integration,* memo 1991–18, Aarhus: Institute of Economics, University of Aarhus.

Austin, Derek 1991: Opening new lines of information, *Banking Technology,* 8, 32–4.

Baldwin, R. 1990: On the macroeconomics of the European monetary union, *European Economy,* special issue *The Economics of EMU,* Brussels: Commission of the European Communities.

Bank of England 1992: The Maastricht agreement on economic and monetary union, 1992, *Bank of England Quarterly Bulletin,* 32, 64–8.

Bannock, Graham 1990: *Taxation in the European Community: the small business perspective,* London: Paul Chapman.

Barclay, Michael J. and Smith, Clifford W. 1988: Corporate payout policy: cash dividends versus open-market repurchases, *Journal of Financial Economics*, **22**, 61–82.

Baron, David P. 1983: Tender offers and management resistance, *The Journal of Finance*, **38**, 331–43.

Beaver, W. H. 1968: The information content of annual earnings announcements, *Journal of Accounting Research*, **6**, 67–92.

Bellamy, C. and Child, G. 1987: *Common Market Law of Competition*, 3rd edn, London: Sweet and Maxwell.

Bensch, Victoria (ed.) 1991: *CELEX Manual*, Brussels: Commission of the European Communities, DG IX.

Benzie, Richard 1992: The development of the international bond market, *BIS Economic Papers*, no. 32, Basle: Bank for International Settlements.

Berkovitch, Elazar and Khanna, Naveen 1991: A theory of acquisition markets: mergers versus tender offers, and golden parachutes, *The Review of Financial Studies*, **4**, 149–74.

Bertrand, Maurice 1992: European integration in a world perspective, *International Social Science Journal*, no. 131, 69–77.

Bierwag, G., Kaufman, G. and Toevs, A. 1983: Duration: its development and use in bond portfolio management, *Financial Analysts Journal*, **39**, 15–35.

Biger, Nahum 1979: Exchange risk implications of international portfolio diversification, *Journal of International Business Studies*, **10**, 64–74.

BIS 1986: *Recent Innovations in International Banking*, Basle: Bank for International Settlements.

BIS 1991a: *Annual Report 1990/91*, Basle: Bank for International Settlements.

BIS 1991b: *International Banking and Financial Market Developments*, Basle: Bank for International Settlements.

Bittner, Claudia 1992: Die EG-Übernahme-Richtlinie aus englischer Sicht: Die Verteidigung der Selbstregulierung durch den Panel on Takeovers and Mergers, *Recht der Internationalen Wirtschaft*, **38**, 182–9.

Black, Fischer and Scholes, Myron 1973: The pricing of options and corporate liabilities, *Journal of Political Economy*, **81**, 637–54.

Block, Stanley B. and Gallagher, Timothy J. 1986: The use of interest rate futures and options by corporate financial managers, *Financial Management*, **15**, 73–8.

Booz Allen 1990: *Study on Obstacles to Takeover Bids in European Community 1990*, Paris: Booz Allen.

Borio, C. E. V. 1990: Leverage and financing of non-financial companies: an international perspective, *BIS Economic Papers*, no. 27.

Bourse de Luxembourg 1990a: *Rapport Annuel 1990*, Luxembourg: Bourse de Luxembourg.

Bourse de Luxembourg 1990b: *L'évolution du Marché 1990*, Luxembourg: Bourse de Luxembourg.

Bownas, Geoffrey 1991: *Japan and the New Europe: industrial strategies and options in the 1990s*. special report 2072, London: The Economist Intelligence Unit.

Brealey, R. A. and Kaplanis, E. C. 1991: *Discrete Exchange Rate Hedging Strategies*, London: London Business School.

Brealey, R. A. and Myers, S. C. 1991: *Principles of Corporate Finance*, 4th edn, New York: McGraw-Hill.

Brennan, Michael J. 1991: A perspective on accounting and stock prices, *The Accounting Review*, **66**, 67–79.

Brennan, Michael J. and Thakor, Anjan V. 1990: Shareholder preferences and dividend policy, *The Journal of Finance*, **45**, 993–1018.

Brittan, Leon 1990: The law and policy of merger control in the EEC, *European Law Review*, **15**, 351–7.

Brittan, Leon 1991: European monetary union: what money for Europe?, *European Business Journal*, **3**, 17–23.

Britton, Andrew and Mayes, David 1990: Obstacles to the use of the ECU: macroeconomic aspects, *The Economic Journal*, **100**, 947–58.

Brown, Keith V. and Smith, Donald J. 1988: Recent innovations in interest rate risk management and the reintermediation of commercial banking, *Financial Management*, **17**, 45–58.

Carré, Hervé and Johnson, Karen H. 1991: Progress toward a European Monetary Union, *Federal Reserve Bulletin*, **77**, 770–83.

Cassen, Bernard 1991: How large is Europe?, *European Affairs*, **5**, 18–21.

CEA 1991: *CEA Activity Report 1990–91*, Paris: Comité Européen des Assurance.

CGCB 1979: *Texts Concerning the European Monetary System*, Brussels: Committee of Governors of the Central Banks of the Member States of the European Economic Community.

CGCB 1992: *Recent Developments in the Use of the Private ECU: statistical review*, Basle: Committee of Governors of the Central Banks of the Member States of the European Economic Community.

Chester, A. C. 1991: The international bond market, *Bank of England Quarterly Bulletin*, **31**, 521–8.

Chiang, Thomas C. 1991: International asset pricing and equity market risk, *Journal of International Money and Finance*, **10**, 349–64.

Choi, F. D. S. 1989: Economic effects of multinational accounting diversity, *Journal of International Financial Management and Accounting*, **1**, 105–29.

Choi, F. D. S. and Levich, R. M. 1990: *The Capital Market Effects of International Accounting Diversity*, Homewood, IL: Business One Irwin.

Choi, F. D. S. and Mueller, G. G. 1978: *An Introduction to Multinational accounting*, Englewood Cliffs, NJ. Prentice Hall.

Chown, John 1992: Commentary on the Ruding Report, *European Taxation*, **32**, 123–8.

Christensen, Jan Schans 1991: *Contested Takeovers in Danish Law: a comparative analysis based on a law and economics approach*, Copenhagen: Gad.

Cobham, David 1991: European monetary integration: a survey of recent literature, *Journal of Common Market Studies*, **19**, 363–83.

Cochrane, John H. 1991: Volatility tests and efficient markets: a review essay, *Journal of Monetary Economics*, **27**, 463–85.

Collins, S. M. 1988: Inflation and the European Monetary System, in Giavazzi, F. et al. (eds), *The European Monetary System*, Cambridge: Cambridge University Press.

Congress of the US 1990: *How the Economic Transformations in Europe will Affect the United States*, Washington DC: Congressional Budget Office, 9–38.

Commission of the EC 1962: *Report of Fiscal and Financial Committee 1962* (Neumark Report), Brussels: Commission of the European Communities.

Commission of the EC 1985: *Completing the Internal Market*, White Paper from the Commission to the European Council, Brussels: COM (85) 310 final, part II, section IV.

Commission of the EC 1990a: One market, one money: An evaluation of the potential benefits and costs of forming an economic and monetary union, *European Economy*, no. **44**, Brussels: Commission of the European Communities.

Commission of the EC 1990b: *Panorama of EC Industry 1990*, Brussels: Commission of the European Communities.

Commission of the EC 1990c: *Guidelines on Company Taxation*, Commission Communication to Parliament and the Council, Brussels: Commission of the European Communities.

Commission of the EC 1991: *Twentieth Report on Competition Policy*, Brussels: Commission of the European Communities.

Commission of the EC (DG XV) annual: *Credit Institutions: Community measures adopted or proposed*, Brussels: Commission of the European Communities.

Cooke, Terence E. 1988: *International Mergers and Acquisitions*, Oxford: Basil Blackwell.

Cooper, Ian A. and Mello, Antonio S. 1990: *Pricing and Optimal Use of Forward Contracts with Default Risk*, London: London Business School.

Cornell, B. and Landsman, W. R. 1989: Security price response to quarterly earnings announcements and analysts' forecast revisions, *The Accounting Review*, **64**, 680–92.

Cornell, B. and Shapiro, A. C. 1987: Corporate stakeholders and corporate finance, *Financial Management*, **16**, 5–14.

Cremona, Marise 1990: The completion of the internal market and the incomplete commercial policy of the European Community, *European Law Review*, **15**, 283–97.

CSEMU 1989: *Report on Economic and Monetary Union in the European Community* (Delors Report), Brussels: Committee for the Study of Economic and Monetary Union.

Culem, C. 1988: The locational determinants of direct investment among industrialised countries, *European Economic Review*, **32**, 885–904.

Cumby, R. 1988: Is it risk? Explaining deviations from uncovered interest parity, *Journal of Monetary Economics*, **22**, 279–99.

Cumby, R. E. and Obstfeld, M. 1981: A note on exchange-rate expectations and nominal interest differentials: a test of the Fisher hypothesis, *The Journal of Finance*, **36**, 697–703.

DeAngelo, H. and Masulis, R. W. 1980: Leverage and dividend irrelevancy under corporate and personal taxation, *The Journal of Finance*, **35**, 453–64.

Dermine, Jean 1990: The specialization of financial institutions: the EC model, *Journal of Common Market Studies*, **28**, 219–33.

Dermine, Jean (ed.) 1991: *European Banking in the 1990s*. Oxford: Basil Blackwell.

Deutsche Bundesbank 1990: The first stage of European economic and monetary union 1990, *Monthly Report of the Deutsche Bundesbank*, **42**, 29–37.

Deutsche Bundesbank 1992a: The Maastricht decisions on the European economic and monetary union, 1992, *Monthly Report of the Deutsche Bundesbank*, **44**, 43–52.

Deutsche Bundesbank 1992b: Financial centre Germany: underlying conditions and recent developments 1992, *Monthly Report of the Deutsche Bundesbank*, **44**, no. 3, 23–31.

Devereux, Michael and Pearson, Mark 1989: *Corporate Tax Harmonisation and Economic Efficiency*, London: The Institute for Fiscal Studies.

Dine, Janet 1990: The Community company law harmonization programme, *European Law Review*, **14**, 322–32.

Dine, Janet 1991 (ed.): *EC Company Law*, London: Chancery Law Publishing.

Donaldson, Gordon 1984: *Managing Corporate Wealth: the operations of a comprehensive financial goals system*, New York: Praeger.

Dornbusch, Rudiger 1991: ECU and the emerging world monetary order, in Vissol, Thierry (ed.), *European Monetary Union in a Turbulent World Economy*, Brussels: De Pecunia, 85–94.

DTI 1989: *Barriers to Takeovers in the European Community*, Department of Trade and Industry, London: Her Majesty's Stationery Office, vols 1–3.

Dufey, Gunter and Srinivasulu, S. L. 1983: The case for corporate management of foreign exchange risk, *Financial Management*, **12**, 54–62.

Dunetz, Mark L. and Mahoney, James M. 1988: Using duration and convexity in the analysis of callable bonds, *Financial Analysts Journal*, **44**, 53–72.

Dunnett, D. R. R. 1991: The European Bank for Reconstruction and Development: a legal survey, *Common Market Law Review*, **28**, 571–97.

Dunning, John H. 1988: *Explaining International Production*, Winchester, MA: Unwin Hyman.

Dunning, John H. 1991: *European Integration and Transatlantic Foreign Direct Investment: the record assessed*, Copenhagen: Institute of International Economics and Management.

Dunning, John and Cantwell, John 1987: *IRM Directory of Statistics of International Investment and Production*, Basingstoke, UK: Macmillan.

Dybvig, Philip H. and Zender, Jaime F. 1991: Capital structure and dividend irrelevance with asymmetric information, *The Review of Financial Studies*, **4**, 201–19.

Eaker, Mark R., Grant, Dwight M., Berry, Michael and Woodard, Nelson 1991: Investment in foreign equities: diversification, hedging and risk, *Journal of Multinational Financial Management*, **1**, 1–21.

Eckl, S. and Robinson, N. J. 1990: Some issues in corporate hedging policy, *Accounting and Business Research*, **20**, 287–98.

ECOFEX 1991: *ECOFEX Directory 1991*, London: ECOFEX Secretariat c/o LIFFE.

Economist 1992: The Danes say no, *The Economist*, 6 June 1992.

Edison, Hali J. and Fisher, Eric O. 1991: A long-run view of the European Monetary System, *Journal of International Money and Finance*, **10**, 53–70.

Ehlermann, Claus-Dieter and Bieber, Roland (eds) 1991: *Handbuch des Europäischen Rechts* (looseleaf), Baden-Baden: Nomos Verlagsgesellschaft.

Eiteman, David K., Stonehill, Arthur I. and Moffett, Michael H. 1992: *Multinational Business Finance*, 6th edn, Reading, MA: Addison-Wesley.

Ellis, J. and Storm, P. M. 1991 (eds): *Business Law in Europe: legal, tax and labour aspects of business operations in the EEC and Switzerland*, Deventer: Kluwer.

Eltis, Walter 1990: Monetary Union: problems that would be solved more easily under the United Kingdom proposal, in Vissol, Thierry (ed.), *Economic and Monetary Union: critical analysis*, Brussels: De Pecunia, vol. II, no. 2–3, 381–8.

Eltis, Walter 1991: The obstacles to European Monetary Union, in Eltis, W. and Johnson, C. (eds), *British Views on EMU*, Brussels: De Pecunia, vol. I, no. 2, 253–73.

Emerson, Christopher 1991: Corporate finance in the 1990s, *Long Range Planning*, **24**, 83–7.

Emerson, Michael, Aujean, Michel, Catinat, Michel, Goybet, Philippe and Jacquemin, Alexis 1988: *The Economics of 1992: the EC Commission's assessment of the economic effects of completing the internal market*, Oxford: Oxford University Press.

Emerson, Michael and Huhne, Christopher 1991: *The ECU Report: the single European currency – and what it means to you*, London: Pan.

Empel, Martijn van 1990: *Financial Services and EEC Law: materials and cases*, Deventer: Kluwer.

Engel, Charles and Rodrigues, Anthony P. 1989: Tests of international CAPM with time varying covariances, *Journal of Applied Econometrics*, **4**, 119–38.

Eun, C. S. and Resnick, B. G. 1988: Exchange rate uncertainty, forward contracts and international portfolio selection, *The Journal of Finance*, **43**, 197–215.

Eun, C. S. and Shim, S. 1989: International transmission of stock market movements, *Journal of Financial and Quantitative Analysis*, **24**, 241–56.

Euroconfidential 1989: *Directory of EEC Information Sources*, Rixensart: Euroconfidential.

Euromoney 1991: *The 1991 Borrower's Guide to Financing in Foreign Markets*, London: Euromoney.

Euromoney 1992: *Guide to European Equity Markets 1992*, London: Euromoney.

Europa 1991: *Europa World Year Book 1991*, London: Europa.

European Taxation 1992: Report of the Ruding Committee: conclusions and recommendations of the Committee of Independent Experts on Company Taxation, *European Taxation*, **32**, 105–22.

Eurostat 1991a: *European Community Direct Investment 1984–1988*, Luxembourg: Eurostat (Unit C3).

Eurostat 1991b: *Money and Finance*, theme 2: economy and finance, series B: short-term trends, Luxembourg: Eurostat.

Eurostat monthly: *External Trade Monthly Statistics*, Luxembourg: Eurostat.

Falthauser, Kurt 1991: Der aktuelle Stand der Harmonisierung der Mehrwertsteueren in der EG, *Steuer und Wirtschaft*, **68**, 324–36.

Fitzgerald, M. Desmond 1983: *Financial Futures*, London: Euromoney.

Fitzgerald, M. Desmond 1987: *Financial Options*, London: Euromoney.

Flood, Eugene and Lessard, Donald R. 1986: On the measurement of operating exposure to exchange rates: a conceptual approach, *Financial Management*, **15**, 25–36.

Fourt, Nicolas 1991: Le Contrat à terme ECU: un outil pour les arbitrages ECU/ECU et ECU/devises européennes, *EBA Newsletter*, no. 7.

Franks, Julian and Mayer, Colin 1990: *Capital Markets and Corporate Control: a study of France, Germany and the UK*, working paper IFA-127-90, London: London Business School.

Frenkel, Jacob A. and Levich, Richard M. 1977: Transaction costs and interest arbitrage: tranquil versus turbulent periods, *Journal of Political Economy*, **85**, 1209–26.

Froot, Kenneth A. and Frankel, Jeffrey A. 1989: Forward discount bias: is it an exchange risk premium?, *The Quarterly Journal of Economics*, **104**, 139–61.

Froot, Kenneth A. and Thaler, Richard H. 1990: Anomalies: foreign exchange, *Journal of Economic Perspectives*, **4**, 179–92.

Fuente, A. and Gardner, E. 1990: *Corporate Income Tax Harmonization and Capital Allocation in the European Community*, working paper 90/103, Washington DC: IMF.

Gaddum, Johan Wilhelm 1992: Europäische Währungsunion, aus der Sicht der Deutschen Bundesbank, *Zeitschrift für das Gesamte Kreditwesen*, **45**, 47–8.

Garman, Mark B. and Kohlhagen, S. W. 1983: Foreign currency option values, *Journal of International Money and Finance*, **2**, 231–7.

GATT 1990: *GATT Activities 1990: annual review of the work of the GATT*, Geneva: General Agreement on Tariffs and Trade.

George, Ken and Jacquemin, Alexis 1992: Dominant firms and mergers, *The Economic Journal*, **102**, 148–57.

Geroski, Paul A. and Jacquemin, Alexis 1989: Industrial change, barriers to mobility, and European industrial policy, in Jacquemin, Alexis and Sapir, André (eds), *The European Internal Market: trade and competition*, Oxford: Oxford University Press.

Geweke, J. and Feige, E. 1979: Some joint tests of the efficiency of markets for forward foreign exchange, *Review of Economics and Statistics*, **61**, 334–41.

Giddy, Ian H. 1976: An integrated theory of exchange rate equilibrium, *Journal of Financial and Quantitative Analysis*, **11**, 883–92.

Giddy, Ian H. 1977: Exchange risk: whose view?, *Financial Management*, **6**, 23–33.

Giovannini, Alberto 1989: National tax systems versus the European capital market, *Economic Policy*, no. 9.

Giovannini, Alberto 1990: *The Transition to European Monetary Union*, Essays in International Finance no. 178, Princeton, NJ.

Giovannini, Alberto and Hines, James R. 1991: Capital flight and tax competition: are there viable solutions to both problems?, in Giovannini, Alberto and Mayer, Colin (eds), *European Financial Integration*, Cambridge: Cambridge University Press, 172–210.

Giovannini, Alberto and Jorion, Philippe 1989: The time variation of risk and return in the foreign exchange and stock markets, *The Journal of Finance*, **44**, 307–25.

Gomard, B. 1990: Possible defensive measures against stock exchange raids in

Denmark, in Maeijer, J. M. M. and Geens, K. (eds), *Defensive Measures against Hostile Takeovers in the Common Market*, Dordrecht: Martinus Nijhoff, 83–9.

Goodhart, Charles 1991: An assessment of EMU, *The Royal Bank of Scotland Review*, no. 170, 3–25.

Goyder, D. G. 1988: *EEC Competition Law*, Oxford: Clarendon Press.

Grauer, F. A., Litzenberger, R. A. and Stehle, R. E. 1976: Sharing rules and equilibrium in an international capital market, *Journal of Financial Economics*, 3, 233–56.

Gros, D. 1987: *On the Volatility of Exchange Rates: a test of monetary and portfolio balance models of exchange rate determination*, Brussels: Centre for European Policy Studies.

Gros, D. and Thygesen, N. 1991: *European Monetary Integration: from EMS to Monetary Union*, London: Longman.

Grossman, Sanford J. and Hart, Oliver D. 1988: One share–one vote and the market for corporate control, *Journal of Financial Economics*, 20, 175–202.

Gyohten, Tyodo 1991: Japan's monetary strategy towards Europe and the ECU, in Vissol, Thierry (ed.) *European Monetary Union in a Turbulent World Economy*, Brussels: De Pecunia, 75–84.

Haberer, Jean-Yves 1991: The new developments in the ECU clearing system and its evolution within the future European Central Bank, *EBA Newsletter*, no. 14, 18–19.

Hailbronner, Kay 1991: Legal-institutional reforms of the EEC: what can we learn from federalism theory and practice?, *Aussenwirtschaft*, 46, 253–64.

Hakansson, Nils H. 1981: On the politics of accounting disclosure and measurement: an analysis of economic incentives, *Journal of Accounting Research*, 19, 1–35.

Haldane, A. G. 1991: The exchange rate mechanism of the European Monetary System: a review of the literature, *Bank of England Quarterly Bulletin*, 31, 73–82.

Hamaekers, Hubert 1992: The EC on the brink of full corporate tax harmonization?, *European Taxation*, 32, 102–4.

Hamao, Yasushi, Masulis, Ronald W. and Ng, Vicort 1990: Correlations in price changes and volatility across international stock markets, *The Review of Financial Studies*, 3, 281–307.

Hansen, J. D., Heinrich H. and Nielsen, J. U. M. 1992: *An Economic Analysis of the EC*, London: McGraw-Hill.

Hansen, Lars Peter and Hodrick, Robert J. 1980: Forward exchange rates as optimal predictors of future spot rates: an econometric analysis, *Journal of Political Economy*, 88, 829–53.

Hanson, T. 1991: *Directory of European Community and Related Databases*, London: European Information Association.

Harris, Milton and Raviv, Arthur 1991: The theory of capital structure, *The Journal of Finance*, 46, 297–355.

Harvey, Campbell R. 1991: The world price of covariance risk, *The Journal of Finance*, 46, 111–57.

Haugen, Robert A. 1990: *Modern Investment Theory*, 2nd edn, Englewood Cliffs, NJ: Prentice Hall.

Hauschka, Christoph 1992: Die Europäische Aktiengesellschaft (SE) im Entwurf der Kommission von 1991: Vor der Vollendung?, *Europäische Zeitschrift für Wirtschaftsrecht*, **3**, 147–9.

Hauser, Heinz and Hösli, Madeleine 1991: Harmonization or regulatory competition in the EC (and the EEA)?, *Aussenwirtschaft*, **46**, 497–512.

Hellwig, Martin 1991: Banking, financial intermediation and corporate finance, in Giovannini, Alberto and Mayer, Colin (eds), *European Financial Integration*, Cambridge: Cambridge University Press.

Herzig, Norbert 1990: Nationale und internationale Aspekte einer Reform der Körperschaftsteuer, *Steuer und Wirtschaft*, **67**, no. 1, 22–39.

Hodder, James E. and Senbet, Lemma W. 1990: International capital structure equilibrium, *The Journal of Finance*, **45**, 1495–516.

Hoffmeyer, Erik 1992: Economic and Monetary Union – a central banker's perspective, *Danmarks Nationalbank Kvartalsoversigt*, **31**, May, 26–31.

Hopt, Klaus J. 1990: The European Insider Dealing Directive, *Common Market Law Review*, **27**, 51–82.

Hottner, Thomas 1992: Einlagenschutz in Europa, *Zeitschrift für das Gesamte Kreditwesen*, **45**, 229–33.

Huang, Roger D. 1987: Expectations of exchange rates and differential inflation rates: further evidence on purchasing power parity in efficient markets, *The Journal of Finance*, **42**, 69–79.

IASC 1989: *Comparability of Financial Statements: proposed amendments to international accounting standards*, London: International Accounting Standards Committee.

IBFD various years: *Guides to European Taxation* (looseleaf), Amsterdam: International Bureau of Fiscal Documentation.

IBFD 1992: The taxation of private investment income, in *Guides to European Taxation*, Amsterdam: International Bureau of Fiscal Documentation.

IMF 1992: *IMF Annual Report*, Washington DC: International Monetary Fund.

Isard, Peter 1990: Corporate tax harmonization and European monetary integration, *Kyklos*, **43**, 3–23.

ISDA 1991: *ISDA Definitions 1991*, London: International Swap Dealers Association.

Israel, Ronen 1991: Capital structure and the market for corporate control: the defensive role of debt financing, *The Journal of Finance*, **46**, 1391–409.

Issing, Otmar 1992: Geldpolitik im Vorfeld der Europäischen Währungsunion, *Deutsche Bundesbank/Auszüge aus Presseartikeln*, no. 34.

Jacobs, Francis Brendan 1991: The European Parliament and Economic and Monetary Union, *Common Market Law Review*, **28**, 361–82.

Jacobs, Otto H. 1991: *Internationale Unternehmensbesteuerung*, München: C. H. Beck'sche Verlagsbuchhandlung.

Jacque, Laurent L. 1981: Management of foreign exchange risk: a review article, *Journal of International Business Studies*, **12**, 81–101.

Jacquemin, Alexis, Buigues, Pierre and Olzhovitz, Fabienne 1989: Horizontal mergers and competition policy in the European Community, *European Economy*, no. 40, Brussels: Commission of the European Communities.

Jacquemin, Alexis and Sapir, André 1989: 1992: a single but imperfect market, in Jacquemin, Alexis and Sapir, André (eds),*The European Internal Market: trade and competition*, Oxford: Oxford University Press, 1–9.

Jaillet, P. 1991: Aspects de l'union économique et monétaire et de la transition, *Revue Marché Commun et de l'Union Européenne*, no. 349, Paris, 518–28.

Jakobsen Svend and Jørgensen, Peter Løchte 1991: *A Comparison of Binomial Term Structure Models*, working paper 91–1, Aarhus: Department of Finance, The Aarhus School of Business.

Jarrell, Gregg A., Brickley, James A. and Netter, Jeffry M. 1988: The market for corporate control: the empirical evidence since 1980, *Journal of Economic Perspectives*, **2**, 49–68.

Jensen, Michael C. 1988: Takeovers: their causes and consequences, *Journal of Economic Perspectives*, **2**, 21–48.

Jensen, Michael C. and Meckling, William H. 1976: Theory of the firm: managerial behavior, agency costs and ownership structure, *Journal of Financial Economics*, **3**, 305–60.

Jessen, Jakob and Frederiksen, Folke Friis 1991: Danske erhvervsvirksomheders gældsgrader i et internationalt perspektiv, *Nationaløkonomisk Tidsskrift*, **129**, 216–35.

Johnson, Christopher 1990: A 10-point plan for European Monetary Union, *De Pecunia*, **2**, no. 2–3, 233–6.

Johnson, R. B. 1981: *Theories of the Growth of the Euro-Currency Market: a review of the Euro-currency deposit multiplier*, Basle: Bank for International Settlements.

Jonas, Bernd 1991: Steuerliche Aspekte bei ausländischen Konzerngesellschaften, *Recht der Internationalen Wirtschaft*, **37**, no. 1, 41–8.

Jorion, Philippe 1992: Portfolio optimization in practice, *Financial Analysts Journal*, **48**, 68–74.

Kaplan, Steven N. 1991: The staying power of leveraged buyouts, *Journal of Financial Economics*, **29**, 287–313.

Kaufold, Howard and Smirlock, Michael 1986: Managing corporate exchange and interest rate exposure, *Financial Management*, **15**, 64–72.

Kendall, Vivienne 1991: The internal market: will the deadline be met?, in *European Community: economic structure and analysis*, London: The Economist Intelligence Unit, 12–18.

Kenen, Peter B. 1992: *EMU after Maastricht*, Washington, DC: Group of 30.

Key, Sidney J. 1989: Mutual recognition: integration of the financial sector in the European Community, *Federal Reserve Bulletin*, **75**, 591–609.

Klein, K. R. 1991: *Die Bankensysteme der EG-Länder*, Frankfurt am Main: Fritz Knapp Verlag.

Knebel, Hans-Werner 1992: Europäischer Finanzbinnenmarkt: Auf dem Weg in ein neues Finanzzeitalter, *Europäische Zeitschrift für Wirtschaftsrecht*, **3**, 149–52.

Koch, Paul D. and Koch, Timothy W. 1991: Evolution in dynamic linkages across daily national stock indexes, *Journal of International Money and Finance*, **10**, 231–51.

Kohl, H. 1991: Faire les Etats-Unis d'Europe, *Politique internationale*, no. 52, Paris, 21–32.

References 229

Kohlhagen, Steven W. 1978: *The Behavior of Foreign Exchange Markets: a critical survey of the empirical literature*, monograph 1978-3, New York: Salomon Brothers Center for the Study of Financial Institutions.
Kuile, B. H. Ter 1991: Legal aspects of fiscal sovereignty within the internal market, *Intertax*, 503-9.
Kulms, Rainer 1990: Competition, trade policy and competition policy in the EEC: the example of antidumping, *Common Market Law Review*, 27, 285-313.
Kupa, Mihaly 1991: The ECU and the East European countries, *EBA Newsletter*, no. 14, 9.
Kwok, Chuck C. Y. 1987: Hedging foreign exchange exposures: independent vs. integrative approaches, *Journal of International Business Studies*, 18, 33-51.
Laboul, André 1992: The new frontiers of insurance and financial services, *The OECD Observer*, no. 173, 16-18.
Lamont, Norman 1991: British objectives for monetary integration in Europe, in Vissol, Thierry (ed.) *European Monetary Union in a Turbulent World Economy*, Brussels: De Pecunia, 25-34.
Lee, Moon H. and Zechner, Josef 1984: Debt, taxes, and international equilibrium, *Journal of International Money and Finance*, 3, 343-55.
Lefebvre, Chris and Lin, Liang-Qu 1991: On the scope of consolidation: a comparative study of the EEC 7th Directive, IAS 27 and the Belgian royal decree on consolidation, *British Accounting Review*, 23, 133-47.
Lehner, Stefan and Meiklejohn, Roderick 1991: Fair competition in the internal market: Community state aid policy, *European Economy*, no. 48, Brussels: Commission of the European Communities, 7-114.
Leigh-Pemberton, Robin 1990: The single market and its implications for Europe's monetary arrangements, *Bank of England Quarterly Bulletin*, 30, 62-7.
Leigh-Pemberton, Robin 1991: European monetary arrangements: convergence and other issues, *Bank of England Quarterly Bulletin*, 31, 516-20.
Leland, Hayne E. and Pyle, David H. 1977: Informational asymmetries, financial structure, and financial intermediation, *The Journal of Finance*, 32, 371-87.
Leonard, John D., Glossman, Diane B., Naschek, Jeffrey B. and Strauss, Rickard 1992: *European Bank Mergers: lessons of experience for the future*, New York: Salomon Brothers.
Lessard, Donald 1989: Corporate finance in the 1990s - implications of a changing competitive and financial context, *Journal of International Financial Management and Accounting*, 1, 209-31.
Liebman, Howard M. and Patten, Russel M. 1991: Review of EC tax developments, *European Taxation*, 31, 364-71.
LIFFE 1991: *Summary of Futures and Options Contracts*, London: London International Financial Futures Exchange.
Lizondo, J. Saul 1991: *Determinants and Systemic Consequences of International Capital Flows*, occasional paper 77, Washington, DC: International Monetary Fund.
Logue, Dennis E. and Oldfield, George S. 1977: Managing foreign assets when foreign exchange markets are efficient, *Financial Management*, 6, 16-22.

Lombard, Odile and Marteau, Didier 1990: *Devisenoptionen*, Wiesbaden: Gabler Verlag.

Louis, Jean-Victor and De Lhoneux, Etienne 1991: The development of the use of the ECU: legal aspects, *Common Market Law Review*, **28**, 335–59.

Louw, André 1991: The ECU and its role in the process towards monetary union, *European Economy*, no. 48, Brussels: Commission of the European Communities.

Lutter, Marcus and Lammers, Brigitte 1990: Hostile takeovers: possibilities and limitations according to German law, in Maeijer, J. M. M. and Geens, K. (eds), *Defensive Measures Against Hostile Takeovers in the Common Market*, Dordrecht: Martinus Nijhoff.

Lux, Michael 1992: Die Rechtsprechung des Europäischen Gerichtshofes zum Antidumpingrecht, 2. Teil, *Recht der Internationalen Wirtschaft*, **38**, 23–43.

Machlup, Fritz 1970: Euro-dollar creation: a mystery story, *Banca Nazionale del Lavoro Quarterly Review*, no. 94.

Madura, Jeff 1992: *International Financial Management*, St Paul, MN: West.

Madura, Jeff and Tucker, Alan L. 1992: Hedging international stock portfolios: lessons from the 1987 crash, *Journal of Portfolio Management*, **18**, 69–73.

Maeijer, J. M. M. and Geens, K. (eds) *Defensive Measures against Hostile Takeovers in the Common Market*, Dordrecht: Martinus Nijhoff.

Makin, John H. 1978: Portfolio theory and the problem of foreign exchange risk, *The Journal of Finance*, **33**, 517–34.

Martin, David 1991: Progress towards European Union: EC institutional perspectives on the intergovernmental conferences – the view of the Parliament, *Aussenwirtschaft*, **46**, 49–66.

Martinovits, Alfred G. 1985: *Currency Know-How*, Whitstable, Kent: AGM Consulting.

Masera, Rainer Stefano 1987: *An Increasing Role for the ECU: A Character in Search of a Script*, Essays in International Finance, no. 167, Princeton, NJ: International Finance Section.

Mast, Hans J. 1989: Die Eigenmittelvorschriften des Cook-Komitees und die Finanzmärkte, *Zeitschrift für das Gesamte Kreditwesen*, **42**, 410–12.

McDonald, Fran and Zis, George 1989: The European Monetary System: towards 1992 and beyond, *Journal of Common Market Studies*, **27**, 183–202.

McDonald, Robert 1991: Enforcing competition policy in the Community, in *European Community: economic structure and analysis*, London: The Economist Intelligence Unit, 1, 19.

Meese, Richard 1990: Currency fluctuations in the post-Bretton-Woods era, *Journal of Economic Perspectives*, **4**, 117–34.

Miller, Merton H. 1977: Debt and taxes, *The Journal of Finance*, **32**, 261–75.

Miller, Merton H. 1988: The Modigliani-Miller propositions after thirty years, *Journal of Economic Perspectives*, **2**, 99–120.

Miller, Merton H. and Modigliani, Franco 1961: Dividend policy, growth and the valuation of shares, *Journal of Business*, **34**, 411–33.

Miller, Merton H. and Rock, Kevin 1985: Dividend policy under asymmetric information, *The Journal of Finance*, **40**, 1031–51.

Miller, Merton H. and Scholes, Myron S. 1978: Dividends and taxes, *Journal of Financial Economics*, **6**, 333–64.

Ministry of Finance 1990: *Statens låntagning og gæld 1990* (Government Borrowing and Debt 1990), Copenhagen: Ministry of Finance.

Modigliani, Franco and Miller, Merton H. 1958: The cost of capital, corporation finance, and the theory of investment, *American Economic Review*, 48, 261–97.

Morgan bimonthly: *World Financial Markets*, New York: J. P. Morgan.

Morland, David and Zenic, Boris 1991: Europe in the 1990s: the M&A wave, *Mergers and Acquisitions International*, 1991, 28–30.

Muray, Roger H. A. 1991: European direct tax harmonization – progress in 1990, *European Taxation*, 31, 74–85.

Nedergaard, Peter 1991: *Conceptualizing the EC Trade Policy: an eclectic framework*, working paper 16–91, Copenhagen: Institute on International Economics and Management.

Neumann, Manfred J. M. and Von Hagen, Jürgen 1991: Conditional relative price variance and its determinants: open economy evidence from Germany, *International Economic Review*, 32, 195–208.

Neven, Damien J. and Röller, Lars-Hendrik 1991: European integration and trade flows, *European Economic Review*, 35, 1295–309.

Nicolaides, Phedon 1991: Investment policies in an integrated world economy, *The World Economy*, 14, 121–37.

Nicolaides, Phedon and Thomsen, Stephen 1991: The impact of 1992 on direct investment in Europe, *European Business Journal*, 3, 8–16.

Noël, Emilie 1991: The new architecture of Europe, *Newsletter of the IPSA*, no. 3.

Nyborg, Kjell G. 1991: *Human Capital and the Market for Corporate Control*, working paper IFA 141–91, London: London Business School.

Obolensky, Ariane 1991: Les emissions en ECUs de la République Francaise, *EBA Newsletter*, no. 7, 8–10.

O'Cléireacáin, Séamus 1990: Europe 1992 and gaps in the EC's common commercial policy, *Journal of Common Market Studies*, 28, 201–18.

OECD 1977: *Draft Convention for the Avoidance of Double Taxation with Respect to Taxes on Income and Capital*, Paris: OECD.

OECD 1983: *Investment Incentives and Disincentives and the International Investment Process*, Paris: OECD.

OECD 1984: *International Investment and Multinational Enterprises*, Paris: OECD.

OECD 1986: *The OECD Guidelines for Multinational Enterprises*, Paris: OECD.

OECD 1987: *Structure and Organization of Multinational Enterprises*, Paris: OECD.

OECD 1990a: *The Export Credit Financing Systems in OECD Member Countries*, Paris: OECD.

OECD 1990b: *Taxation and International Capital Flows*, Paris: OECD.

OECD 1991a: *Industrial Policy in OECD Countries: annual review 1991*, Paris: OECD.

OECD 1991b: *Strategic Industries in a Global Economy: policy issues for the 1990s*, Paris: OECD.

OECD 1991c: *Financial Market Trends*, no. 49, Paris: OECD, 28–48.

OECD 1991d: Regulations on ownership linkages between banks and insurance companies, *Financial Market Trends*, no. 49, Paris: OECD, 45–8.

OECD 1991e: *Systemic Risk in Securities Markets*, Paris: OECD.

OECD 1992a: *Banks under Stress*, Paris: OECD.

OECD 1992b: *Insurance and Other Financial Services: structural trends*, Financial Market Trends no. 51, Paris: OECD, 31–8.

Officer, Lawrence H. 1976: The purchasing-power-parity theory of exchange rates: a review article, *IMF Staff Papers*, **23**, 1–60.

Oliver, Peter and Baché, Jean Pierre 1989: Free movement of capital between the member states: recent developments, *Common Market Law Review*, **26**, 61–81.

Ommeslaghe, P. Van 1991: Le règlement sur le contrôle des opérations de concentration entre entreprises et les offres publique d'acquisition, *Cahiers de droit européen*, **27**, 259ff.

OOPEC 1978: *Treaties Establishing the European Communities: treaties amending these treaties, documents concerning the accession*, Brussels: Office for Official Publications of the European Communities.

OOPEC 1991: *Directory of Community Legislation in Force and Other Acts of the Community Institutions*, Brussels: Office for Official Publications of the European Communities.

Orbañanos, Miguel Angel Arnedo 1991: The role of the ECU in Eastern Europe, *EBA Newsletter*, no. 14, 7–8.

Patel, J. 1990: Tests of purchasing power parity as a long-run relation, *Journal of Applied Econometrics*, **5**, 367–80.

Petersmann, Ernst-Ulrich 1991: Constitutionalism, constitutional law and European integration, *Aussenwirtschaft*, **46**, 15–48.

Pezet, Jean-Louis 1991: Contrat à terme sur obligations en ECU et options sur la contrat à terme, *EBA Newsletter*, no. 7, 37–8.

Poitras, Geoffrey 1988: Arbitrage boundaries, treasury bills, and covered interest rate parity, *Journal of International Money and Finance*, **7**, 429ff.

Pomfret, Richard 1991: What is the secret of the EMS's longevity?, *Journal of Common Market Studies*, **29**, 623–33.

Poos, Jacques 1991: Milestones on the Eurotrack, *European Affairs*, **5**, 55–6.

Pope, Peter F. and Peel, David A. 1991: Forward foreign exchange rates and risk premia – a reappraisal, *Journal of International Money and Finance*, **10**, 443–56.

Raad, Kees van 1991: The 1977 OECD model convention and commentary – selected suggestions for amendments of the articles 7 and 5, *Intertax*, 497–502.

Ramirez, Gabriel G., Waldman, David A. and Lasser, Dennis J. 1991: Research needs in corporate finance: perspectives from financial managers, *Financial Management*, **20**, 17–29.

Rasmussen, Hjalte 1989: *The European Community Constitution*, studies from the Institute of European Market Law, Copenhagen: Handelshøjskolens Forlag.

Raymond, Arthur J. and Weil, Gordon 1989: Diversification benefits and exchange-rate changes, *Journal of Business Finance and Accounting*, **16**, 455–65.

Rivera, Juan M. 1989: The internationalization of accounting standards: past problems and current prospects, *The International Journal of Accounting*, **24**, 320–41.

Roberts, A. C. R. and Wiseman, R. M. 1990: Possible defensive measures against stock exchange raids in the UK, in Maeijer, J. M. M. and Geens, K. (eds),

Defensive Measures against Hostile Takeovers in the Common Market, Dordrecht: Martinus Nijhoff.

Rodriguez, Rita M. 1979: Measuring and controlling multinationals' exchange risk, *Financial Analysts Journal*, **35**, 49–55.

Roll, Richard 1986: The hubris hypothesis of corporate takeovers, *Journal of Business*, **59**, 197–216.

Roll, Richard 1992: Industrial structure and the comparative behavior of international stock market indices, *The Journal of Finance*, **47**, 3–41.

Ross, Stephen A. 1977: The determination of financial structure: the incentive-signalling approach, *The Bell Journal of Economics*, **8**, 23–40.

Ross, Stephen A. 1988: Comment on the Modigliani-Miller propositions, *Journal of Economic Perspectives*, **2**, 127–33.

Ross, Stephen A., Westerfield, Randolph W. and Jaffe, Jeffrey F. 1990: *Corporate Finance*, 2nd edn, Homewood, IL: Irwin.

Roth, Kendall and Ricks, David A. 1990: Objective setting in international business; an empirical analysis, *International Journal of Management*, **7**, 13–19.

Rudolf, Bernd 1989: Die Eigenkapitaldefinition in Europa, *Zeitschrift für das Gesamte Kreditwesen*, **42**, 404–8.

Rutterford, Janette 1985: An international perspective on the capital structure puzzle, *Midland Corporate Finance Journal*, **3**, 60–72.

Salojarvi, Liisa 1991: The ECU as a financial instrument: an international investor point of view, *EBA Newsletter*, no. 7, 26–8.

Scaperlanda, A. and Balough, R. 1983: Determinants of US direct investment in the EEC, *American Economic Review*, **59**, 558–68.

Schaefer, Stephen M. 1989: *The Regulation of Banks and Securities Firms*, London: London Business School.

Schlesinger, Helmut 1992: Einige Bemerkungen zum Vertragswerk über die Europäische Wirtschafts-und Währungsunion, *Deutsche Bundesbank/Auszüge aus Presseartikeln*, no. 37.

Schonewille, Peter H. 1992: Some questions on the Parent-Subsidiary Directive and the Merger Directive, *Intertax*, no. 1, 13–20.

Sekely, W. S. and Collins J. M. 1988: Cultural influences on international capital structure, *Journal of International Business Studies*, **19**, 87–100.

Shah, S. 1989: The market in currency options, *Bank of England Quarterly Bulletin*, **29**, 235–41.

Shapiro, Alan C. 1991: The economic import of Europe 1992, *Journal of Applied Corporate Finance*, **3**, 25–36.

Shapiro, Alan C. and Titman, Sheridan 1985: An integrated approach to corporate risk management, *Midland Corporate Finance Journal*, **3**, 41–56.

Sharpe, William F. 1970: *Portfolio Theory and Capital Market*, New York: McGraw-Hill.

Sharpe, William F. and Alexander, Gordon J. 1990: *Investments*, Englewood Cliffs, NJ: Prentice Hall.

Shefrin, Hersh M. and Statman, Meir 1984: Explaining investor preference for cash dividends, *Journal of Financial Economics*, **13**, 253–82.

Sinn, Hans Werner 1987: *Capital Income Taxation and Resource Allocation*, Amsterdam: North-Holland.

Siragusa, M. and Subiotto, R. 1991: The EEC merger control regulation: the Commission's evolving case law, *Common Market Law Review*, **28**, 877–934.

Smith, Clifford W., Smithson, Charles W. and Wakeman, Lee Macdonald 1988: The market for interest rate swaps, *Financial Management*, **17**, 34–44.

Smith, Martin and Farquharson, Melanie 1990: The EEC merger regulation, *The Journal of International Securities Markets*, **4**, 315–22.

Snape, Richard H. 1991: International regulation of subsidies, *The World Economy*, **14**, 139–64.

Soenen, Luc A. 1979: A portfolio model for foreign exchange exposure management, *Omega*, **7**, 339–44.

Solnik, Bruno H. 1977: Testing international asset pricing: some pessimistic views, *The Journal of Finance*, **32**, 503–12.

Solnik, Bruno H. 1978: International parity conditions and exchange risk: a review *Journal of Banking and Finance*, **2**, 281–93.

Sørensen, Peter Birch 1990: *Tax Harmonization in the European Community: problems and prospects*, Copenhagen: Institute of Economics, University of Copenhagen.

Sørensen, Peter Birch 1991: *Coordination of Capital Income Taxes in the Economic and Monetary Union: what needs to be done?* working paper 17–91, Copenhagen: The Copenhagen School of Business.

Srinivasulu, S. L. 1983: Classifying foreign exchange exposure, *Financial Executive*, **51**, 36–44.

Stegemann, Klaus 1991: The international regulation of dumping: protection made too easy, *The World Economy*, **14**, 375–405.

Steiner, Claus 1992: Die europäische Banken als unternehmensgläubiger, *Zeitschrift für das Gesamte Kreditwesen*, **44**, 1144–8.

Steinherr, Alfred 1990: Roles for the ECU in the process of achieving European Monetary Union, *The Journal of International Securities Markets*, **4**, 359–70.

Stiglitz, Joseph E. 1988: Why financial structure matters, *Journal of Economic Perspectives*, **2**, 121–6.

Stonehill, Arthur and Dullum, Kaare 1990: Corporate wealth maximization, takeovers, and the market for corporate control, *Nationaløkonomisk Tidsskrift*, **128**, 87ff.

Strivens, Robert 1992: The liberalization of banking services in the Community, *Common Market Law Review*, **29**, 283–307.

Swoboda, Alexander K. 1968: *The Euro-Dollar Market: an interpretation*, Essays in International Finance no. 64, Princeton, NJ.

Thadden, Ernst-Ludwig von 1990: On the efficiency of the market for corporate control, *Kyklos*, **43**, 635–58.

Thiemann, Bernd 1992: Kann die ECU die DM verdrängen?, *Zeitschrift für das Gesamte Kreditwesen*, **45**, 51–4.

Thömmes, Otmar 1990: Harmonization of enterprise taxation in the EC, *Intertax*, 208–14.

Thomson, Ian 1989: *The Documentation of the European Communities: a guide*, London: Mansell.

Thurley, Keith and Wirdenius, Hans 1991: Will management become 'European'? Strategic choice for organizations, *European Management Journal*, **9**, 127–33.

Tichy, Gunther 1990: Die wissenschaftliche aufarbeitung der 'Merger-Mania': neue erkenntnisse für die wettbewerbspolitik?, *Kyklos*, **43**, 437–71.

Tietmeyer, Hans 1990: Voraussetzungen eines Europäischen Zentralbankensystems, *Aussenwirtschaft*, **45**, 301–11.

Tietmeyer, Hans 1991: Reunification and beyond: Europe's economic union must be built on solid foundations, *European Affairs*, **5**, 6–11.

Tietmeyer, Hans 1992: Europe in the world economy, *Deutsche Bundesbank/ Auszüge aus Presseartikeln*, no. 33, 1–4.

Tomsett, Eric 1992: The impact of EC tax directives on US groups with European operations, *Bulletin for International Fiscal Documentation*, **46**, 123–33.

Tondkar, Rasoul H., Adhikari, Ajay and Coffman, Edward N. 1990: An analysis of the impact of selected EEC directives on harmonizing and filing requirements of EEC stock exchanges, *The International Journal of Accounting*, **25**, 127–43.

Toth, A. G. 1990: *The Oxford Encyclopaedia of European Community Law. Vol. 1: Institutional Law*, Oxford: Clarendon Press.

Trojan-Limmer, Ursula 1991: Die Geänderten Vorschläge für ein Statut der Europäischen Aktiengesellschaft (SE), Gesellschaftsrechtliche Probleme, *Recht der Internationalen Wirtschaft*, **37**, 1010–17.

Tsiang, S. C. 1959: The theory of forward exchange and effects of government intervention on the forward exchange market, *IMF Staff Papers*, **7**, 75–106.

Ungerer, Horst 1989: The European Monetary System and the international monetary system, *Journal of Common Market Studies*, **27**, 231–48.

Ungerer, Horst, Evans, Owen, Mayer, Thomas and Young, Phillip 1986: *The EMS: recent developments*, occasional paper 48, Washington, DC: IMF.

Van Horne, James C. 1989: *Financial Management and Policy*, Englewood Cliffs, NJ: Prentice Hall.

Van Hulle, K. 1989: *Harmonisation of Company and Securities Law*, Tilburg: Tilburg University Press.

Venit, James S. 1990: The 'merger' control regulation: Europe comes of age . . . or Caliban's dinner, *Common Market Law Review*, **27**, 7–50.

Verchère, Ian 1991: *The Investor Relations Challenge: reaching out to global markets* special report 2188, London: The Economist Intelligence Unit.

Veugelers, Reinhilde 1991: Locational determinants and ranking of host countries, *Kyklos*, **44**, 363–82.

Vignes, Daniel 1990: The harmonization of national legislation and the EEC, *European Law Review*, **15**, 358–74.

Walter, Ingo and Smith, Roy C. 1990: Economic restructuring in Europe and the market for corporate control, *The Journal of International Securities Markets*, **4**, 291–313.

Walter, Ingo and Smith, Roy C. 1991: *Investment Banking in Europe after 1992*, Oxford: Basil Blackwell.

Ward, Martin, Wright, Mike and Robbie, Ken 1991: Corporate restructuring and the development of management buy-outs in Europe, *European Business Journal*, **3**, 26–40.

Warren, Manning Gilbert 1990: Global harmonization of securities laws: the achievements of the European Communities, *Harvard International Law Journal*, **31**, 185–232.

Wentz, Rolf-Christian 1979: Wechselkursrisikokonzepte und Devisenkurssicherung, *Zeitschrift für Betriebswirtschaft*, **49**, 906–32.

Wils, G. 1991: The concept of reciprocity in EEC law: an exploration into these realms, *Common Market Law Review*, **28**, 245–74.

Winters, L. Alan 1991: International trade and '1992': an overview, *European Economic Review*, **35**, 367–77.

Wright, Mike, Robbie, Ken and Thompson, Steve 1991: Corporate restructuring, buy-outs, and managerial equity: the European dimension, *Journal of Applied Corporate Finance*, **3**, 47–58.

Zuleeg, Manfred 1990: Der Rang des Europäischen im Verhältnis zum nationalen Wettbewerbsrecht, *Europarecht*, **25**, 123–34.

Index of Subjects

Index of Authors

Printed and bound by CPI Group (UK) Ltd, Croydon, CR0 4YY

16/04/2025

14658825-0002